CONCEPTS IN LEARNING

WILLIAM L. MIKULAS

Department of Psychology
University of West Florida

1974
W. B. SAUNDERS COMPANY
Philadelphia, London, Toronto

W. B. Saunders Company: West Washington Square
Philadelphia, Pa. 19105

12 Dyott Street
London, WC1A 1DB

833 Oxford Street
Toronto, Ontario M8Z 5T9, Canada

Concepts of Learning   ISBN 0-7216-6327-3

Last digit is the print number: 9   8   7   6   5   4   3   2   1

DEDICATION

*To my parents, who are responsible for my
existence and started me learning.*

*To Benita, who makes existence pleasurable
and shares in my learning.*

*To everyone who is interested in the nature of
existence and learning.*

preface

I have several objectives in writing this book. First, I want to show the reader how basic principles in the psychology of learning are applicable in varying degrees from the physiological level through complex human behavior. Most learning texts omit physiological material and minimize discussions of applications of learning principles to problems of human behavior. However, the physiological literature suggests relationships and constraints that are relevant to much of learning. Similarly, attempts to apply learning principles to various practical problems have suggested new interrelationships among learning variables, pointed out inadequacies in current psychological models, and provided a proving ground for the relevance and pragmatic aspects of our knowledge of the learning process.

In attempting to trace learning phenomena and principles across the various levels, I have organized the material somewhat differently from other texts. For example, where another text might have chapters devoted to such topics as verbal learning and behavior modification, in this text these topics have been broken down into their constituents and are discussed under general principles such as contiguity, holding mechanisms, and feedback. I hope such an organization is a useful one, both for the reader just entering the field of the psychology of learning and for the reader who has learned about the field using a different approach.

A second objective of this book is to provide the reader with a brief overview of the various ways in which different learning phenomena are conceptualized by different theorists, as opposed to selecting for the reader what *I* consider the best explanation for any phenomenon. Although such an approach may be slightly more difficult for the reader, I believe it will provide him a greater breadth of perspectives both for understanding the current state of learning and for better assimilation of future findings and theories.

The emphasis of this book is more on concepts and ideas than on specific laboratory experiments. Specific experiments are discussed to the extent that they are unique or critical experiments, differentiate various points of view, or illustrate important ideas. This book thus will supplement texts that stress discussions of the methodology of learning or emphasize experiments.

For people interested in applications of learning principles to problems of human behavior, particularly clinical problems, the psychology of learning offers a number of conditioning-based theories and therapies, such as behavior modification, to name but one. As powerful as I believe these approaches to be, they are far from adequate in explaining the complexities of human behavior. As these learning-based models expand, they must take into account such things as learning-genetic interactions, the nature and source of individual differences in conditioning, and predispositions for certain types of learning. From here we can develop the type of "personality theory" that is both experimentally based and useful to the learning-oriented practitioner in delineating the relevant variables for therapy. I suspect that the development of such models is both highly desirable and inevitable. Therefore I have included a chapter on personality that covers some of the existing research and thoughts related to such models.

The final chapter, on behavior, cognitions, and consciousness, deals with how such subjective phenomena as consciousness, cognitions, and general awareness relate to the relatively mechanical-behavioral model of man developed in the earlier chapters. Some of the issues raised in this chapter are the basis for many of the major controversies in psychology and philosophy. Many of these issues cannot currently be resolved satisfactorily, and the assumptions one psychologist makes about them may lead him in directions quite different from those followed by another psychologist who makes different assumptions.

I would like to thank the following people who made comments on various parts of an early draft of the book: John DeLorge, Bruce Dunn, Jay Isgur, and Jack Keller.

WILLIAM L. MIKULAS

contents

chapter one

what is learning?

Psychology is the science of the behavior of organisms and related mental events. To completely understand the behavior of any organism we must interrelate many different factors, including genetic background, the role of instinctual behavior, physiological abnormalities (as in the nervous system), and nutrition, to name just a few. Generally, however, the major influence on the behavior of a complex organism, particularly man, is the types of experiences he has encountered, that is, what he has learned; for a man's learning experiences are by far the most important determinant of the way he acts and thinks. Therefore, anyone who wishes to optimally understand, predict, or alter human behavior needs to learn about learning. This is true for everyone, whether he be a teacher, parent, psychologist, therapist, or someone seeking to better understand himself. Learning deals with changes in an organism's behavior as it adapts to its physical and social environment. But what exactly is learning?

A college student quietly listens to a lecture and on a later test repeats back some of the professor's information. A 5 year old boy has acquired many of the mannerisms of his father, although no attempt was made to teach the child these behaviors. Most Americans find mouth-to-mouth kissing enjoyable, while many Orientals find it revolting. Because of some bad childhood experiences with dogs, a grown woman now has an intense, irrational fear of dogs. Some people like corn and dislike spinach; for others it is the other way around. One person can make fine distinctions about a particular wine, while another person can tell only that the wine is red and sweet. A cat learns to jump off the forbidden sofa when it hears its owner at the front door. These are all examples of learning and the question is what they have in common. That is, what is this phenomenon of learning that includes such disparate types of events? Kimble (1961, p. 10) raises the same question:

> Changes of behavior of the sort we call learning range from the simplest modifications of the simplest organisms, to the most impressive contributions of human intelligence. Learning is basic to the development of athletic prowess, of tastes in food and dress, and of the appreciation of art and music. It contributes to ethnic prejudice, to drug addiction, to fear, and to pathological maladjustment. It produces the miser and the philanthropist, the bigot and the patriot, the coward and the hero. In short, it influences our lives at every turn, accounting in part for the best and the worst in each of us. Can such a range of influences be encompassed by a single concept such as learning?

DEVELOPMENT OF A DEFINITION

In developing a definition of learning, a number of distinctions must be made. The first distinction is between "learning" and "performance." *Performance* is what the organism actually does—its behaviors. It includes overt motor behavior as in shaking hands, verbal behavior as in talking, and physiological behavior such as a change in heart rate. Performance can always be observed and measured. *Learning*, on the other hand, refers to behavior potential. Learning specifies what the organism is *capable* of doing, whereas performance specifies what the organism actually does. Learning can never be studied directly; we can only make theoretical inferences about learning based on performance.

As we will see, learning is just one of the variables affecting performance. Other variables include such things as motivation and fatigue. Consider the following case: a fifth-grade boy, although he attended school regularly, often did not adequately answer the teacher's questions. Based on this poor performance the teacher argued that the boy was far below normal in learning capabilities and suggested he be put into a special class for slow learners. The author then instigated a program in which by answering questions correctly in class the boy earned points that could be exchanged for special privileges at home. Very soon the boy became one of the best students in the class. It appeared that he had been *learning* all the time in class, but what he had learned had not previously been expressed in *performance*. The introduction of the point system provided the *motivation* for the learning to be more evident in the performance.

A second distinction is that most learning refers to a relatively permanent change in behavior potential. A standard assumption is that learning involves a more or less permanent change within the organism.

Once something is learned it is permanently stored in memory. Apparent loss of learned information is assumed to be due not to a deficit in *storage*, but to a deficit in *retrieval*, i.e., getting the information out of storage. If you can't remember something you learned, it is assumed the information is still in your memory storage, but you are having trouble retrieving the information from storage. The associative interference theory, which will be discussed later, argues that a major problem in retrieval is interference from other learned material.

Hypnotists often assume that memories are permanent and that hypnosis is a tool to facilitate retrieval. Similarly, many clinical psychologists believe that memories are permanent but that psychological factors such as repression keep them from reaching consciousness. Psychoanalytic procedures such as word association and dream analysis may facilitate retrieval.

Earlier we spoke of memories as being "relatively permanent." This is to allow for the fact that with age there is a deterioration of the nervous system. Since the nervous system is involved in learning, such a deterioration may result in loss of some stored information. For example, there is no regeneration of neurons (nerve cells) in the central nervous system (brain and spinal cord) of man. Around the time of birth, man has all the brain neurons he will ever have, and as these neurons die naturally throughout life, they are not replaced. However, since memories appear to be stored in more than one place in the brain, the effects on the memory system of a loss of a few neurons may be fairly small.

Most definitions of learning include a phrase like "learning occurs as a result of *practice*." Although another word such as "experience" might be used in place of "practice," the idea is that somehow the organism is an active participant in the learning experience. Exactly what the concept "practice" includes and does not include is far from clear. In the next chapter it is suggested that memories might be transferred biochemically from the brain of one animal to the brain of another animal. If this is true, it might not be considered practice and therefore memory transfer would not be learning.

But what is practice? In our example of the student learning while listening to a professor's lecture, what is the student practicing? When a mouse learns a task in one trial, such as not to jump off a platform onto an electrified grid floor, what is the mouse practicing? These are difficult questions.

There is also an extensive literature on *observation learning* (also called "modeling" and "imitation") in which animals acquire behaviors simply by observing another animal perform the behavior. For example, John and his associates (1968) showed that cats observing other cats correctly performing the task could learn to jump a hurdle in response to a buzzer to avoid shock, or to press a bar in response to a light stimulus to receive food. Much of human behavior, particularly children's, is acquired through observation learning. Children model or imitate many of the behaviors of their parents, movie or television personalities, and important peers. Students model teachers, clients model therapists, and golfers model the golf pro. Much of how we behave consists of combining diverse bits of behavior we have modeled from other people. But what sort of practice is taking place during modeling or observation learning?

Practice by itself is not sufficient for learning, for practice alone may simply produce fatigue or extinction, resulting in a decrease in the probability of the response. Kimble (1961, p. 6) therefore suggests defining learning in terms of "reinforced practice," where reinforcement is some event which strengthens learning. But the necessity for some type of reinforcement for learning is still debatable, so perhaps we should leave it out of our definition for the present.

Although far from adequate, our definition of learning is as follows: *Learning is a relatively permanent change in behavior potential which occurs as a result of practice.*

LEARNING AND MOTIVATION

Where learning provides the repertoire of responses than an organism might make, motivation is one of the main variables that determine which responses will be made and with what intensity. Motivation is difficult to define since, like learning, it is not directly observable but can only be indirectly measured through performance. However, basically *motivation* refers to temporary states that tend to activate behaviors. Two main categories of motivation are drives and incentives. *Drives* refer to general energizers of behaviors. A food-deprived rat is often said to have a hunger drive that energizes those behaviors which lead to food. *Incentives* refer to expectations of rewards following specific behaviors. Based on past experiences in a maze, a rat develops an "expectation" that he will find food pellets if he goes to a particular part of the maze.

Drives can be divided into *specific* drives and *non-specific* drives. *Specific drives* energize the organism toward a small class of goals or objectives. A thirst drive energizes the organism toward the goal of something to drink, not toward some other goal such as sex. A common trap when studying human behavior is explaining the behavior by postulating an associated drive. Thus a social psychologist or anthropologist might try to explain man's warlike behavior in terms of a drive or instinct to defend and expand his territory. Or a personality theorist might try to account for large parts of human behavior in terms of drives such as power-striving. Such approaches that explain complex learned behavior by postulating a few drives have very limited scientific usefulness because of their oversimplification. Also, labeling a phenomenon does not explain it. Most learning theorists try to minimize the number of drives they must postulate (e.g., thirst, hunger, release of sexual tension, needs in terms of stimulus complexity, avoiding pain) and explain most behavior in terms of what the organism learns to do in various situations associated with basic drives. Most unlearned drives are based on biological needs such as food.

A *non-specific drive* receives input from a number of different drive sources such as hunger and thirst, and theoretically energizes all behaviors the organism is involved in. However, specific drives and the drives feeding into a non-specific drive have associated with them *drive stimuli* — stimuli specific to the individual drives — as stomach contractions may be associated with a hunger drive. These drive stimuli help cue the animal to the appropriate goal (e.g., food if hungry), whereas the non-specific drive is assumed to energize whatever behaviors are selected or cued.

Some theorists deal only with specific drives, and some, often under the influence of B. F. Skinner, do no more than describe the deprivation procedures (e.g., "the pigeon is 23-hours food deprived"); they see no need to postulate any types of drives. Other theorists, often under the influence of Clark Hull, describe behavior in terms of a non-specific drive with the behaviors guided by the specific drive stimuli. Neal Miller has suggested that deprivation procedures produce drive stimuli which, if intense enough, result in a general drive (Miller & Dollard, 1941).

The relationships between learning and motivation are very complex (Bolles, 1970; Brown, 1961; Kimble, 1961, Chap. 13), but to a large extent performance is the interaction of learning and motivation. Theorists differ in terms of the relative weight they give to motivational variables and learning variables when explaining performance. For example, in clinical practice the Freudian approach accounts for performance primarily in terms of motivational constructs, while behavior modification includes a clinical approach that emphasizes the role of learning in explaining performance.

Hull was the first major theorist to give equal importance to learning and motivation (Bolles, 1970, p. 5). This can be seen in the following formulation from Spence (1960), who expanded on Hull's basic model:
$$R = f\,[(D + K)\,H]$$
D stands for the non-specific drive, K stands for the effects of incentives, and H is the learned habit. Although Spence's theory is more complex than the above formulation, and varies with the type of learning situation, we can see that Spence considers performance (R) to be some function (f) of the product of motivation (D + K) and learning (H).

Figure 1–1 shows an often found inverted-U relationship between motivation and performance. That is, performance is usually best at some intermediate level of motivation and decreases as motivation is

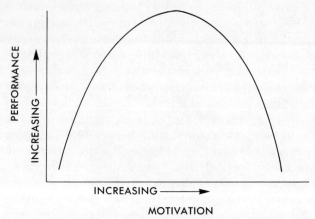

Figure 1–1   *A common relationship between motivation and performance.*

increased or decreased. For example, consider the effects on test-taking of general arousal, a motivational variable that corresponds to the amount of excitement within the person. If arousal is too low, as when the person is tired and uninterested in the test material, performance on the test will probably be below optimum. Performance will similarly be poor when arousal is too high, as when the person has excessive test anxiety. Optimal performance requires some intermediate level of arousal.

A common finding (Broadhurst, 1957) is that the point of optimal motivation varies with the complexity of the task; within limits the more difficult the task, the lower the optimal amount of motivation. This supports the *Yerkes-Dodson law* proposed 70 years ago (Yerkes & Dodson, 1908). This law suggested that there is an optimal intermediate level of motivation for learning, which decreases as problem difficulty increases.

Practically, it is often very difficult to divide variables into those that affect learning and those that affect motivation. Many variables probably affect both learning and motivation to various degrees. Those variables that might affect only learning or only motivation are hard to discriminate since we can only measure performance, which is some unknown interaction of learning and motivation.

Another problem in separating learning and motivation is that learning affects motivation and motivation may affect learning. The primary way in which learning affects motivation is through learned drives and learned incentives (to be discussed in Chapter 5). Basically what is meant here is that much of motivation is acquired. Man's striving for approval and recognition is not innate, but is based on the learned value of approval and recognition.

The effects of motivation on learning are not always clear. Although motivation affects when learning takes place, it is debatable whether motivation affects the memory itself. There are some suggestions that motivation may affect the availability and retrieval of memories (Weiner, 1966). For example, Weiner has done a series of experiments (Weiner, 1967; Weiner & Walker, 1966) in which subjects learn sets of consonants. The consonants (e.g., 3 consonant letters called "trigrams") are presented with a background color which tells what the subject will later receive for correct recall. Thus one color might mean the subject will get one cent for later correct recall, while another color means five cents. By controlling for variables such as how much the subject can rehearse (review his learning) between trials, Weiner argues that later better recall of high incentive consonants (e.g., 5 cents) over lower incentive consonants (e.g., 1 cent) is due to the effect of the incentive on the retention of the memory, rather than on the original learning. There needs to be much more research in this area.

In Chapter 4 we will suggest a way that motivation might influence learning by affecting the neural activity responsible for formation of the memories. If there is some active process (called "consolidation") responsible for whatever physiological change underlies the storage of learned material, then perhaps motivational variables might affect this process.

SENSITIZATION AND HABITUATION

Occasionally an organism, simply as a result of his responding to a specific class of stimuli, will have a change in his tendency to respond to these stimuli. The change may be an increment (sensitization) or a decrement (habituation). The changes are non-associative; they do not result from any learned association, but occur simply as a result of reacting to the stimuli. That is, the changes do not require the animal to learn associations between stimuli or associations between stimuli and responses, as is implied in many forms of learning. The issue is whether we wish to include such phenomena under our concept of learning. Some theorists would not include them, since they want all learning to be associative. However, following Razran (1971), these will be included as simple forms of learning, there being no reason to restrict learning to associative processes alone. In the discussion that follows the reader should keep in mind that there is no concensus on the definitions of sensitization and habituation, with many theorists meaning significantly different things by the same terms.

According to Razran (1971, p. 58) *sensitization* can be defined as "a more or less permanent increment in an innate reaction upon repeated stimulation." This increased reactivity "is manifested in two behavioral modes: (a) increases in incidence and magnitude and decreases in latency and threshold of reactions, and (b) pseudoconditioning, or new reactions to originally inadequate stimuli" (Razran, 1971, p. 78). These are described below.

The following is an example of the first type of sensitization: a dog is given electric shocks in the hind leg. These shocks produce a muscular response in the leg. Although we keep the intensity of the shock constant, we might find that after a few shocks the dog's response is more pronounced (increase in magnitude) and occurs faster (decrease in latency) after the shock comes on. This increment in the response is sensitization. Similarly, after a few shocks the number of times the dog actually responds to the shock might increase (increase in incidence) and the minimum intensity of the shock necessary to produce the response might decrease (decrease in threshold).

Pseudoconditioning, the second type of sensitization, refers to the strengthening of a response to a previously neutral stimulus through the repeated elicitation of the response by a *non-associated* stimulus. That is, the stimulus which elicits the response is not paired (non-associated) with the neutral stimulus. Between trials of shocking the dog we might present to the dog a tone. At first the tone does not elicit the shock-produced response; it is a neutral stimulus. But after eliciting the leg-response by shock a number of times, we might find that the dog now occasionally responds to the tone, even though the tone and shock were never systematically paired. This increasing of the leg-response to the tone is an example of pseudoconditioning.

We could have produced a similar effect by pairing the tone and shock, presenting first the tone and shortly thereafter the shock. After a few such pairings, the dog would respond to the tone. But this is an example of associative learning (respondent conditioning to be discussed later), based on systematic pairing of stimuli. For true pseudoconditioning we must assume that the effect is not due to any associative learning. An interesting question is whether many of the types of learning we assume to be associative (because we experimentally present stimuli in what appears to be an associative context) can be more readily reduced to pseudoconditioning.

Habituation can be defined as "the decrement and disappearance of innate reactions through nonassociative repeated reacting" (Razran, 1971, p. 56). If suddenly a cement mixer starts going outside your window, you may startle and orient to the sound. After a while your reactions to the sound will decrease. This is an example of habituation. Razran sees habituation as the lowest level of learning, manifested fully in protozoa and in reactions mediated by just two neurons (nerve cells). For example, many protozoa will contract to mechanical stimulation (being touched), but will habituate if the stimulation is presented immediately after the animals have expanded.

Similar to sensitization and habituation is *adaptation,* the adjustment of a sense organ to the stimulus environment. When you first go into a darkened movie theater you have trouble seeing in the dark. But after a short time your visual system adjusts to the dark (dark adaptation) and you can see better. Similarly when coming out of the dark theater into bright lights your visual system must readjust (light adaptation). Although adaptation involves changes in responses (visual responses in this example), the changes are not specific to a small class of stimuli as in sensitization and habituation, but rather are sensory changes generally involving an entire sense modality. Therefore adaptation will not be included as an example of learning.

OTHER NON-LEARNING PERFORMANCE VARIABLES

Here we will consider four other variables that affect performance, but which are not included under learning: fatigue, maturation, senescence, and stimulus change.

Fatigue is a decreased capacity to respond due to previous responding. It is a physiological condition of cells and organs. A rat might learn to run a complex maze for a food pellet. After a number of such trials, the rat's running speed may decrease or the rat may stop running altogether. This may simply be the result of the rat's being tired, i.e., fatigue. We wouldn't want to say that the rat has forgotten the route through the maze or that it has learned not to run. Some visual perception phenomena are also explained in terms of fatigue of retinal cells, owing to chemical changes.

Maturation is change which occurs through the biological processes of growth. Much of human motor development, such as learning to walk, requires a certain amount of maturation. A child can't be taught to walk until maturation provides the necessary development of muscles and nerves. The type and sequence of pre-walking behaviors the child goes through are primarily due to maturation processes. Maturation and learning obviously interact, but it is important to recognize them as separate processes. The fact that we suddenly see a new behavior in an organism, such as some type of sexual behavior, does not mean that the organism just learned it. Rather the organism may have just reached the stage of maturation necessary for this behavior.

At the other end of the developmental continuum from maturation is *senescence* – deterioration with old age. In humans this is generally accompanied by a reduced capacity to process and retain new information and to recall recent memories. Such deficits appear to have a physiological basis correlated with aging and should not be attributed to learning phenomena.

When something is learned, it is often learned to a specific set of stimuli. The behavior will occur to other stimuli (*stimulus generalization*), but only to the extent that the new stimuli are similar, from the organism's point of view, to the original stimulus. The more similar the stimulus is to the original, the more probable and the stronger the behavior. Thus if an organism learns a behavior in one situation and we change this situation (*stimulus change*), decrements in the behavior may be due to generalization phenomena, and not to learning variables. Thus stimulus change may produce changes in performance that do not necessarily reflect changes in learning.

The stimuli to which the behavior is learned include not only external stimuli but also various internal states of the organism, such as level of deprivation or chemical states as might result from drugs. This is referred to as *state-dependent learning* (Overton, 1969).

In the earliest state-dependent learning experiment, Girden and Culler (1937) gave dogs a curare type drug which to a large extent paralyzes muscles. They found that conditioned autonomic and muscular responses learned while the dog was drugged disappeared in the nondrugged state, but reappeared when the dog was drugged again. That is, the response was learned to a set of stimuli including those produced by the drug. They could even train a dog to make one response to an external stimulus while drugged and a different response to the same stimulus when not drugged.

Thus it is possible that a student who uses amphetamines to stay up all night studying for an exam might find much of his learning is tied to drug-produced stimuli. When not on the drug much of the learned information might be difficult to recall. Similarly, a mental hospital which provides therapy to the patients while the patients are on drugs such as tranquilizers may find poor generalization of some of the therapeutic effects to the non-drugged state.

Stimulus change is often useful when trying to establish new behaviors. A married couple might have a number of interpersonal problems. These problem behaviors then become associated with the stimuli of the home so that now the stimuli tend to produce the behaviors. A marriage counselor, after establishing a program of desirable behaviors with the couple (perhaps while they live in a place other than home), could utilize stimulus change in the home. The couple might be instructed to rearrange their furniture, buy some colored lights, change their time and place of eating, dress differently, buy new paintings, and so forth. This way, it is hoped, the home stimuli become associated with the new desired behaviors.

The preceding discussion covered a number of variables that affect performance, but which are not to be included in the concept of learning. Our final definition of learning was as follows: Learning is a relatively permanent change in behavior potential which occurs as a result of practice, and does *not* include behavioral changes due to motivation, sensory adaptation, fatigue, maturation, senescence, or stimulus change.

MEASURES OF LEARNING AND RETENTION

Remembering that we can not measure learning, but only performance, the question is what measures of performance should we use. The following are a few of the common response measures that are presumed to reflect learning:

1. *Response probability.* How likely is it that the response will occur in a given situation? (How probable is it that the elementary student will know the sum of 6 plus 7 after covering this sum once in class?)

2. *Response latency.* How long does it take the response to occur to the stimulus situation? (How quickly can you remember the definition of "pseudoconditioning" given earlier?)

3. *Response duration.* How long does the response keep going? (How long does the rabbit keep his eyelid closed when being trained to blink his eye to a tone?)

4. *Response amplitude.* How strong is the response? (How hard does the dog turn the wheel to avoid shock?)

5. *Trials to extinction.* How many times does the response occur after the learning contingency has been removed? (How many times does a rat continue to press a bar which it learned to press for food after pressing of the bar no longer yields food?)

Unfortunately there is little correlation among the various response measures, all of which are supposedly measures of the same "learning." The reason for this is not clear. Perhaps other variables that affect performance cloud the actual correlations, or perhaps only a couple of the measures actually reflect learning. Probably the error is in assuming that one type of learning underlies all the measures. It might be more profitable to think of learning within each separate measure. Logan (1956) has suggested a *micromolar theory* of learning in which even different response values of the same response system are treated as being entirely different responses. That is, we can think of an organism learning to make a response of a certain range of rates, a certain range of amplitudes, and so forth. If this is the case, then the rate and amplitude are also learned and are not independent measures of learning. For example, a rat might learn to press a bar at a certain rate and with a certain amplitude. The rate and amplitude then are learned and cannot be taken as measures of learning itself.

Given the response measures listed above, some are used more with some response systems than others. For many autonomic responses, such as heart rate, amplitude and latency are common measures. For some skeletal responses, such as pressing a bar, probability and trials to extinction are common measures, while for others, such as running a maze, latency is often used.

In studying human verbal learning three popular measures of retention are recall, recognition, and savings. *Recall* is the subject's ability to reproduce previously learned material without additional cues. (What is the German word for train station?) *Recognition* is the subject's ability to identify the correct response from a limited set of alternatives. (Which of the following five German words means train station?) *Savings* refers to how much faster the subject can learn material for the second time as opposed to the amount of time it took the first time. All of these are assumed to be measures of memory. But a subject can recognize correctly when he can't recall and relearn faster when he can't recognize. What does this mean for the concept of memory? Are these measures of different types of memories, measures of different sensitivities for the same memory, or measures requiring different types of retrieval processes?

In applied situations it is important to recognize the independence of response measures that appear to measure the same learning. Consider a therapy program in which a person is to learn to overcome some particular fear. The fear can be measured in terms of the person's verbal report (what he says about his fear), his overt motor fear behavior (how he acts in the feared situation), and relevant physiological measures such as heart rate. The problem is that all of these measures can be controlled independently of the others (Lang, 1969). Thus the therapist might conclude, on the basis of physiological measures, that the subject has learned to overcome the fear, when in fact there is no change in the overt motor behavior.

Unfortunately, many change agents, particularly therapists and counselors, rely almost exclusively on the subject's verbal report as a measure of learning. But verbal report is very easy to change without affecting other response systems.

WHAT CAN LEARN?

Given that we have some idea about what learning is, the next question is *what* is capable of learning. The answer to this question depends to a large extent on the definition of learning. Some theorists in their definition of learning put in the requirement of a central nervous system. With such a requirement, one-celled animals by definition are not capable of learning. But it is probably desirable not to build such biases into definitions.

There is no question that complex animals such as cats and rats are capable of learning. So let us ask what is the simplest organism that appears capable of learning according to the definition of learning given earlier.

The simplest animals, of course, are protozoans, one-celled animals. Most of the research has involved paramecia, and most of the controversy has centered on the experiments by Beatrice Gelber (see discussion in McConnell & Shelby, 1970). Paramecia generally avoid platinum wires lowered into their cultures. However, Gelber reported that if she baited the wire with bacteria (food for paramecia), the paramecia would approach and cling to the wire. Learning seemed to occur in that, after a number of such bacteria trials, the paramecia would then cling to the bare wire, even 10 hours after the last bacteria trial.

Critics of these experiments generally try to explain the effect as being an artifact of the bacteria introduced into the paramecian culture. For example, in the presence of the bacteria food in the fluid surrounding the wire, the paramecia will cling to any nearby structure, which in this case just happens to be the wire. There is also some question as to whether paramecia can even perceive the wire except through chemical contamination of the surrounding fluid. The issue of whether paramecia actually learn in this situation is far from settled.

Earlier we quoted Razran (1971) as arguing that habituation is manifested fully in protozoa (e.g., habituation to contraction-producing mechanical stimuli). To the extent that these results hold up, and since we include habituation as learning, it appears that protozoa are capable of simple learning and perhaps also of the more complex associative learning described by Gelber.

An even more controversial issue is whether plants can learn. Enough people consider such an idea absurd that most studies on plant learning remain unpublished. Unfortunately, because of such biases and the lack of a series of well-designed and replicated studies, little can be said about plant learning at this time. However, one representative, unpublished study will be given as an example.

Armus conditioned the plant Mimosa pudica, a sensitive plant that closes its leaves and droops its stem on contact. The plant will close its leaves when put in darkness, but not as fast as when the stem of the plant is struck. The conditioning, then, consisted of turning off the illumination lamp and two minutes later striking the main stem of the plant. The measure of learning was the latency of the folding up of the leaves. It was reported that the plant "learned" to close up its leaves faster to the offset of the lamp, even on test trials when the stem was not struck. Control plants which had their stems struck one-half hour before light offset did not show such learning. During extinction, when the light offset was no longer paired with stem-striking, the latency of the conditioned plants returned to the level of the control plants.

Rather than decide in advance whether something can learn we should merely see if it fits into our definition of learning. This procedure, however, often yields unsettling results. For example, we all assume that linseed oil can't be capable of learning. But consider the following: linseed oil when exposed to light will turn gummy. If we expose it to some illumination, but not enough for there to be a noticeable effect, we find upon later illumination that it turns gummy faster than if it hadn't been previously exposed. Did the linseed oil "remember" its first exposure and did it "learn" to turn gummy faster? It might be argued that this fits our definition of learning, unless we pass it off as something akin to sensory adaptation or maturation. This raises an important general point: There does not exist a concept or definition of learning that includes all phenomena generally held to be learning and that excludes all non-learning phenomena. This, of course, reflects theoretical differences among researchers, but it also reflects the basic ambiguity surrounding a concept as basic and broad as "learning."

UNLEARNED BEHAVIORS

Unlearned behaviors basically can be divided into two groups: reflexes and instincts. A *reflex* is a simple, unlearned, and immediate response to specific stimulation. For example, the patellar reflex is the knee kick that occurs when the tendon just below the knee is tapped. Reflexes depend on maturation. Many of them are absent in the newborn human and only occur later with maturation.

An *instinct*, on the other hand, is a more complex, unlearned sequence of responses. A phenomenon which illustrates instinctive variables is *imprinting*, the attachment of a behavior pattern to a specific stimulus purely as a function of exposure to the stimulus at a critical time. For example, newly hatched ducks will follow whatever moving object (within certain dimensions) they happen to see during the imprinting time, the maximum time being between 13 and 16 hours after birth (Hess, 1959). This moving object generally is the mother duck, which is why you often see a mother duck followed by a row of ducklings. But it could be a human if the mother duck is absent. Naturalist Konrad Lorenz had ducks imprint on him and follow him about.

For our purposes, the importance of understanding unlearned behaviors is to keep from confusing them with learned behaviors. A lot of effort could have been wasted trying to determine how ducklings learn to follow their mother, when the behavior is primarily instinctual. Unfortunately, behaviors don't neatly divide into the categories of learned and unlearned; rather, there is a complex interaction between the two. For example, the feeding behavior of a sea gull chick is primarily instinctual but requires a certain amount of learning. Hailman (1969) summarizes it as follows:

> The newly hatched gull chick begins life with a clumsily coordinated, poorly aimed peck, motivated by hunger and elicited by simple stimulus properties of shape and movement provided only by a parent or sibling. The chick cannot recognize food, but by aiming at the bills of its relatives and missing, it strikes food and rapidly learns to recognize it. As a result of the reward embodied in the food, the chick comes to learn the visual characteristics of the parent. Through practice in pecking its aim and depth perception improve steadily. The chick also learns to rotate its head when begging from the parent, and thus its begging peck and feeding peck become differentiated.

In the case of young human children there is some debate about how much of their behavior can be accounted for in terms of instinctual components. However, as the person gets older, learning becomes more and more prominent. In adult humans it is probable that instinct has little or no effect on most of behavior. That is, with the exception of reflexes, learning and related performance variables seem sufficient to account for most adult human behavior.

SOME THEORETICAL ISSUES

This section will briefly discuss four theoretical issues that have been the basis of many theoretical arguments over the years. The issues are far from resolved and have generated extensive literatures (Goldstein, Krantz, & Rains, 1965; Hilgard & Bower, 1966).

S-S vs. S-R Learning

One issue concerns the nature of what is learned. Some theorists argue that learning is based on associations between stimuli (S–S learning), while other theorists claim learning is based on associations between stimuli and responses (S–R learning). Consider a rat learning a maze or a person learning his way across a new town. The S–S theorist would explain the learning in terms of associations between significant stimuli: the rat associates the food reward with stimuli of the alleyway to the right. The person learns that the correct route across town passes the firehouse and then curves toward Keller's racetrack. The S–S associations then chain together in what Tolman (one of the classic S–S theorists) called a *cognitive map*. The rat's cognitive map is a chain of S–S associations that lead from the start box to the goal of the maze. According to the S–R theorist, on the other hand, the rat and human are learning to make specific responses to stimuli at choice points. The rat learns to turn left at the corner with the peeled-off paint. The person learns to turn left just after Isgur's tennis courts.

The main problem with the S–S approach is that it doesn't have a response system built into it. That is, how do associations between stimuli cause the organism to make some response? It was along this line that Guthrie (one of the classic S–R theorists) accused Tolman of leaving the rat "buried in thought" in the maze. S–S theorists often respond that the translation of learning into action is a performance issue – not a learning issue.

A problem with the S–R approach is that it is not always easy to divide the world into stimuli and responses. Consider a paired associate learning task in which the subject is required to learn associations between nonsense syllables (e.g., CIH-GEX) so that when he is later presented with the first of the two paired associates (CIH) he will respond with the second (GEX). Here CIH is considered, by S–R theorists, to be a stimulus to which the subject makes the response GEX. But it is known (Ekstrand, 1966) that if we present the subject with GEX, he can often respond with CIH (this is called a *backward association*). Does this mean that the response GEX to the stimulus CIH suddenly became a stimulus GEX for a response CIH? Or does it mean that while the subject was learning the response GEX to the stimulus CIH he was also learning the response CIH to the stimulus GEX? Either way the distinction between stimulus and response becomes a little hazy.

Historically there were numerous debates between S–R and S–S theorists. These debates often took the form of the S–S theorists posing problems for S–R theory, and the S–R theorists modifying and expanding S–R theory to handle these problems. Because of this, S–R theory evolved significantly more than S–S theory and currently has a greater influence on psychology. However, both orientations can adequately explain learning phenomena as expressed in behavior.

It may be that differentiation between the two approaches, which remains unresolved on the behavioral level, might someday be resolved at the physiological level. For example, there are areas in the cortex of the brain that receive input from different sensory modalities (e.g., polysensory neurons) but are not connected with response mechanisms. If we can show learning to take place in such an area, it would be S–S learning, not S–R learning. Similarly, other areas of the brain have anatomical links between sensory nerve centers and motor fiber tracts that lead to responses. Such areas might be a seat of S–R learning.

Contiguity vs. Reinforcement

The second issue is based on the question of what is necessary for learning. A contiguity theorist (see Chapter 5) argues that learning requires only that the learned elements occur together in time. Thus an

S–S contiguity theorist says learning is an association between stimuli based on the stimuli occurring together in time. A reinforcement theorist (see Chapter 6), on the other hand, claims that contiguity is not sufficient; there must also be some event, called a "reinforcement," which has some strengthening effect on the learned association. For example, an S–R reinforcement theorist would say that an organism learns to make responses to stimuli. The responses that are learned are those that occur contiguously with the stimuli *and* are reinforced. These positions will be discussed later.

It has been the task of reinforcement theorists to find sources of reinforcement in *all* applicable learning situations; this has often been a difficult, and sometimes strained, task. But, as will be seen, almost any stimulus can become a learned source of reinforcement, so the clever theorist can almost always postulate some source of reinforcement.

In Chapter 6 it will be seen that events identified as reinforcements (such as food to a hungry rat, or money to a person) do have a facilitative effect on performance. This effect is called the *empirical law of effect*. But is the effect only on performance or is it also on learning? A reinforcement theorist who holds that reinforcement has a necessary facilitative effect on learning is said to hold the *theoretical law of effect*. Contiguity theorists, then, have been required to explain the empirical law of effect while denying the theoretical law of effect.

All-or-None vs. Incremental Learning

How long does learning take? The all-or-none position suggests that one trial of learning is sufficient, that the association is either learned at full strength or is completely absent. The incremental position suggests that the learned association builds up in gradual increments during learning trials.

It seems obvious that performance changes are incremental. Doesn't the rat still make some mistakes in a complex maze even after a perfect trial? Doesn't the student have to go over and over the formulas for organic compounds until he has learned them? All-or-none theorists reply that although learning may appear incremental at the *molar* level, it is, in fact, all-or-none at the *molecular* level. That is, at the very simplest level, the molecular level, very simple responses become connected to very simple parts of the whole stimulus complex in an all-or-none fashion. These stimuli and responses are so basic that it is often practically impossible even to identify them. At the more complex molar level the stimuli we observe are really composites of many molecular stimuli, while molar responses are composites of molecular responses. Thus the apparent incremental change in the molar response is due to a change in the number of constituent molecular responses, which were acquired in an all-or-none fashion.

For example, a rat learns to press a bar in a test apparatus in order to receive food. At the molar level the response of pressing the bar in the apparatus gradually improves with each rewarded trial. However, at the molecular level this improvement is explained in terms of more and more of the molecular responses that compose the response of pressing the bar becoming connected with molecular stimuli of the test apparatus.

Also noted by the all-or-none theorists is the fact that many psychological experiments involve averaging together the results from several animals. This often obscures the particular learning patterns of the individual animals, and the averaged data may give a greater impression of incremental learning than the individual records would.

Saltz (1971) has proposed a model of learning in which a learned association achieves near maximum strength during the first trial in which the subject attends to the two elements to be associated, or at least early in training if not the first trial. In time what develops is *boundary strength,* a resistance to interference from other material. According to this model, learning is basically all-or-none, but retrieval improves incrementally as the learned material becomes less affected by the interfering effects of other material at the time of retrieval.

One or More Kinds of Learning

How many different kinds of learning are there? Can we reduce all learning to one particular model, such as S–R, reinforcement, incremental learning? Or will we find more than one basic type of learning? Since learning at the molecular level is so difficult to observe, there is no agreement on how many different types of learning there are. Some theorists argue for one kind of learning, some for two kinds, and occasionally someone argues for more than two. At one time Tolman (1949) suggested six types of learning.

Of the people who suggest that there are two basic types of learning, the most popular version is that one type is S–S contiguity learning and the other is S–R reinforcement learning. As will be seen later, the first is usually associated with what will be called respondent conditioning and the latter with operant conditioning.

In the next chapter we will look at some of the physiological changes that may underlie learning.

SUMMARY

We can never observe learning directly. We can only observe the *performance* of an organism — what it does. Numerous factors affect this performance, *learning* and *motivation* being two of the most important. Learning is a "behavior potential": how the organism is potentially capable of behaving if other factors do not alter performance. The effects of learning are believed to be relatively permanent. Once information is learned, it goes into *memory storage*, where it may stay for the lifetime of the organism. However, even though the information is there, there may be difficulty in retrieving it from the storage, which is a cause of forgetting.

The range of phenomena included in the concept of learning makes learning difficult to define. The proposed definition states that "learning is a relatively permanent change in behavior potential which occurs as a result of practice." Other factors which also produce changes in behavior but are not considered to be part of learning include *motivation, sensory adaptation, fatigue, maturation, senescence,* and *stimulus change.* It is often very difficult to separate learning variables from non-learning variables, particularly since these two classes of variables interact in very subtle ways. It is obvious that all complex animals are capable of learning, but there is no agreement on what is the simplest organism capable of learning. It seems that one-celled animals are possibly capable of at least some simple forms of learning, but there is great controversy over whether plants can learn.

Learning is measured via performance, with measures such as *response probability, response latency, response duration, response amplitude,* and *trials to extinction.* Brief mention was made of the following theoretical issues in learning: *S-S vs. S-R, contiguity vs. reinforcement, all-or-none vs. incremental learning,* and the question of whether there are one or more kinds of learning.

SUGGESTED READINGS

Deese, J., & Hulse, S. H. *The Psychology of Learning.* New York: McGraw-Hill, 1967.

Hall, J. F. *The Psychology of Learning.* Philadelphia: Lippincott, 1966.

Hilgard, E. R., & Bower, G. H. *Theories of Learning.* New York: Appleton-Century-Crofts, 1966.

Kimble, G. A. *Hilgard and Marquis' Conditioning and Learning.* New York: Appleton-Century-Crofts, 1961.

Marx, M. H. (ed.). *Learning: Processes.* New York: Macmillan, 1969.

Razran, G. *Mind in Evolution.* Boston: Houghton-Mifflin, 1971.

physiology of learning

There must be some physiological changes associated with learning and responsible for long term memories. Currently the popular place to look for such changes is in the central nervous system (brain and spinal cord). Since the central nervous system (CNS) appears to be responsible for perceiving and classifying stimuli and for sending out motor directives, it is a logical locus for learning, which involves such stimuli and responses. A few of the theoretical approaches will be discussed here under the following classifications: (a) neuronal-synaptic models, (b) RNA-protein models, (c) glial models, and (d) non-connectionistic theories.

NEURONAL-SYNAPTIC MODELS

The main building block of the CNS is the *neuron:* the nerve cell and its processes (dendrites and axon). All information that passes through the CNS, relevant to incoming stimuli and outgoing responses, as well as all mediation within the CNS, is carried by neurons and passed from neuron to neuron. Within the neuron, information is transmitted electrically (as the result of flows of ions through the neuron's surrounding membrane). Pribram (1971a, p. 15) distinguishes two types of electrical effects in the neuron: nerve impulse unit discharges and graded slow potential changes. The first type, the nerve impulse unit discharge, occurs when the excitation coming into a neuron exceeds some value, called the *threshold.* The neuron fires, and a wave of electrical activity (*action potential*) moves down the neuron toward the next neuron. The second type of electrical activity, graded slow potential changes, refers to the small, fluctuating electrical potentials within a neuron. These slow potential changes are more sensitive to non-neuronal influences, such as from the chemicals surrounding the neuron.

Neurons may influence each other if the neurons are simply close enough together so that the electrical-chemical activity of one interacts with and influences the electrical-chemical activity of the other. Such a connection between neurons, which does not involve any specific structures, is called an *ephaptic junction*. Perhaps more important for learning is the *synapse*, a specific structure for transmitting the activity of one neuron to the next. When a neuron fires, the action potential moves through the neuron to the synapse, where it activates the *synaptic knob*. This structure of the synapse contains a number of small sacs of chemicals called *synaptic vesicles*. When the neuron is fired these vesicles move within the synaptic knob to the space between the neuron and the next neuron; this space is known as the *synaptic cleft*. The chemicals, released from the vesicles into the synaptic cleft, travel across to the next neuron. Therefore these chemicals are called *transmitter substances*, for they transmit chemical changes from one neuron to another. Depending on the type of chemical it is and the nature of the synapse, the transmitter substance will produce either an excitatory or an inhibitory effect on the next neuron. This second neuron will then fire only when the sum of excitatory effects it receives from many different neurons minus the sum of the inhibitory effects exceeds the threshold for that neuron.

Figure 2–1 shows a schematic of an idealized neuron. All neurons have many dendrites which primarily receive information from other neurons via synapses, a cell body, and a single axon with many branches

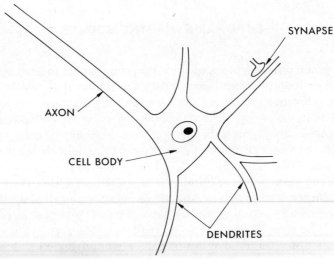

SYNAPSE

AXON

CELL BODY

DENDRITES

Figure 2–1 *Schematic drawing of a neuron.*

that carry the information to the next neurons. (For more detail on neurons see Eccles, 1957, 1964; Ochs, 1965.)

There are about 10 billion neurons in the human brain, each of which communicates with hundreds of other neurons. The number of synapses on any neuron may be in the thousands. Eccles (1965, p. 18) suggests that there could be as many as 10,000 synapses on a single neuron. This great complexity of interactions is one of the reasons that neuronal systems are popular theoretical bases for behavior and learning. A general problem is to explain how the nervous system can be flexible enough for continuous learning, but inflexible enough to store memories for the lifetime of the organism. Another problem is that there is probably no regeneration of neurons in the CNS of a mature organism; once a neuron dies, it is not replaced. Thus neuronal theories of learning must be careful about the types of growth postulated to occur in the CNS.

Most neuronal-synaptic theories of learning (e.g., Eccles, 1964, 1965; Hebb, 1949) assume that learning is based on physiological changes that permit some neurons to fire other neurons more easily. Currently most such theories assume the change to occur in the synapse between neurons. For example, it might be postulated that with learning, the relevant neurons grow closer together at the synapses so that it is easier for the transmitter substances to cross the synaptic cleft and affect the next neuron. Or a theory might be based on learning making the relevant synaptic transmission more effective, perhaps due to some chemical change in the synapse.

Thus according to a very oversimplified neuronal-synaptic model of learning, when a person learns to associate a particular song with the image of the recording artist singing it, learning involves something like the following: There is a set of neurons corresponding to hearing the song and another set corresponding to the image of the singer. Since these two sets of neurons are fired simultaneously (you see the singer as you hear the song), neuronal-synaptic changes occur between the neurons that connect the two sets of stimulated neurons. Now when one set of neurons is fired (you hear the song on the radio), there is a tendency for the other set to fire (you get a visual image of the singer). Such a theory is a *connectionistic* theory, since it is based on specific connections between specific neurons.

Eccles (1964, 1965) and other synaptic theorists have drawn heavily from a phenomenon called *posttetanic potentiation*, first observed by Lloyd (1949). This refers to an effect of very rapid stimulation (*tetanic stimulation*) on a simple nervous preparation. For example, a common preparation is a reflex pathway in the spinal cord of an animal. Here the firing of one set of neurons (the dorsal root fibers) has a tendency to fire some associated neurons (the ventral root fibers). If tetanic stimulation at a rate of about 300 stimulations per second is applied to the first set of neurons, it results in an enhanced ability (i.e., lowered threshold) of the first set of neurons to fire the second set. This enhanced ability lasts for several minutes after the tetanic stimulation is terminated, and thus the effect is called posttetanic potentiation (PTP). PTP is then suggested to be a model of how learning might occur by synaptic changes following continued stimulation.

At first Eccles suggested that the effects of tetanic stimulation were due to a swelling or growth of the neuron in the area of the synapse. However, as Grossman (1967, p. 837) argues, "the proposed swelling does not, per se, increase the size or number of the vesicles containing the humoral transmitter substance which presumably is responsible for the propagation of impulses across the synapse." In light of this, Eccles by the mid-1960's was putting more emphasis on changes in the chemical transmission mechanism of the synapse.

There are a number of problems in using PTP as a model of learning. First is the fact that the changes are usually only seen after about 10,000 stimulations. But learning may require only one trial. Thus it is necessary to postulate some process (perhaps the reverberatory circuits discussed in Chapter 4) that is started by a single learning trial, but keeps going until the neurons are fired 10,000 times. It may be that there is no such process that naturally produces PTP in intact animals. A second problem is that the effect of PTP is only temporary, making it necessary to add other mechanisms to explain long term memories. A third problem is that the effects of PTP may not be specific enough to explain learning. That is, PTP appears to involve all the synapses of the fired neurons, which means an increased tendency to fire the hundreds or thousands of neurons that might synapse with the tetanic stimulated neuron. This effect then is probably too diffuse for learning. Learning more probably would involve only synaptic changes between a few select neurons, and thus only a few of the synapses of a neuron. To accomplish this more limited specificity some theorists (e.g., Hebb, 1949) assume that for learning to occur and produce the required synaptic changes *both* neurons to be associated must be fired together.

Although most synaptic theories talk about learning in terms of positive changes such as growth at the synapse, learning might also involve negative changes such as a shrinkage in contact area at the synapse. One paper (Rosenzweig, Møllgaard, Diamond, Bennett, 1972) suggests that the "structural synaptic changes underlying learning and memory storage need not be of a single form, but rather may take one or more of these four forms: (a) increase in number of synapses, (b) increase in size of contact areas, (c) decrease in number, and (d) decrease in size of contact."

Deutsch (1968, 1971) has done a series of experiments designed to investigate chemical changes in the synapses that might underlie learning. He investigated those synapses in which the transmitter substance appeared to be acetylcholine (ACh). When released, ACh leaves the synaptic vesicles of one neuron, crosses the synaptic cleft to the next neuron, and has an excitatory effect on this second neuron. Then the ACh is broken down by the enzyme acetylcholinesterase (AChE). This prevents too much ACh from building up and interfering with future synaptic transmission. Deutsch used a variety of drugs, including drugs that interfere with ACh activity by blocking the receptor sites that ACh stimulates, drugs that produce similar effects as ACh but are resistant to being broken down by AChE, and drugs that inhibit the functioning of AChE. By manipulating the dosages of different drugs that enter the synapses and different learning variables, Deutsch mapped out the types of synaptic changes that correlate with learning. A problem with any such research that utilizes drugs is that the effect of the drug may not be due to the reason suspected but may merely be an artifact of some other effect of the drug. The drug may be producing some side effect that the researcher is not aware of and thus may produce misleading results.

From his research Deutsch concluded that learning involves changes in the efficiency with which synapses transmit messages. He suggests that this increased transmission efficiency is due to an increase in the sensitivity of the receptor neuron to respond to the transmitter substance. This sensitivity increases for some time after initial learning and then declines. The rate of initial increase depends on the amount of learning. The decline in sensitivity may correspond to forgetting.

RNA-PROTEIN MODELS

Besides neuronal-synaptic models, another approach to the physiology of learning and memory has centered around specific molecules that may store learned information. First let us consider an oversimplified model of how proteins are produced: In the nucleus of a cell is *DNA* (deoxyribonucleic acid), which contains the genetic information. DNA is a long chain in the form of a double helix, similar to a spiral staircase. A major constituent of the DNA is a *base* (a nitrogenous base) which comes in one of four types. DNA molecules differ in the particular sequence of these bases that occur in a long string along the DNA. Since the sequence of these bases probably determines which proteins will eventually be produced, including genetic characteristics, the sequence is called the *genetic code*.

With the DNA as a pattern or template, a form of *RNA* (ribonucleic acid), called *messenger RNA,* is formed in the nucleus. Having received the genetic code about which proteins to produce, the messenger RNA moves into the cytoplasm of the cell. Here the messenger RNA synthesizes proteins from amino acids brought to it by a different type of RNA called *transfer RNA*. These proteins are complex molecules that are the basis for all living cells.

Although the above DNA-RNA-Protein sequence is fairly well established (although in a much more complex form), the relation to learning is quite speculative. Since behavior depends on what neurons fire and in what patterns, physiological theories of learning must include variables related to neuronal firing. There are basically two such relationships to be considered here. First, some of the proteins produced will affect the cell metabolism of the neurons and hence their firing pattern and/or they might affect some other aspect of neural transmission such as by directly affecting the transmitter substance. Second, there is evidence, discussed below, that neural firing affects the synthesis and type of RNA. These relationships are shown in Figure 2–2.

A theory of learning then might be as follows: A learning experience results in certain neurons firing. This neural activity affects RNA (or perhaps DNA), which in turn alters the type of protein synthesis, which then affects future firing of the neuron. Probably no one holds such a simple theory, but many theories have something similar to this at their core. DNA models, RNA models, and protein models will now be discussed separately as possible explanations of memory storage. Memories, however, may be more complex than any of these proposed storage systems. Memory storage may involve a number of different components, such as RNA plus proteins plus neuronal chemistry.

DNA is seldom considered as the site of memory storage, for two reasons. First, there is some question as to whether DNA ever changes or is influenced by neural activity, which appears to be a necessary prerequisite for memory storage. The second reason is that if DNA were to be changed it might hinder DNA's prime function, the eventual production of very specific proteins. The cells might be able to afford to use some RNA and proteins for memory storage, but perhaps not the number that would result from changes in the DNA.

There have, however, been some DNA theories of learning. Gaito (1963) suggested that DNA might be the seat of memory. He dealt with the above problems by suggesting that the DNA of nerve cells might be different from the DNA usually studied by the biochemists (such as from the liver and pancreas). Gaito, however, later abandoned this theory. Griffith and Mahler (1969) have proposed what they call a DNA-ticketing theory of memory. They suggest that the sequence of nucleotides that

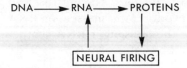

Figure 2–2 *Possible biochemical relationships in learning.*

compose DNA may be modified by enzyme activity which may produce changes in the bases away from the original four types. These base changes then alter the function of the DNA and the type of protein synthesized, which may then affect the firing of the neuron.

Most of the research and theories, however, have centered around RNA and related proteins (Booth, 1967; Gaito & Bonnett, 1971; Glassman, 1969; Gurowitz, 1969; Horn et al., 1973; Ungar, 1970). There is an abundance of RNA in brain cells, and this RNA is very responsive to neural activity. That is, if a particular area of the brain is activated, either artificially stimulated directly or because the animal is involved in a task utilizing this brain area, there is an increase in the amount of RNA synthesized in this area. As the stimulation becomes excessive there may be a decrease in the RNA. Pevzner (1966) and Gaito and Bonnett (1971) provide the following summary: With moderate stimulation (sound, electrical, vestibular) there is an increase in RNA in the appropriate brain area. With excessive stimulation (revolver shot, fatigue, electroshock) there is a decrease in the amount of RNA. Similar relationships should also hold for the related proteins (Gaito & Bonnett, 1971).

But a simple increase in the amount of RNA is probably not specific enough to justify RNA as a memory molecule. Rather it seems necessary to look for qualitatively different changes in RNA molecules as a function of the specific learning experiences. This is what Hyden attempted to do in a series of classic experiments.

In the first experiment (Hyden & Egyhazi, 1962) an experimental group of rats was trained to walk up a wire at a 45-degree angle to the floor. The behavior involved in such a task depends on the vestibular nucleus, a group of neurons concerned with balance. A second group of rats, the functional control group, was slowly rotated in a centrifuge to control for the vestibular stimulation the first group experienced. A third group, the no-treatment control group, was not given any special treatment. Following the treatments, an analysis on all rats was made of the RNA in the nuclei of cells (Deiter's cells) in the vestibular nucleus. For the first two groups, the experimentals and the functional controls, but not for the no-treatment controls, the vestibular stimulation resulted in an increase in the amount of RNA. But there were differences in the relative amounts (ratios) of the different bases making up the RNA of the two groups. Climbing the wire resulted in the production of RNA with ratios of the bases making up the RNA different from those of the RNA resulting from the centrifuge spinning. This suggests that different learning experiences might be coded in terms of the bases of the RNA.

Associated with neurons are non-neural cells called *glia* or glial cells. A later experiment (Hyden & Egyhazi, 1963) showed that the types of RNA changes found in the neurons of the vestibular nucleus could also be found in the glia associated with these neurons.

Although very important and suggestive, there are a number of problems with these experiments. First, it is not clear whether the experimental rats can really be said to be learning to climb the wire, for they learned to do it very quickly, with some of the rats performing perfectly on the first trial. Second, the experimental groups and the functional control groups may not be equated on the amount of vestibular stimulation. Actively walking up a wire may produce a different amount of stimulation of the vestibular nucleus than is produced when the rats are passively being rotated. Third, a sensory nucleus, such as the vestibular nucleus, seems an improbable site for storing memories. Finally, the different effects observed disappear after 24 hours. Hence we need some other mechanism to account for long term memories.

Some of the above problems were avoided in another experiment (Hyden & Egyhazi, 1964). Rats were first trained to reach for food with one paw. Then they were forced to use the other paw to get the food (transfer of handedness). Studies of those parts of the cortex associated with the different paws showed changes in the bases of the RNA with the transfer of handedness.

Over the years Hyden has suggested a number of models relating his experiments to the molecular basis of learning and memory. He has described one of his more recent models as follows:

> *At learning,* a sequence of events leads to a fixation of memory. Information-rich modulated frequencies, field changes, transcription into messenger RNA in both neuron and glia, synthesis of proteins in the neuron, give a biochemical differentiation of the neuron-glia unit in millions, a readiness to respond on a common type of stimulus.
>
> *At retrieval,* it is the simultaneous occurrence of the three variables: electrical patterns, the transfer of RNA from glia to neurons, and the presence of the unique proteins in the neuron, which decide whether the individual neuron will respond or not. (Hyden, 1970, p. 116.)

Gaito and Bonnett (1971) have questioned whether Hyden's experiments show that learning results in any changes in the base ratios of RNA or whether it is merely an artifact of increasing the quantity of one type of RNA, with a particular base ratio, over other types of RNA. In other words, learning results in an increase in total RNA in the relevant brain areas, which increase may involve different RNA with different base ratios. Perhaps learning experiences cause a greater production of one type of RNA than of another. Since Hyden's analyses generally involve pooling all the RNA from one area, the changes in base ratios of RNA may be due to the differential production of one type of RNA rather than to a change of the base ratios of RNA within any particular RNA molecule. Gaito and Bonnett conclude that there currently is "*no* conclusive evidence to indicate that qualitatively different RNA and/or protein species are synthesized during learning and other behaviors."

If RNA is related to learning in some way, then perhaps injections of RNA could facilitate learning. Cameron and Solyom (1961) reported that they could improve learning and retention in senile humans by giving them yeast RNA. Later reports, although often somewhat confusing and contradictory, seemed to support this general finding. However, there are a number of problems with this research (cf. Sweet, 1969).

The main problem is that the effect may simply be due to a general stimulant effect. The RNA (perhaps through the intermediary of serum uric acid) might simply improve *performance*, not *learning*, by increasing the amount of overall stimulation. If this is true, then the effect could be produced by a whole range of stimulant drugs unrelated to RNA. This seems to be the case.

Even if the effect is somewhat specific to RNA, it may not be the RNA itself but some of its breakdown constituents (e.g., nucleotides) that produce the effect. Perhaps learning and memory optimally require a certain level of supply of nucleotides, and some senile humans go below this level. Thus by providing the extra needed nucleotides (or whatever constituents), learning and memories are improved. If this is the case then such injections might help only those people whose level of supply has fallen below the ideal level and would not help people with normal levels.

In 1955 Thompson and McConnell reported the conditioning of planaria (flatworms). Weak electric shock causes the planaria to contract their bodies. When the shock was paired with a light, the planaria eventually learned to contract to the light alone. (This is a form of respondent conditioning to be discussed in Chapter 5.) Later McConnell (1962), using the planaria, began the controversial *memory transfer* experiments. These experiments involve training one animal on a specific task and then seeing if the animal's memory of this task can be biochemically transferred to some extent to another animal. McConnell began by conditioning some planaria to contract to light. These planaria, called donors, were then chopped into small pieces and fed to untrained cannibal planaria, the recipients. Control recipients were fed untrained donors. All recipients then were conditioned to contract to the light. The recipients that ate trained donors learned faster than recipients that ate untrained donors, making more correct responses from the first day of conditioning. This suggested to McConnell that perhaps some of the memory of the donor was biochemically transferred to the receiver. It appeared that RNA might be the molecule responsible for the transfer.

These experiments evoked considerable controversy (cf. McConnell & Shelby, 1970). Some people could not replicate the effects, and there were debates about experimental procedures. A popular argument is that it is not learning that is transferred, but only sensitization. For example, Hartry and associates (1964) reported that they could get the same cannibalism effect if the donor had any of a number of treatments such as exposure to light alone. Thus they argued that all that is transferred is a sensitivity to respond to certain stimuli. Therefore the reason the experimental recipients learn faster is that they have a sensitivity to simply respond more to the stimuli involved in the conditioning task.

In addition to arguments about Hartry's procedures, there are problems with the general sensitization argument. First, learning has been defined in this book as including sensitization. Thus, by this definition, it makes no sense to say that no learning is transferred, only sensitization. Second, as will be seen in one example below, there are many transfer experiments that suggest that something more complex and specific than sensitization is being transferred.

In the mid-1960's Danish and American investigators began reporting memory transfer studies with rats. In one of the first studies Fjerdingstad and associates (1965) trained rats in a two-alley runway to approach a light. After training, these donors were sacrificed, their brains removed, and the RNA extracted from their brains. This RNA was then injected into naive recipient rats. Control recipients either received no RNA or received RNA from naive rats. All recipients were then trained on the light approach task, with the experimental recipients learning faster than either set of controls.

Albert (1966) trained rats on an avoidance task where the rats on cue had to escape from one compartment to another to avoid shock. The rats were trained with the cortex of one hemisphere or half of the brain made temporarily non-functional through a procedure called *spreading depression*. Spreading depression occurs when the cortex is stimulated by certain forms of electrical, mechanical, or chemical stimulation which inhibit or depress the normal electrical activity of the cortex. This depression effect spreads from the point of stimulation through the cortex of that hemisphere. In Albert's experiment the spreading depression restricted the cortical part of the memory to form only in the unaffected hemisphere. After training, Albert extracted part of the cortex of the rats. For the experimental group he extracted the area that appeared to be involved in the memory of the avoidance task. For the control rats he extracted a different part of the cortex. The RNA from each cortical area was extracted and injected back into the cavity around the stomach area of the same rat from which it was taken. The spreading depression was then switched from the untrained hemisphere to the trained hemisphere, and the rats were retrained on the avoidance task. Thus each rat had to relearn the avoidance with the half of the brain that was nonfunctional during the first learning, plus each rat had some of his own RNA injected back into him. The results of the experiment were that the experimental rats, who received RNA from a trained area of cortex, relearned much faster than the control rats.

Braud and Braud (1972) trained donor rats to choose the larger of two circles. The rats' brains were then extracted, homogenized, and injected into recipient rats. The recipients were then given a choice between two circles, the larger of the two circles the donors had been trained on plus a still larger circle. The recipients, without training, had a significantly greater tendency to choose the larger of the two circles presented to them. Control rats showed no significant preference. This suggests that responding to a relationship between stimuli (always pick the larger) can be transferred biochemically. Sensitization to specific stimuli cannot account for this result. Perhaps there is sensitization to the larger-smaller relationship, but this is a more complex form of sensitization than most sensitization explanations usually suggest.

Many experimenters have not been able to replicate the memory transfer experiments and/or do not believe the reported results. Luttges and associates (1966), for example, reported unsuccessful attempts at demonstrating memory transfer. Also, when radioactively labeled RNA was injected into the stomach cavity, where RNA is often injected in transfer studies, there was no evidence that any significant amount got to the brain. Debates about why transfer studies are not replicated generally center around subtleties of training procedures and methods of extracting the active material.

The issue of the active material is fairly complex. Most of the RNA extracts used in transfer studies are impure, containing DNA and proteins, and perhaps peptides and other substances which might account for the transfer effect. Thus the effect may have nothing to do with RNA but rather may depend on some "impurity." Perhaps the effect is based on some constituent of RNA after RNA is broken down. If one of these alternatives is true, it may not matter whether RNA molecules can reach the brain from the stomach cavity.

Protecting the brain is a functional barrier called the *blood brain barrier*, which keeps some substances from passing from the blood into the brain. It is often suggested that RNA molecules are too big to pass through this barrier, and that RNA injected into the body of an animal will not get to the brain. But it is not clear whether the blood brain barrier will always stop RNA (Albert, 1966).

A conceptual problem for memory transfer experiments is to explain how the RNA molecules (or whatever the active ingredient is), after reaching the brain of the recipient rat, are able to find and affect exactly those neurons that are related to the specific behavior or tendency being transferred. This is particularly difficult in light of the fact that although the brains of two different rats show a number of similarities of organization, they are also very different in many respects.

Best (1968) has proposed the following theory to account for the problems just discussed: Each genetically determined neuron is identified with a specific code which is part of its DNA. This identifier can be coded into other molecules, such as messenger RNA and polypeptide molecules, which then affect the efficacy of synapses by interacting with similarly coded proteins. Thus each molecule can only facilitate the one neuron which it matches in code. Transfer effects, then, depend on the injected molecules affecting (perhaps indirectly) specific neurons with matching codes.

Recently many theorists have been giving more emphasis to proteins as possible memory molecules. An early protein model of memory was suggested by Katz and Halstead (1950). According to this model, learning results in proteins that are capable of reproducing themselves. Some of these replicas then become part of the membrane of the neuron ("membrane organization"), which facilitates the neuron's ability to affect adjacent neurons. Memory traces were assumed to be composed of evolving protein lattices interrelating various neurons. In terms of things learned since 1950 we now see that Katz and Halstead made a false assumption about proteins serving as templates for the reproduction of other proteins. However, with changes the theory might still be viable.

The more recent experiments have primarily utilized drugs, such as puromycin, that are assumed to disrupt protein synthesis but which do not interfere with RNA synthesis. If such a drug given to an animal after a learning experience disrupts the memory of the experience, this suggests that the memory is stored in proteins rather than in RNA.

The first series of such experiments was begun by Flexner and his associates in 1962 (Flexner et al., 1962). Mice were trained to avoid shock in a Y-maze. After learning they were injected with puromycin, which appeared to disrupt the memories. Similar effects of protein blocking agents on learning have been reported for goldfish (Agranoff, 1967).

Later, however, Flexner and Flexner (1968) reported that the puromycin-disrupted memories recover over time, and that the recovery can be facilitated with injections of saline. This recovery suggests that the effects of puromycin are more on the expression of the memory than on the storage per se. Or, as Booth (1970, p. 25) suggested, the original effects of puromycin might have been on retrieval or on the subjects' ability to be frightened, or both.

Unfortunately, the effects of drugs such as puromycin are not as clean as often assumed, but are often quite diverse. More information on the direct and indirect effects of such drugs is necessary for our understanding of research such as the above.

DNA, RNA, and proteins, with their complex sequences of bases and other constituents, appear to have enough complexity and storage space to store learned information. But there are some general problems:

RNA and most proteins are quite short lived, the average life span for a protein being about 8 hours. Therefore any theory that attempts to explain long term memory in terms of RNA and/or proteins requires some type of system that perpetuates those types of molecules or other physiological changes that are assumed to underlie long term memory.

It also may be that there are several different stages of learning, each with different properties and physiological substrates. RNA and proteins may be involved in only one stage of learning in a sequence of stages.

GLIAL MODELS

Associated with neurons are non-neural cells called glia. In man's brain there are 5 to 10 times as many glial cells as neurons. Glia provide structural support, aid in the metabolism of the neurons, help maintain the water–salt balance, and aid the transmission from the blood in the capillaries to the neurons. By affecting the metabolism of the neuron, glia can affect the firing rate of the neuron, and thus might be involved in learning. However, neuronal theories are in vogue, and most theorists emphasize neurons instead of the more numerous glia. Some exceptions are noted in the following paragraphs.

As mentioned above, Hyden and Egyhazi (1963) found RNA changes in glia similar to those found in the related neurons. In Hyden's theorizing he generally considers the neuron and its glia as a metabolic and functional unit involved in learning.

Galambos (1961) also saw the glia and neurons working together as functional units. He suggested that the glia might be "genetically charged to organize and program neuron activity" and thus provide the basis for memory. To a large extent, then, the neurons "merely execute the instructions glia give them." According to this model, glia receive impulses, organize them somehow, and in some way give order to the neural activity. To Galambos the relationship of glia to the brain is like that of a program to a computer. Galambos also suggests that glia might be capable of some electrical activity, such as slow wave activity.

NON-CONNECTIONISTIC THEORIES

Other approaches to the study of the physiology of learning have emphasized the electrical properties of the nervous system. Electrodes on the skull of the subject, as with an *electroencephalogram* (EEG), can measure gross electrical activity of the brain. Such measures are good for identifying general states of the organism, such as how aroused it is. More localized information can be obtained by lowering fine electrodes into the brain itself. These electrodes can then measure the electrical activity of a small group of neurons or even of a single neuron. By recording under what situations neurons fire and the pattern of their firing we can attempt to map out the function of the neurons and the changes in them that correlate with learning. Electrodes in the brain can also be used to electrically (or chemically) stimulate and fire specific neurons in order to study their function.

Using such procedures, a variety of studies (John, 1961; Morrell, 1961) have investigated phenomena such as the following: the conditioning of specific brain waves as measured by the EEG, changes in the electrical activity of specific brain areas with different stages of learning, the effects on learning of the electrical stimulation of specific brain areas, and the effects on learning of electrical currents of different polarity.

E. Roy John and his co-workers (John, 1961, 1972) ran a series of learning experiments in which they used lights that flickered at specific frequencies. They chose frequencies within the range to which the brain can respond. That is, when a flickering light is presented to an organism, groups of neurons in the brain, particularly in the visual system, may tend to fire in a pattern that corresponds to the flicker frequency. By investigating the neurons that fire to a specific pattern, an attempt is made to discover what information is being carried by these neurons.

For example, in one experiment (John et al., 1969) cats were trained on a task in which they discriminated between two frequencies of light flicker. For one frequency (V_1) the cats pressed the right lever for food. For the other frequency (V_2) the cats pressed the left lever to avoid being shocked. After the cats were well trained, they were exposed to a novel stimulus (V_3) with a frequency midway between V_1 and V_2. Electrical activity (averaged evoked potentials) was recorded from various brain areas such as the visual system (visual cortex, lateral geniculate). These recordings showed that specific and different wave shapes were elicited by V_1 and V_2. When V_3 was first introduced, the cat generalized and made the response appropriate to V_1 or V_2. The wave pattern recorded during this presentation of V_3 was thus similar to that recorded during V_1 or V_2, depending on which response was made. If the cat, when presented with V_3, pressed the right lever (the response learned to V_1), the electrical activity to V_3 would be similar to that of V_1. If the cat pressed the left lever, the V_3 activity would correspond to the activity caused by V_2.

It thus appears that the pattern activity of the visual system to the novel stimulus V_3 depends in part on whether the cat "interprets" the stimulus as being an example of V_1 or V_2. The experimenters concluded that "the shape of the evoked potential released by a novel stimulus during generalization is not solely determined by the actual physical stimulus but contains an endogenous component which varies depending upon the meaning attributed by the animal to the signal."

On the basis of experiments like the one above, John (John 1967,

1972) has proposed a *statistical configuration theory* of learning. Following a learning experience the relevant neurons are involved in a coherent pattern of activity. Neurons always have some baseline activity, but the learning causes the relevant neurons to now fire in a coherent pattern. This activity is assumed to result in a common change in cellular chemistry, which increases the probability that the next time the neurons fire they will display the coherent pattern. Memory, then, is stored as the probability of coherence of neural firing. A memory is recorded in terms of electrical patterns from many neurons, like the patterns that flicker-frequency V_3 first elicited in the generalization study. According to this theory, "remembering" and "thinking" are subjective experiences corresponding to the release of the electrical wave-shape representing a specific memory. An important point is that the memory requires a particular *pattern* of activity, but does not necessarily require the participation of any specific neurons. All that is needed is enough of the neurons to produce sufficient patterned activity for memory.

John's theory is an example of a *non-connectionistic theory* since it does not depend on specific connections, as, for example, do most neural-synaptic theories. A non-connectionistic theory of learning is one whose postulated physiological base does not depend on fixed specific neuronal or molecular connections. Most such theories, often in the tradition of Karl Lashley, explain learning in terms of a physiological organization with interchangeable constituents. Pribram (1971a, p. 9), in discussing his approach to non-connectionistic theories, assumes that "certain interactions important to the organization of behavior and the psychological processes occur in brain tissue, and that these interactions cannot be specified solely in terms of permanent associative connections among neurons." Non-connectionistic theories do not disregard synaptic relationships, as such relationships obviously impose some order and restrictions on the brain. Non-connectionistic theories merely argue that learning cannot be reduced to a specific set of synaptic connections between specific neurons, but rather involves a more general organization.

A number of arguments are offered in favor of non-connectionistic theories. One set of arguments hinges on the apparent plasticity of sensory and response systems. A person can easily learn to respond to a relationship between stimuli (e.g., always choosing the smaller of two things) regardless of which stimuli are presented on each trial. A person who has learned to write with his right hand can still write to a certain extent if a pencil is put into his mouth, even though this is an entirely different response system. These examples illustrate that people don't learn simple associations (or connections) between specific stimuli and responses. Perhaps, then, the generalized nature of learning is easier explained by non-connectionistic theories.

Another argument relates to the often reported recovery of function following brain ablation (i.e., situations where parts of the brain have been destroyed or removed). Following such an operation or accident the organism may lose some function that was associated with the part of the brain that was destroyed. With time, the organism often regains this function. If the function depends on some past learning, the recovery of function suggests that the memory was stored in a number of different places and/or that the memory was stored in a non-connectionistic fashion and could afford the loss of some specific neurons.

Pribram (1969, 1971a, 1971b) has offered an interesting non-connectionistic model of the brain based on parallels with a form of photography called *holography.* One way to do holography is to take a light source from a laser and split it in two. One part goes directly to a photographic film, while the other part is reflected from the object being photographed onto the film. The film then contains a record, called a *hologram,* of the interference patterns of the two beams of light. If the hologram is then illuminated with a similar light, it will recreate the object photographed. The recreation is extremely lifelike, with definite three dimensional aspects to it. When looking at a scene from a hologram, the viewer, by moving his head, can see the photographed objects from different angles, including looking around and behind objects.

Pribram suggests that images and memories may be stored and produced by processes similar to those of holography: Neural activity produces momentary wave fronts which result in interactions between different wave fronts. These interactions, or interference patterns, might be recorded by some biochemical change in a manner similar to a hologram.

An interesting property of holography is that almost the entire original scene can be reproduced from just a piece of the hologram. If memories are stored as holograms, this phenomenon might correspond to the brain's ability to retrieve a whole item of information from any of a number of different pieces of the information. One of the mysteries of human memory is how we can retrieve information so quickly on the basis of just a few related cues.

Another aspect of holography is that an enormous amount of information can be stored in a small area, with the same part of a hologram involved in entirely different information systems. If the brain works in this way, this would explain how we have the flexibility and information storage necessary for learning.

All of the different models discussed above (neuronal-synaptic models, RNA-protein models, glial models, and non-connectionistic theories) are currently very speculative and probably too simplified to completely account for the complex process of learning. (It should be noted, however, that these models are much more intricate than was presented here.) That is, although many of the models are quite complex, they are probably not as complex as the physiological processes underlying learning. But this is a relatively new and incomplete field of study that is rapidly advancing. Future research findings may help us to integrate the different models, add new constructs, and gradually evolve a model for the physiology of learning and memory.

MEMORY TRACES

Between 1917 and 1950 Lashley searched for a place where a memory trace or *engram* was localized. His general approach was to train experimental animals on specific learning tasks and then to make localized cuts or ablations in the cortex. Cortical destruction in some areas could disrupt the learning or retention of a specific activity (e.g., destruction of parts of the visual cortex might impair some visual tasks). But Lashley was looking for areas where his destruction of the brain would disrupt an engram — a learned association — and not merely simple activities. In 1950 he reported his failure to find such an engram by his procedures (Lashley, 1950).

Lashley suggested that the reason for his failure to find an engram was due to the multiple representation of memories. That is, memories might be stored in more than one place, so that destruction of one memory site would not eliminate all copies of the memory from storage. Another interpretation is that memory systems are too complex to be reflected by the surgical and experimental procedures used by Lashley. Perhaps more extensive cortical and subcortical destruction or more sensitive tasks might have shown more positive results.

Evidence in favor of localized memory traces has been offered by Penfield (Penfield, 1954; Penfield & Jasper, 1954). Penfield's experiments involved the electrical stimulation of the temporal lobe (along the side of the head) of the cortex of humans. The subjects would then report what subjective experience they had when electrically stimulated in different parts of this cortex. Penfield found that many stimulations seemed to produce recollection of old, and often forgotten, memories. The memory might be a specific visual image or the hearing of a specific sound, or both. These memories included all of the original associations and emotions attached to the memories. The effect of the stimulation seemed to include in the memory everything the person was aware of at the time of original learning. Stimulation of the same area of cortex on successive days always produced the same general experience. The subject could, however, by shifting his attention, pick out slightly different details each time.

This suggests that the brain may work something like a tape recorder, except that where the tape recorder records only sound on the tape, the brain records sound, visual images, emotions, and all other inputs on its "tape." Memories then, whether occurring naturally or because of electrical stimulation of the brain, involve playing back some part of the brain's tape.

There are some complexities, however, in interpreting Penfield's findings. First, although Penfield produced memories by stimulating the cortex, most memories probably involve subcortical components (those parts of the brain beneath the cortex). For example, when a memory elicits an emotion in a person, it is hard to understand neurophysiologically how such an effect could occur without participation of subcortical areas known to be involved in the particular emotion. A second complication is that the electrical stimulation might not be stimulating specific memory traces, but may be stimulating some more general mechanism which in turn produces the memory.

Interhemispheric Transfer

The brain of man is divided into two halves, or hemispheres. The left hemisphere influences the right side of the body, whereas the right hemisphere is more concerned with the left side of the body. The two hemispheres are almost mirror images of each other in appearance and function. Most functions served by some area in one hemisphere also occur in a similar place in the other hemisphere. Thus the brain is highly redundant, which has obvious advantages in terms of protection from the results of brain injury. We might expect then that memory systems might also be redundant between hemispheres.

There are some exceptions to the functional symmetry of the hemispheres. One is that in the more complex animals, such as monkeys and man, one hemisphere is stronger, or *dominant* to the other hemisphere. In most humans the left hemisphere is dominant to the right. Hence there are more right-handed people than left-handed because the left hemisphere primarily controls the right side of the body.

Another major difference between the hemispheres is that in most humans, after the first couple of years of life, the "speech center" of the brain is primarily localized in the left hemsiphere. Thus damage to this area, such as from a stroke, is harder to recover from because of the lack of equivalent functioning in the right hemisphere.

The hemispheres differ in a number of other functions, many of which favor one hemisphere or the other. The reader is referred to the articles by Kimura (1973) and Ornstein (1973) for further information in this area.

Many nerve fibers, and bundles of nerve fibers called *commissures*, connect the two hemispheres. The *corpus callosum,* or *great cerebral commissure,* is the main commissure interconnecting the hemispheres. It appears that a major function of the corpus callosum is the transmission of information from one hemisphere to the other. From the perspective of learning this raises the following questions: Let us assume, as many theorists do, that equivalent memory traces are often laid down in the two different hemispheres. Does this mean that memories are laid down in both hemispheres simultaneously or is the memory laid down in one hemisphere and then transferred (as by the corpus callosum) to the other hemisphere, or is learning a combination of both these processes? Perhaps which of these alternatives occurs depends on the nature or difficulty of the learning task. The process of information going from one hemisphere to the other is called *interhemispheric transfer*.

The most popular way of studying interhemispheric transfer utilizes the procedures of *spreading depression*, described earlier, in which waves of depressed electrocortical activity are induced to spread through the cortex of one hemisphere. There are several advantages to spreading depression: First, it is an easy way to make the cortex of a hemisphere largely non-functional, particularly with respect to learning. Second, it stays fairly well restricted to the hemisphere in which it is induced, leaving the other hemisphere normal. Third, the effect is reversible, dissipating over time. Although spreading depression primarily affects the cortex, it also affects some subcortical areas (e.g., the thalamus and hypothalamus). It should also be kept in mind that although spreading depression may disrupt interhemispheric transfer at the cortical level, it may have little effect on any transfer at the subcortical level.

The type of experiment used on interhemispheric transfer is as follows: An animal is trained on a learning task with one hemisphere (the left, for example) depressed by spreading depression. If the animal is later tested on the same task with the left hemisphere functional and the right one depressed, it will behave as if it had never learned the task, for the learning was restricted to the right hemisphere which is now non-functional. However, if after the learning with the left hemisphere depressed the animal is allowed a few trials on the task with both hemispheres functional, the animal when later tested with the right hemisphere depressed shows retention of the learning. It seems that the trials with both hemispheres functional allowed the information from the right hemisphere to transfer to the left hemisphere.

Russell and Ochs (1963) trained rats to press a bar under unilateral spreading depression (applied to one side or hemisphere). They found evidence for some interhemispheric transfer if they allowed the rat one rewarded trial with both hemispheres functional. Just letting the rat sit with both hemispheres functional did not result in any transfer. They also reported no transfer if the rat was not rewarded on the one trial (other studies have not shown the necessity for the reward).

Schneider (1967) has questioned the interpretations of the interhemispheric transfer studies and has proposed an alternative stimulus generalization explanation. He argues that unilateral spreading depression provides very pronounced stimuli to which the response is learned. The apparent loss of memory when spreading depression is shifted to the other hemisphere, then, is simply due to the large shift in stimuli. Schneider suggests that learning is not affected, because it could be stored subcortically. For example, suppose a rat with spreading depression on the left hemisphere is trained to turn left in a T-maze. The effects of the spreading depression are that the right side of the rat's body feels differently and provides different sensory cues (e.g., from paralyzed muscles). So the rat in learning to turn left in the maze may be learning to turn in the direction opposite this different side of its body. If spreading depression is now shifted to the right hemisphere, causing the left side of the body to feel different, the rat might now turn to the right, away from the strange side of the body. Its turning right, when it was "supposed to" turn left, might look like a memory failure when, in fact, it is only due to a change in the stimuli.

Schneider and Ebbesen (1967) redid the Russell and Ochs study, but included another group. All rats were trained to bar-press with unilateral spreading depression. Then the first group, as in the Russell and Ochs study, was given a single rewarded trial with neither hemisphere depressed. The second group, however, received the rewarded trial with the trained hemisphere depressed. Both groups were then tested for bar-pressing with the trained hemisphere depressed. Although both groups showed a greater tendency to bar-press following the one rewarded trial than they did before this trial, the increase was more for the second group (the one with the trained hemisphere depressed). This fits Schneider's theory, for the second group had more experience (the rewarded trial) pressing the bar in the presence of the stimuli resulting from shifting the spreading depression from one hemisphere to another.

As we can see from the preceding examples, the conclusions to be drawn from interhemispheric transfer studies are still uncertain. Schneider's studies have shown the important stimulus aspects of spreading depression and how some of the effect can be explained in terms of stimulus generalization. In this sense spreading depression is another variable affecting the organism's state as in state-dependent learning. But, as originally suggested, spreading depression might also disrupt the formation of cortical memory traces. Future research will have to separate the different effects of spreading depression to clarify exactly how it works.

Split-Brain Studies

If the corpus callosum *is* involved in transmitting information from one hemisphere to the other, a simple way of investigating this is by severing the corpus callosum. Such preparations, called *split-brain studies*, generally also involve severing other connections, such as other commissures and sometimes the optic chiasm. Subcortical connections, and thus possible subcortical transfer, is left intact.

The idea of split-brain studies is to separate the two hemispheres so that they can be trained separately. Since the left half of the visual field feeds the right hemisphere and the right half feeds the left hemisphere, the experimenter can control what information gets to which hemisphere by where in the visual field he presents the information. If, because the corpus callosum is cut, the hemispheres cannot exchange information, it is as if the hemispheres are two brains learning independently. Although most of the earlier experiments were done on infrahumans, the discussion below will deal only with humans, describing some of the work done by R. W. Sperry and his associates (Gazzaniga, 1967; Sperry, 1968).

The main reason for cutting the corpus callosum in humans is that this surgery appears to decrease the spread and occurrence of epileptic seizures. The operation does not produce any noticeable change in the person's temperament, personality, or general intelligence. However, split-brain humans do appear to have some deficits in short term memory; they fatigue more quickly in mental tasks, and they often favor the right side of the body (the side controlled by the dominant hemisphere).

Generally the two hemispheres of the split-brain human learn the same things. As both eyes usually see about the same thing and both ears hear about the same thing, generally both hemispheres receive about the same input. It is only in special situations where the hemispheres can be given different inputs that differences can be observed.

Since in humans speech-related functions are generally and primarily localized in the left hemisphere, information presented only to the right hemisphere cannot be responded to verbally. For example, if a split-brain human is shown a picture of a pencil in his left visual field (which feeds to the right hemisphere) and then asked what he saw, he will verbally insist he saw nothing. For the left hemisphere with the speech functions has no information of anything being seen. However, if the person is asked to point with his left hand to what he saw, he will point to a pencil. For although the right hemisphere can't "speak," it *can* point a finger. Or if a funny picture is presented to the right hemisphere, the person may laugh but not be able to verbalize what is funny.

Similarly, consider a split-brain human whose left hemisphere sees (in the right visual field) a question mark, while the right hemisphere sees a dollar sign. If the person is now asked to draw with his left hand what he saw (keeping his left hand out of sight while he draws) his left hand draws a dollar sign. If he is then asked what he just drew, he will say that he drew a question mark.

The split-brain studies suggest that the two hemispheres of a split-brain person can learn independently. Later it will be suggested that there might even be two independent streams of consciousness. The studies also suggest that a function of the corpus callosum is to transfer learned information from one hemisphere to the other.

The split-brain human, if given two simple tasks, each of which can be handled by a single hemisphere, can do two different tasks at the same time. With more complex tasks it is often better if both hemispheres work together.

One hemisphere may try to cue the other hemisphere in on the correct response. In one task a red or green light was presented to the subject's right hemisphere and the subject then had to verbally (i.e., using his left hemisphere) guess what color he saw. The left hemisphere verbally guessed a response (at a chance level x) even though the right hemisphere presumably knew the correct answer. After a while, however, it appeared that whenever the right hemisphere would hear the left hemisphere say an incorrect guess, the right hemisphere would make the person frown and shake his head. Perceiving the head motion, the left hemisphere would realize that it had made a mistake and would change its answer.

WHERE TO NOW?

The first two chapters of this book have tried to provide some idea of what learning is and have indicated possible physiological mechanisms underlying learning. In the chapters that follow we will trace the role of learning from input to output. We will start with a description of how learning affects what we perceive in our environment (Perception and Learning). This perceived information is then traced through several stages (Information Holding Mechanisms) on the way to storage. After investigating some mechanisms of learning (Stimulus Contiguity, Feedback) we will show how learning is expressed in the personality of the person (Personality). Finally we will discuss the role of consciousness in learning and speculate on what role consciousness actually serves in man's behavior (Behavior, Cognitions, and Consciousness).

SUMMARY

There must be some physiological changes that are associated with the learning process and that underlie memory storage. Most current researchers look for such changes within the central nervous system, for it is this network of neurons that is largely responsible for processing information and producing behavior. Four categories of physiological theories of learning were discussed: *neuronal-synaptic models, RNA-protein models, glial models,* and *non-connectionistic theories.*

The major assumption of *neuronal-synaptic models* is that learning involves a change in the neurons which makes it easier for some neurons to influence the neural transmission of the neurons with which they have connections or synapses. Such models are popular because neurons are the units of the central nervous system which apparently underlie behavior and because the billions of neurons in the human brain are interwoven in a vastly complex web which seems intricate enough to account for the complexity of human learning and behavior.

RNA molecules are involved in the production of proteins, some of which affect neural transmission. Changes in RNA molecules and proteins have been shown to be correlated with learning. Thus proponents of *RNA-protein models* of learning suggest that memories are stored in specific molecules of RNA or proteins or both. One set of controversial experiments offered in support of RNA models is the *memory transfer experiments.* These involve training one set of animals on a task, extracting their RNA and injecting it into a second set of animals, and demonstrating that some memory was transferred with the RNA. Currently there are many complications with this type of research, and theories of the RNA-protein models and exactly how they work are still in dispute.

Glial cells are cells that support the activity and functioning of the neurons, and in this capacity they can affect the firing activity of neurons. A glial theory of learning, then, would postulate that memories are stored in glial cells and are expressed in terms of the glial cells' influence on neurons. Essentially no-one advocates a glial model of learning, although the glial cells have been incorporated into other physiological models. Ultimately a physiological explanation of learning will probably involve some combination of neurons, glia, RNA, and proteins.

Non-connectionistic theories of learning postulate that learning is not based on specific connections between specific neurons, but rather depends on coherent patterns of electrical activity of groups of neurons. Thus memory is recorded in terms of an electrical pattern. One advantage to non-connectionistic theories is that they allow for the possibility of specific neurons being destroyed without necessarily impairing memory, so long as other neurons can still produce the required patterned activity.

Considerable research has been directed toward identifying exactly where *memory traces* are stored. Some animal research has involved selectively destroying parts of the brain in an attempt to obliterate memory traces. Such attempts have not been successful in localizing memory traces, suggesting to some researchers that specific memories may be stored in several different places. Electrical stimulation of some areas of the human brain has caused the subjects to recall specific memories, perhaps because the stimulation somehow activated a memory trace. There is also evidence suggesting that information stored in one hemisphere of the brain may be transferred via nerve fibers to the other hemisphere, where the information is then also stored. Severing these nerve fibers produces a *split brain* where the two hemispheres learn things independently to some degree.

SUGGESTED READINGS

Deutsch, J. A. (ed.) *The Physiological Basis of Memory.* New York: Academic Press, 1973.

Grossman, S. P. *A Textbook of Physiological Psychology.* New York: Wiley, 1967.

Gurowitz, E. M. *The Molecular Basis of Memory.* Englewood Cliffs, N.J.: Prentice-Hall, 1969.

John, E. R. *Mechanisms of Memory.* New York: Academic Press, 1967.

Ungar, G. (ed.) *Molecular Mechanisms in Memory and Learning.* New York: Plenum Press, 1970.

perception and learning

The real world, as man currently perceives it, is a complex mass of potential stimuli: various sound and light waves speeding by, molecules of different odors drifting in the air, hot and cold sources producing varying interactions of temperatures, and things to be touched, to name just a few. Man is limited by the capabilities of his sense organs and central nervous system to being able to perceive only an extremely small percentage of these stimuli. Man's visual spectrum covers only a small part of the electromagnetic continuum. Dogs can hear sounds that man misses, and many animals can smell things that man cannot detect. Other things cannot be perceived because they are too small, too far away, too fast, and so forth. Thus man perceives the world through very small windows. He can, however, enlarge his scope somewhat with mechanical devices such as microscopes, infrared photography, slow-motion photography, and amplifiers.

Another source of stimuli is from man's own body, such as from some internal organs, muscles, and substances in the blood. Again, whole sources of stimuli are outside of man's conscious sensory capabilities. For example, try to perceive the activity of your spleen.

Given the range of stimuli that man can potentially perceive, what explains why he receives some stimuli and not others at any given time? Part of the answer lies in the properties of the stimuli themselves. Some stimuli simply push their way through the windows. It is fairly probable that a sudden loud noise or a bright light will be perceived in some fashion. This chapter, however, is concerned with the interaction between learning and the sensory-perceptual-attention mechanisms that select, filter, and interpret the stimuli. Figure 3–1 shows a model of this interaction. Some of the potential stimuli are selected and perceived and sent

45

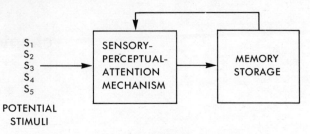

Figure 3-1 *Memory influence on perception.*

into memory storage. This memory storage then affects the later selection and interpretation of stimuli.

In the 17th and 18th centuries, philosophers debating about how our mind comes to have certain ideas often divided into two camps—the nativists and the empiricists. *Nativists,* such as Descartes, argued that man is born with the ability to perceive certain basic phenomena. The *empiricists,* such as Locke and Berkeley, argued that man *learns* to perceive. Thus the nativists stressed that learning depended on perception, whereas the empiricists stressed that perception depended on learning. Most theorists now reject both of these two extremes and emphasize the continually evolving interactions between perception and learning.

There are many examples of man's learning to perceive. The first time a person looks through a microscope at a slide of part of the brain, he perceives very little of what he might later *learn* to see in the same slide. The Russian missile bases on Cuba were discovered by a man who had learned how to identify them from aerial photographs, whereas other observers of the photographs did not see them (Gibson, 1969, p. 8). The wine connoisseur has learned to perceive fine discriminations in the taste, smell, and color of various wines.

A key question is whether learning ever affects the way an object is *initially* perceived or whether it affects only some later stage in the processing of the information obtained from the object. Does the wine actually *taste* different to the wine connoisseur, or has he simply learned to do more (make different responses) to the same taste that most of us experience? Perhaps learning doesn't affect the original *perception* of the object, but rather affects what type of *information* about the object can be retrieved from short and long term information storage centers (see Chapter 4). Perhaps these retrieval processes affect what parts of the information go into the person's consciousness. Alternatives such as these may be greatly expanded depending on the number of stages assumed to exist in the processing of information. The point is that although it is clear that learning interacts with the information-processing system, it is seldom clear at what point in this system learning has its effect. One of the early stages in the system is attention.

ATTENTION

Of all the stimuli a person is capable of perceiving, he attends to some stimuli at the expense of others. Considerable research (Norman, 1969, Chap. 2) has been devoted to determining the variables that affect attention. Consider the "cocktail party phenomenon." A room is filled with people talking to each other in small groups. Thus for any one person there are many voices and sounds impinging on his ears. Yet he is able to filter out of all this noise the conversation of the person he is talking to, and selectively attend to this conversation alone. The person can also easily switch his selective attention so that he tunes in on the conversation of two people nearby or to the words of the music in the background. Such selective attention is a truly remarkable process, which, as Norman (1969, p. 14) points out, has not been duplicated by electronic devices.

Since we can't attend to all possible stimuli, it is important that we attend to those stimuli that are important to us at the time. But how do we know if a stimulus is important if we don't first perceive it? Such reasoning usually leads to discussions of different levels of perception. For example, at a basic, probably non-conscious level, stimuli are processed and some decision mechanism or filter determines which stimuli will be further attended to. A different level of perception then might deal only with these selected stimuli. But on what basis does the decision mechanism or filter pick some stimuli over others? Part of the answer is past learning. What is important to the person now usually depends on prior learning experiences. An experienced automobile driver has learned what stimuli should be attended to for efficient and safe driving. Thus we see one place where learning and perception interact: memory storage partially determines what stimuli will be attended to.

A similar argument can be made for the phenomena of perceptual vigilance and perceptual defense. *Perceptual vigilance* refers to the hypothesis that events of particular importance to the individual are easier for him to perceive, while *perceptual defense* refers to the hypothesis that it may be possible for an individual to *not* perceive some events which are psychologically unpleasant. Although there is controversy about these phenomena, they may, to some extent, involve processes similar to those described above for selective attention. That is, some decision mechanism, influenced by memory storage, must first classify stimuli as important or dangerous before perceptual vigilance or perceptual defense can occur. Perhaps at one (non-conscious) perceptual level a stimulus is perceived, interpreted, and classified as dangerous. On the basis of this classification the stimulus is not permitted into the perceptual level that involves consciousness, so that the person has no subjective experience of ever having perceived the stimulus at all.

Phenomena such as hysterical blindness (functional blindness due to psychological rather than physiological factors) may often be extreme cases of perceptual defense. Consider the man who has a series of tragic experiences such as the death of his wife and loss of his job. Many of the stimuli that he encounters, such as things that remind him of his wife, will elicit excessive anxiety in this man. If the anxiety is strong enough, the decision mechanism may, via perceptual defense, stop certain stimuli from entering consciousness. In the extreme, with many stimuli eliciting an unbearable degree of anxiety, the decision mechanism may simply shut almost all visual stimuli from consciousness. This, then, would be a case of hysterical blindness, for although there is nothing anatomically wrong with the man's visual system, he is, to a large extent, functionally blind. Such an explanation is, of course, oversimplified, but perceptual defense may be a significant factor in cases of hysterical blindness.

The next question is how learning affects the perception of stimuli that *are* attended to.

THEORIES OF PERCEPTUAL LEARNING

From the stimuli attended to, man constructs some idea of his environment. Although some of the processes involved in this construction may be innate, many appear to be learned, and this learning how to perceive is called *perceptual learning*.

There are basically two theoretical approaches to perceptual learning. The first emphasizes that the environment supplies most of the needed information for perception; perceptual learning is described in terms of learning how to effectively use information from the environment. (This is the approach of E. J. Gibson.) The second approach sees the environment as supplying inadequate information, and therefore views perceptual learning in terms of learning to make extrapolations from this limited information. This is the approach of the transactionalists and theorists such as Bruner. These two approaches are, of course, different points along a continuum of theories on how much information is supplied by the environment. Research will have to tell us which points on this continuum offer the best explanation of perceptual processes in different situations.

A few examples of the two approaches will be given below. (For a more complete coverage see Gibson, 1969.) Keep in mind that the specific experiments and arguments given with each theory are not unique to that theory but could be interpreted differently to fit a different theory.

Gibson's Theory.   Gibson's (1969) theoretical position, a perceptual differentiation theory, is that perceptual learning is learning to extract information out of the sensory data of the environment. The environment is seen as supplying an abundance of information. To make sense of the sensory input a person must learn how to respond to *distinctive features* of the stimuli. For example, when a young child first hears people speaking to him it probably sounds like an undifferentiated mass of meaningless sounds. With time the child learns to pick out distinctive features, basic sounds that he can use to discriminate words, meanings, and other aspects of the language.

Perceptual learning, then, according to Gibson, has two components: First, the person must learn what the distinctive features are (e.g., according to what criteria does a good wine differ from a bad wine?). Second, the person must learn how to use the distinctive features to discriminate different relevant objects. At the start of a task a person might already be able to identify the distinctive features. If so, then perceptual learning is facilitated, as the person has only to learn how to use these features. Memory of an object is conceived as being stored in terms of distinctive features and invariant patterns, as opposed to just an unanalyzed copy of the stimuli.

Learning to identify and to respond to distinctive features involves processes such as abstraction, filtering out irrelevant variables, and selective attention. *Abstraction* involves distinguishing common elements or relationships. For example, in language learning we learn to identify (abstract out) certain basic sounds independent of differences in pitch, loudness, or speed. *Filtering out irrelevant variables* is learning to ignore those parts of the stimulation that are not essential to the required perception, as pitch might be irrelevant to the understanding of some parts of language. *Selective attention*, according to Gibson, refers to the exploratory activity of the sense organs, such as turning the head toward a sound or rolling a liquid over the tongue.

Let us consider the implications of Gibson's theory in a practical situation: teaching. To facilitate perceptual learning, the teacher should emphasize distinctive features, for example, through the use of clearly contrasting examples. This technique would apply equally to elementary children learning to read, to high school students learning to discriminate among the sounds of different musical instruments, and to a medical student learning to make sense out of electroencephalogram records. First the teacher would help the students to identify some of the distinctive features; for example, pointing out cues for the student to discriminate between the string instruments. Then through the systematic use of contrasting examples the students would be given practice using the distinctive features to make the required discriminations.

Transactional Theory.   An example of a theory that emphasizes extrapolations from limited information is *transactional theory* (Ittelson & Cantril, 1954). Perception is considered to be dependent on the person's past transactions with the environment; it is an active process of interpretation of environmental events in terms of the person's purpose, values, and past learning (e.g., expectations and assumptions). A stimulus pattern on the retina could have come from a variety of different objects; hence there are a number of different possible "perceptions." The actual perception that the person has thus depends on his past learning: how functional and useful were the different possible perceptions in the past?

A number of impressive demonstrations were generated in support of transactional theory (Ittelson & Kilpatrick, 1951). One of the more outstanding of these is the trapezoidal window. This is a trapezoid frame with window-like panes in it and shadows painted on it to make it look like a window (a schematic is given in Figure 3–2). When seen in the proper setting a person can perceive the window in at least two different ways: (1) It could be seen for what it is, a trapezoid-shaped window; or (2) It could be perceived as a rectangular shaped window seen from an angle. Because most people's transactions with windows in the past have been primarily with rectangular windows, the trapezoid window is generally perceived as a rectangular window.

Now consider what happens when the window is slowly rotated about the post shown attached to the middle of the base of the window. If the person perceived the window as being a trapezoid, he would simply see a rotating trapezoid. But he perceives the window as a rectangle. A rotating trapezoid does not produce the same types of retinal images as a rotating rectangle would. In order to fit the actual retinal images into the rectangle "hypothesis," the person's perception becomes distorted. What he immediately sees is an oscillating window whose speed,

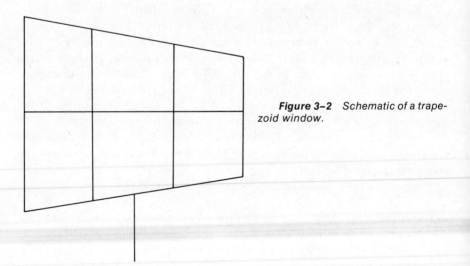

Figure 3–2 *Schematic of a trapezoid window.*

shape, and direction of turning seems to keep changing. It may seem to slowly move around in one direction and then to suddenly dart around in the other direction. If a rod is hung through the window pane, it often appears to move in a direction opposite that of the window. Sometimes the rod appears to bend, break, or pass through solid parts of the window. Thus in order to maintain seeing the trapezoidal window as a rectangle, most people will literally perceive the window and rod as doing things that they know are impossible. For instance, this author always sees these perceptual effects even though he "knows" the window is a trapezoid and "knows" it is turning at a constant rate.

The transactionalists have made a good case for the influence of learning on perception. However, as Gibson (1969, p. 45) pointed out, they have not included a clearly formulated explanation of how this learning takes place.

Categorization. Some theorists, such as Bruner (1958), have conceived of perception as influenced by categorization. The categories by which things are classified are generally a result of learning. Thus when some object or event is first perceived it is classified according to a system of categories. The final perception then depends on how the sense data were categorized at the time they were first perceived. Any difference between the actual object or event and the category under which it was classified may result in a distortion in the perception of the object or event, in order to make it fit the category. This "distortion" may often be nothing more than the selective perception of some features of the object over other features. Also, differences between categories and environmental events may produce modifications of the categories.

Consider playing cards in which the colors of the suits are reversed: spades and clubs are red, while hearts and diamonds are black. These cards do not fit into the card categories of an experienced card player. If quickly shown a red ten of spades, the card player's perceptual system tries to map the sense experience into a category such as black spades, red hearts, or red diamonds, but there is no category for red spades. Thus the person might misperceive the red ten of spades and perceive it as the black ten of spades or the red ten of hearts. In an experiment with such cards, Bruner and Postman (1949) identified two frequent types of errors: dominance reactions and compromise reactions. A *dominance reaction* occurred when the subject forced the suit to match the color or the color to match the suit. Perceiving the black five of hearts as the red five of hearts is a dominance reaction. In a *compromise reaction* the subject perceives some compromise between the actual object and a dominance reaction. For example, a red spade might be perceived as a purple spade (purple being a compromise between red and black), or as a black spade with red edges.

The author has introduced such a color-reversed deck into bridge games with experienced bridge players. The usual response by the players when they first pick up the cards is that there is something funny or unpleasant about the cards, but they don't know exactly what it is. Many players play an entire hand without seeing what is actually different about the cards. Such players often have trouble sorting the cards into suits, suddenly noticing that they have five suits in their hands. Even when the color reversal is noticed, following suit during the play of the hand is often difficult. This author still gets a slightly unpleasant feeling from looking at such cards as a black jack of diamonds. On the other hand, the author's wife, who does not play cards (and hence does not have as set a group of categories) never had any trouble immediately seeing the cards as they actually were.

As another example of categorization, consider prejudice. The roots of prejudice are many and varied. Aronson (1972, p. 180) lists four basic causes of prejudice: (1) economic and political competition or conflict, (2) displaced aggression, (3) personality needs, and (4) conformity to existing social norms. From the perspective of the preceding discussion it could be argued that an important variable in many cases of prejudice is the type of categories the prejudiced person uses in perceptually classifying people.

Consider a person with the following three categories for automobile drivers: good male drivers, bad male drivers, and bad female drivers. Now assume that a female driver passes by this person, but so fast that he doesn't get a clear look at the sex of the driver. Assume also that the female driver displays particularly good driving skills. Because our prejudiced person has no category for good women drivers (she's a black queen of hearts in his world), he misperceives the situation and perceives the driver as being male (a dominance reaction).

We can see how such a categorization argument can be applied to many forms of prejudice. Bruner (1958, p. 86) suggests, "We see a Negro sitting on a park bench, a Jew or Texan changing a check at a bank window, a German dressing down a taxi cab driver, and allocate each experience to an established and well-memorized stereotype: lazy Negro, mercenary Jew, rich Texan, bullying German." Now there are many reasons why a black might be sitting on a park bench, few of which are because he is lazy. Perhaps he is on a break from a ten-hour-a-day job. But if the prejudiced person has only one category for blacks, a category that includes being lazy, then the prejudiced person's perception of the black may be distorted. Worse still, when this person remembers the scene of the black in the park, his memory includes all of the distortions he originally added to the perception. Such a person perpetuates his own prejudice because his misperception and distorted memories are proof to him of the validity of his stereotypes.

This type of distortion is illustrated in an early study that Allport and Postman (1945) did on rumors. (Please remember that the study is

30 years old, and some of the specific findings might be different today, although the psychological processes are assumed to be the same.) In their study they would show one subject a picture which he would describe to a second subject, who then told a third subject, and so forth. This way the experimenters could observe the types of changes that took place as the story was passed on. Some of the results could be interpreted in terms of our categorization model. One picture was a subway scene that included a white man holding a razor while arguing with a black man. In over half of the final stories the black ended up holding the razor. Perhaps for many of the people a razor during an argument better fit the black category than the white man category. In some cases the number of blacks increased to four or "several."

Although the preceding examples might be fairly extreme, it can be argued that everyone has a limited number of categories and so must be misperceiving some events. One purpose of education then is to increase the number of categories a person has and uses in order to decrease the amount of misperception.

The Hebbian Model.   Hebb (1949) offered a provocative theory of perceptual learning in his book *Organization of Behavior*. The theory suggests that there are neural representations that correspond to environmental stimuli, and that learning involves neuronal associations between such representations. According to Hebb, simple visual perception can be broken down into small units such as lines and angles. With learning, these basic units form into simple figures and then into more complex perceptions. Hebb explains this learning in terms of associations between neural units. For example, one set of neurons might respond to a particular angle, while another set responds to a particular line. The perception and memory of a figure that includes this angle and line require a learned association between the two sets of neurons. In other words, we start seeing very simple things and gradually learn to be able to see more complex perceptions.

In developing his theory, Hebb drew heavily on the work of the German ophthalmologist von Senden (1960). Von Senden studied adults who had been virtually blind since birth and then were suddenly given sight by an eye operation such as removal of cataracts. Hebb distinguished two processes of perceptual development: *figural unity,* the simple detection of an object against its background, and *identity,* identifying an object as a member of class of objects. Von Senden's patients, when given sight, were generally capable of figural unity, but seldom capable of identity. They could fixate on objects and follow moving objects with their eyes, but at first could not identify objects. In the beginning the patients relied a lot on color. If the shape of an object were changed but the color left the same, the patients often still identified the object as being the same.

Although von Senden's subjects could detect a square or triangle against its background, they could not at first tell one from the other unless they counted the number of corners. Similarly they could not tell which of two sticks was longer unless they felt the sticks. Even when they learned to identify some objects by sight, a change in the physical orientation of the object might make it unknown again. With time the subjects learned how to visually identify more and more objects, but for many of the subjects their visual skills never became "normal." Two years after the operation one patient could identify only four or five faces.

Hebb argued that the type of perceptual learning seen with von Senden's subjects corresponded to what occurs with normal infants. The advantage of von Senden's subjects is that they could verbalize what was taking place. Although correspondences between von Senden's patients and infants may exist, there are too many differences to enable us to draw any firm conclusions. For example, von Senden's subjects may have experienced some side effects when suddenly given sight (e.g., dazzle of bright lights or cramps in eye muscles) that impaired their visual progress, which wouldn't be the case in a normal infant. It should also be remembered that von Senden's subjects had spent their entire lives learning to interpret the world through sense modes other than vision. Thus it would be expected that these other learned responses related to handling the environment would interfere with the acquisition of new visual responses. In fact, many such patients often prefer their old sense modes to their now confusing vision. Another possibility is that there are certain *critical periods* in human visual development similar to the critical period discussed in the first chapter regarding imprinting. That is, there might be certain critical periods in the development of an individual in which he is particularly predisposed for some type of learning, such as perceptual learning. If this critical period is bypassed, as with von Senden's subjects, the learning may be significantly more difficult.

Later support for theories such as Hebb's came from the neurophysiological studies of Hubel and Wiesel (Hubel, 1963). Using recording electrodes in the visual cortex of cats (striate area of the occipital cortex), they studied what types of external visual stimuli would cause different nerve cells to fire. They found some cells that maximally fired to simple lines presented at one orientation to the eye, while other cells fired maximally to lines at other orientations. Some cells fired to movement of a stimulus in one direction in the visual field, but not to movement in the other direction. This type of cell function appears to be innate in that it can be demonstrated in newborn kittens.

Hubel and Wiesel categorized the nerve cells they studied into two basic groups: simple cells and complex cells. *Simple cells* are ones that respond only to line stimuli of a specific orientation and position, while *complex cells* are more general in what they respond to. Hubel and Wiesel suggest that complex cells receive input from a number of simple cells.

For example, one simple cell might respond only to a dark vertical line in a specific part of the left visual field, and another simple cell might respond only to a dark vertical line in part of the right visual field; whereas a complex cell that receives input from these two simple cells might respond to the vertical line in either place. With more simple cells feeding into a complex cell we can imagine a complex cell that responds to a vertical line anywhere in the visual field. As complexity of the cell increases, we might find a cell that fires to figures of triangles if it gets the right input from cells that respond to horizontal lines plus cells that respond to slanted lines of a certain orientation.

It is easy to see how we could slowly build up a model of vision this way with more and more complex cells. Such a model could be compatible with Hebbian theory, as Hebb also sees perceptions building up from simple components such as those of simple cells. Such models, however, go far past the basic findings of Hubel and Wiesel, and hence should be considered quite speculative. We also have to be careful to not construct a model of perception that simply provides firing neurons to correspond to visual stimuli. A model of perception must be more flexible in order to include such intricate phenomena as visual illusions and the effects of learning on the interpretation of sensory events.

VISUAL ILLUSIONS

Gregory (1966, Chap. 9; 1968) has shown how past learning might account for a number of visual illusions. Consider the illusions given in

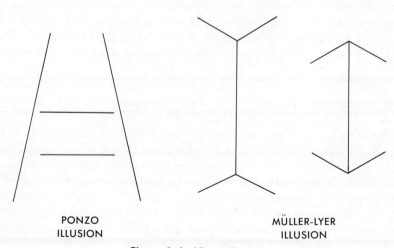

PONZO
ILLUSION

MÜLLER-LYER
ILLUSION

Figure 3-3   *Visual illusions.*

Figure 3-3. In the *Ponzo illusion* the top of the two horizontal lines usually looks longer, although both lines are actually the same length. In the *Müller-Lyer illusion* the shaft of the first "arrow" with the ends turned out usually appears longer than the shaft of the second arrow with the ends turned in.

Gregory suggests that both illusions suggest depth to the viewer, and that those features of the figures "assumed" to be more distant appear larger. The Ponzo illusion corresponds to experiences the viewer has had with similar figures, such as railroad tracks. Our experience with railroad tracks has taught us that when our eye gets the image of the Ponzo illusion, the top of the figure is actually farther away from us than the bottom. Hence the top of the two horizontal lines is farther away, but both lines produce the same sized image on the retina. If two objects produce the same sized retinal image and one object is farther away, the farther object must be larger, and often will appear larger. So the argument is that somewhere in the perceptual processing of the Ponzo illusion the actual retinal images are compared with information about how far away the different parts of the figures are, and the results of this comparison determine our subjective experience of the relative sizes of the different figure parts. And it is past learning that affects the distance estimation.

Similarly the Müller-Lyer illusion might be explained in terms of our past experience with corners of rooms and buildings. If you look at the inside corner of a room, the line edges formed by the walls, ceiling, and floor, you will see a three-dimensional representation of the Müller-Lyer arrow with the ends turned out. Note that in this situation the shaft of the arrow is the part farthest away. Now if you look at the outside corner of a flat-roofed building, such as a phone booth, the line edges form a three-dimensional example of the arrow with the ends turned *in*. Here the shaft is the nearest part of the figure. If we look at the illusion, both shafts produce the same retinal image. But the one shaft is "assumed" to be the nearest part of the figure, while the other shaft is "assumed" to be the farthest part. Therefore we perceive the farther shaft to be larger.

If these illusions can be explained by the depth they suggest, why don't the illusions look more three-dimensional? This is probably because the figures are printed on paper which superimposes a two-dimensional effect, but not a strong enough effect to offset the illusion. If instead the Müller-Lyer figures are constructed out of wire, painted with luminous paint, and viewed with one eye (to avoid stereoscopic depth information) in the dark, then they do look three-dimensional, like corners.

We have now seen a number of ways in which learning might affect perception. The next question is how the particular language a person learns affects his perception.

THE WHORFIAN HYPOTHESIS

The Arabs have a multitude of different ways of naming camels, and the Hanunoo people in the Philippines have names for 92 different varieties of rice (Bourne et al., 1971, p. 285). Do these languages affect the way the person actually perceives and thinks about his environment? In other words, does learning a language affect later perception of the world? Is the Arab's perception of camels different from ours, or does he just use the available information differently?

Whorf offered an interesting theory relative to these questions, called the *Whorfian hypothesis* or the *linguistic relativity hypothesis* (see Bourne et al., 1971, Chap. 13; Carroll, 1956). According to this theory, language is not simply a medium of communication and thought. In addition to these generally accepted functions of language, Whorf contends that the structure and semantics of any particular language mold the way a person perceives, understands, and responds to his environment. Similar to the process of categorization, language provides a *framework* for the person's perception and storage of information. According to Whorf we dissect nature along lines laid down by our native language.

For example, Whorf noted that English grammar tends to divide sentences into noun phrases and verb phrases. He suggested that an effect of this grammar was that English speaking people have a tendency to analyze all of their experiences in terms of one of two categories — things or actions. (If your counterargument is that this is the only or best way to divide experiences into categories, then you are proving Whorf's point.) Whorf spent considerable time studying the Hopi Indians, and many of his examples come from these studies. It appeared to Whorf that the Hopi did not have tenses for their verbs. From this Whorf concluded that the Hopi perception of the world must then be timeless. The Hopi language also had no word for imaginary space, which suggested to Whorf that the Hopi could not even imagine something like a missionary's hell. However, many of Whorf's conclusions about the Hopi have since been questioned.

Although the Whorfian hypothesis may be true to some extent, there are too many confounding variables to determine its exact status. Consider the problems in showing how language affects thinking. First of all, most of what we know about another person's thinking processes comes from what the other person tells us, and so we are using the person's *language* as a measure of the effects of language on thinking. This boils down to showing the effects of language on language, which isn't too revealing. Secondly, there is the complication that most of thinking revolves around language. (Try to "think" about some topic without using words.) Therefore language must affect thinking, since it is one of the components of thinking.

But our question is whether language affects *perception*. Does one of the Hanunoo people, who can discriminate 92 varieties of rice, literally see rice differently than we do? Perhaps not. It may be that the importance of rice to these people plus their greater experience with different types of rice simply allows them to make more and finer judgements. The fact that they have more words for rice than we do in English simply reflects their ability to make more discriminations. That is, rice "looks" the same to them as it does to us, but they know more things to look for and have more words to classify what they see.

Thus one of the Hanunoo can code in one word (one of the 92 varieties) a lot of information about the rice. When he tells one of his friends which variety of rice he is dealing with, considerable information is exchanged. An English speaking person who knew what to look for might be able to code the rice with all of the same information, except that instead of a single word, his identification of the rice might involve a number of short descriptive phrases. One-word coding, being more efficient after you have mastered the coding process, may facilitate learning, remembering, and thinking about rice. But that is quite different from saying that the original perception is affected. So at this time we can't say whether language affects original perception and/or only affects other processes, such as how the information is coded. The distinction between perception and coding is also far from clear.

In a relevant experiment, Brown and Lennenberg (1954) categorized a set of color discs according to "codability." A color disc with a high codability score was one which most of their subjects gave the same name (e.g., "red"), while a disc with a low codability score was one given many different names and descriptive phrases (e.g., "dirty reddish green"). Next, a different set of subjects was shown some of the individual discs and had to match each color with one of the discs from a large display of all the color discs. When these subjects had to find one disc at a time, it made no difference whether the disc was of high or low codability. However, when the subjects were asked to find four discs simultaneously, they were faster and more accurate at finding discs of high codability. When looking for just one disc the subjects simply kept a picture of the disc in their mind as they scanned the display of discs. Doing four at a time, however, depended more on how the subjects coded the colors.

Gibson's (1969) position on language and perception is that the person first learns to perceive objects and their features and later learns names for these objects, as opposed to Whorf's position that language affects the original perceptual development. Gibson questions whether perceptual learning is appreciably affected by language categories, although she does allow that perceptual learning can be facilitated by calling attention, as with language, to distinctive features of the objects.

SET

The discussion in this chapter has shown that stimuli do not fall on passive receivers. Rather, each person is predisposed to perceive stimuli in specific ways. This predisposition has sometimes been referred to as *set*, an ambiguous, generic term that encompasses a range of variables, including past experiences, motives, context, rewards, and instructions (see Dember, 1960, Chap. 8; Haber, 1966). In fact, the concept of set includes everything discussed so far in this chapter.

Think about the answer to the following question before reading further: Why are 1972 pennies worth almost twenty dollars? The answer is that you need two thousand pennies for twenty dollars and so you are only twenty-eight cents short. Most people have some trouble with this question because they are in the set of perceiving 1972 as a date, not as a number of pennies. But is this effect really on the *perception* of the 1972 or is it on some other stage in the processing of the concept of 1972, or possibly both? This is a key, and as yet unanswered, question.

The next example will illustrate how set-like effects can affect problem solving processes. Quickly answer the following question before reading further: If *polk* is pronounced *poke* with the *l* silent, and *folk* is pronounced *foke*, also with a silent *l*, how do you pronounce the white of an egg? Most people who answer quickly do not realize the white of an egg is the albumen, not the yolk, for they are in the set of words ending in *lk* or *ke*.

Figure 3–4 gives two other examples of set. Read each example fairly quickly and then go back and look for the set. The following are the answers for those who want them: In the first example the word "the" is printed twice, but most people read over one of the "the's" because "bird in the hand" is such a common phrase. In the second example the last word may be read as a Scottish name because of the set established by the first three words, but it can also be the common word "machine."

Let us now consider how set can influence people's perceptions in a classroom situation. Kelley (1950) used students in a college psychology class. The experimenter came into the class one day and told the students that their regular instructor was to be replaced by a substitute

Figure 3–4 Examples of set.

for the day. The students were then given a written description of the substitute. However, the descriptions were not all the same. Half of the descriptions referred to the substitute as being a rather cold person, while the other half were the same except the word "warm" was used instead of "cold." During the class that the substitute taught, the students who got the "warm" description participated more in class discussion with the substitute than did the students who got the "cold" description. After the class, the "warm" description students evaluated the substitute higher than did the "cold" description students, in terms of being more considerate, better natured, and so forth. All students were in the same classroom with the same substitute, but, according to the set they were in as a result of the written descriptions, they perceived the substitute differently and interacted with him differently. The substitute's actual personality and teaching style, of course, affected the students' ratings and perceptions in an absolute sense, but set made the difference between the two groups of students. It is easy to see how this type of phenomenon takes place all the time in classrooms, as students tell other students what they think or have heard about a particular teacher. Similarly, people perceive and respond differently to political figures (or anyone else for that matter) and to their speeches, depending on their particular "set."

Set also affects a teacher's perception of his students. Rosenthal and Jacobson (1968) told elementary school teachers that they had a test that would identify "spurters"—sudden fast learners. In fact, the students they identified as spurters were chosen randomly; thus any difference between spurters and non-spurters was purely due to the set of the teachers' minds. Over time, the "results indicated strongly that children from whom teachers expected greater intellectual gains showed such gains." The teachers also described the spurters as being happier, more curious, more interesting, more appealing, better adjusted, more affectionate, less in need of social approval, and as having a better chance of being successful in later life. The non-spurters also improved intellectually, but the more they improved, the less favorably they were rated by the teachers. This effect of set was powerful, particularly on first grade teachers.

How did the teachers' sets influence the students' intellectual gains? Rosenthal and Jacobson argue that it was not simply that the teacher spent more time with spurters but that the effect lay in more subtle interactions: "Her tone of voice, facial expression, touch and posture may be the means by which—probably quite unwittingly—she communicates her expectations to the pupils. Such communication might help the child by changing his conception of himself, his anticipation of his own behavior, his motivation or his cognitive skills."

Other researchers (e.g., Clairborn, 1969) have criticized the methodology of Rosenthal and Jacobson and have failed to replicate their findings. O'Leary and Drabman (1971) conclude that "At most, the evidence demonstrating such an effect is equivocal, and the teacher's behavioral changes that result from receiving a 'false' expectation are quite variable." However, Rosenthal and others (Rosenthal, 1973) have demonstrated this type of phenomenon in enough situations that it appears to be a legitimate and powerful effect in at least some circumstances.

Keeping Rosenthal and Jacobson's theory in mind, consider what might be happening to students classified as slow learners, problem students, or special education students. Suppose a student does something that could be perceived as either creative curiosity or bothersome digression. The "spurter" might be rewarded and encouraged, whereas if the teacher is in the set of thinking of the student as a problem student, the student might be verbally punished and discouraged. What a shame this would be if the behavior had elements of curiosity that could have been encouraged.

Those who work with teacher training try to minimize such effects of set by discouraging the labeling of students and encouraging well-specified behavioral objectives and systematic keeping of behavioral records. That is, if the teacher decides exactly which behaviors should be encouraged and which should be discouraged (regardless of who does them) and how he can *objectively* determine which kind of behavior has occurred in a given situation, then the effects of set will be dramatically reduced.

Many clinicians utilize *projective tests* to aid in the personality assessments of their clients. These tests consist of relatively unstructured stimuli that the client must organize or interpret in some way. For example, the person might be shown an inkblot and asked to tell what it looks like. The assumption is that the responses that the subject makes to the projective test are some measure of his personality. Unfortunately such responses might be affected by set. The clinician could, although subtly and unintentionally, influence the subject's set so that the subject will respond to the projective test in ways that fit the clinician's expectations or theoretical bias. It is possible that many clinical phenomena, such as the types of symbols that a person reports as having occurred in his dreams, are influenced by set.

As mentioned earlier, we cannot at this time say for sure whether set affects the original perception or some later stage of information processing, or perhaps both. Haber (1966) discusses two contradictory hypotheses about set: (a) set affects the percept of the stimulus *while* the person is actually viewing it, and (b) set affects the *report* of the stimulus *without* affecting its percept. Haber summarizes as follows: "This review must conclude inconclusively with respect to a choice between the two hypotheses. Some evidence exists to support each of them, and some exists which favors one over the other. But there is none that supports one while disproving the other." It does appear, however, that learning is a major variable affecting set, and that set may affect perception. This suggests again the possibility that learning plays a role in perception. Next we will consider how learning and perception interact in the learning of verbal material.

PERCEPTION AND VERBAL LEARNING

Different types of verbal material vary in their ability to elicit images. Does this image-eliciting ability affect how easily the material can be learned and remembered? This is the question investigated by Paivio (1969). Paivio classified verbal stimuli along a dimension from concrete to abstract. A concrete stimulus, such as the word "house," is more likely to evoke images than an abstract stimulus such as the word "truth." (Say each of these words to yourself and see which elicits more images.) Paivio suggests that concrete stimuli derive their meaning through association with specific objects and events as well as through association with other words. Learning of concrete material, then, could utilize the images or verbal associations, or both. Abstract stimuli, on the other hand, derive their meaning largely through associations with other words. Thus learning of abstract material would primarily utilize verbal associations.

Paivio often used a form of *paired associate learning* of noun pairs. Paired associate learning involves presenting the subject a number of paired items that the subject must learn to associate together. In Paivio's task the subject, when presented with the first noun of a pair (the stimulus), had to learn to say the second noun (the response). Paivio found that learning was faster if the stimulus noun was concrete than if it was abstract. For example, it is easier to learn an association to the word "house" than to the word "truth." Paivio suggests that images serve as "conceptual pegs" to which responses can be conditioned. That is, concrete nouns elicit more images than abstract nouns, and these images form the basis for learned associations. If given the pair "house—dog" the subject can easily conjure a scene involving a house and a dog, which facilitates learning and/or memory. It is not so easy with the pair "truth—dog." Thus a person learns images to certain stimuli and these images facilitate later learning that involves the stimuli.

Paivio showed that the effects of noun-imagery were greater on the stimulus side than on the response side. Although having a concrete response noun might yield better learning than an abstract response noun, it is more important to have a concrete stimulus noun. The effects of noun-imagery were also found to be relatively independent of how meaningful the material was to the subject, i.e., how many associations the subject already had to the specific material. Although meaningfulness and noun-imagery often go together, in Paivio's tasks the imagery had a greater effect on learning.

The rest of this discussion of verbal learning centers on how the subject encodes stimuli. Whether or not this should be called "perception" depends on the definition of perception. This author includes under perception *all* processes of cataloguing information. Memory and retrieval processes begin after this. Others have defined perception so that its domain stops earlier in the information processing.

Consider paired associate learning in which the subject is presented with one or more pairs of items and must learn to associate the members of the pair. Paivio's task above was a form of paired associate learning. Another task might have pairs such as LUF–ZIJ, where the subject must learn to make the response ZIJ when presented with the stimulus LUF. A critical part of paired associate learning must be learning to tell the stimuli apart, a process called *stimulus discrimination*. Early theories of paired associate learning (e.g., Gibson, 1940) emphasized the role of stimulus discrimination. Now this emphasis has shifted somewhat to how the subject encodes the stimuli.

According to *stimulus encoding theory* the subject translates stimuli into forms that are easier to use in the current task. A visual stimulus might be coded into a verbal phrase and stored verbally. Or the stimulus LUF might be encoded as "love" for easier processing. Martin (1971) has argued that "a major portion of learning is perceptual learning – learning an effective identifying response to the nominal stimulus situation." Let us say that a person learns one set of paired associates and then has to learn another set which consists of the same stimuli but different responses. (This two-stage learning is referred to as the A-B, A-C paradigm.) According to Martin the subject in learning to do this might learn to code the stimulus differently the second time; that is, he might make a different identifying response to the same stimulus.

COMPLEXITY

Perception, learning, and motivation all come together in explanations for animals' (including humans) apparent need for sensory complexity. Animals strive for variety, novelty, and complexity in their environments even though such striving does not seem to serve any immediate biological need. There is a vast literature on such phenomena (Berlyne, 1960; Dember, 1960, Chap. 8; Eisenberger, 1972; Fiske & Maddi, 1961), which includes the following examples. Bees prefer those flower shapes with the longest outline with respect to surface area. Some fish will learn mazes just to look in a mirror. In mazes with many correct paths to the goal, rats vary their paths and often prefer those paths with greater variety. Rats will also learn a simple maze where the reward is the opportunity to explore another maze. A rat will press a bar simply to turn a light on and then will press another bar to turn it back off again. Monkeys like to handle objects, and show preference for the more heterogeneous objects. Monkeys will also open windows or pull levers to see outside their cages, and will keep doing this, particularly if the environment keeps changing. Coming home from work, a man might decide to take a different, perhaps even longer route, just for a change in his routine. Women rearrange their living room furniture for similar reasons. Teachers find that almost any significant change in the classroom (painting the walls, installing new blackboards, introducing a new audio-visual device, making new seating arrangements) seems to improve learning for a while. In Chapter 7 we will see how need for variety might be a major personality variable.

Phenomena such as those just noted have been described under many names: exploration, novelty, curiosity, stimulus change, and stimulus satiation. Is there something common to all these phenomena, some theoretical construct under which they all fall? One answer to this question centers on stimulus complexity and animals' attempts to experience a certain degree of complexity: a novel stimulus is often more complex than a familiar stimulus. Exploration and curiosity are simply attempts to increase the stimulus complexity of the environment. Unfortunately there is no good independent measure of complexity, although there have been attempts to measure it in terms of information theory, conflict, or specific stimulus attributes. A useful way of thinking about complexity, following Dember (1960, p. 352), is that "the more complex stimulus is the one the individual can do more with: it affords more potential opportunities for responding than does the less complex stimulus." Most experiments, however, simply use stimuli that intuitively differ in complexity. We are nowhere near the point where we can take *any two* stimuli, particularly if they are of different sense modalities, and say that for a given organism one stimulus is more complex than the other.

To explain the effects of stimulus complexity many theorists use the concept of arousal. *Arousal* is a general excitatory process—a nonspecific drive—perhaps related to the activity of the reticular formation, a neural system in the brain stem. Although most studies measure arousal in terms of some physiological phenomenon (skin resistance, pupil size, EEG, heart rate, respiration, blood pressure), there is poor correlation among changes in the various measures. This raises the questions of which measure is best and whether there is more than one type of arousal.

Many theories have been offered to interrelate complexity, arousal, and behavior (see Eisenberger, 1972). A few of these will be mentioned under the following categories: minimum arousal theories, arousal induction theories, and optimal arousal theories.

Minimum Arousal Theories.   The general orientation of minimum arousal theories is that arousal is a measure of deviation from an optimal state, so the less arousal there is, the better. Arousal might be produced by many different variables, including states of deprivation and noxious stimulation. Malmo (1958) suggested that drives could be broken down into general arousal plus a directional component. Since reduction in the drive was considered by Malmo to be rewarding, Malmo would be a minimum arousal theorist.

Dember (Dember, 1960; Dember & Earl, 1957) describes a *pacer theory* of complexity that doesn't mention arousal per se, but that can be considered akin to arousal theories. According to this theory each animal has a preferred level of stimulus complexity. The animal will seek out that stimulus situation whose complexity is near his preferred level. Being forced to attend to stimuli that are too complex, or not complex enough, causes emotional disturbance. A *pacer* is a stimulus whose complexity is slightly higher than the animal's complexity level. When an animal interacts with a pacer the preferred complexity level of the animal moves toward that of the pacer. Thus the animal's complexity level keeps rising as its experience with pacers increases.

A baby's complexity level is very low at first. He is very content with low complexity stimuli that might bore an adult, and can be overwhelmed by fairly complex stimuli that are pleasing to an adult. To "protect" himself, the baby might not attend to complex stimuli or he might screen them out early in perceptual processing. As the baby grows and encounters pacers, his complexity level rises and he seeks stimuli of greater and greater complexity.

Rather than speaking of a single complexity level for each animal, Dember suggests that there may be different complexity levels for different types of stimuli. Thus a person's complexity level for music might be significantly higher than his complexity level for literature, probably because in his life he has had more experience with music and thus encounters more music pacers.

Pacers are usually pleasing because they are different enough to be not boring, but are not so complex that they are disrupting. Humor often involves situations that are somewhat unexpected, but not so strange that we strain to make sense of them. Beethoven is said to have remarked that in music everything must be at once surprising and expected.

Although pacer theory emphasizes the continual rise in complexity levels, one wonders if complexity levels ever decrease. Are there negative pacers which when encountered lower the animal's complexity level? It may be that although an animal's complexity level along some dimension generally rises, it does fluctuate back and forth, including many short term decreases.

If we assume, as some theorists after Dember have done, that discrepancies between an animal's complexity level and the stimulus complexity produce arousal, then pacer theory is a minimum arousal theory, for animals work for minimum discrepancies between their complexity level and that of stimuli.

Pacer theory assumes that if the complexity of the stimulus situation is too far from the animal's preferred level, there will be emotional disturbance. Chimps are frightened by a model of a chimp's head without a body. They have always seen heads on bodies; a head without a body is too complex. Human infants are often distressed if they hear a strange sound coming from a familiar face or a familiar voice coming from a strange mask. Many unpleasant experiences with hallucinogenic drugs such as LSD result from the person's being overwhelmed by sensory and thought experiences unfamiliar to him.

The effect of stimuli of too little complexity may be simply boredom. In more extreme situations, such as sensory deprivation, the effects are more pronounced. *Sensory deprivation* is not so much the depriving a person of stimuli as it is a drastic reduction in stimulus complexity. In some of the first studies (Bexton, Heron, & Scott, 1954), college students were paid to stay in a room lying in a bed. To reduce visual complexity their eyes were covered with translucent goggles. Auditory complexity was reduced by the person keeping his head in a U-shaped foam rubber pillow and hearing the hum of the air conditioner. Tactile complexity was reduced by having the person wear cotton gloves and cardboard cuffs that extended beyond the fingers. The students stayed this way 24 hours a day with time out only to eat and go to the toilet. Most subjects lasted only two to three days, although a few were able to last longer.

The effects of sensory deprivation on the subjects were quite disturbing. The subjects were restless, often displaying constant random motion. Their feelings vacillated between anger and mirth. Perhaps most distressing was that they could not think clearly for any length of time. It appears that the functional organization of the mind that we call rational thinking requires a certain amount of environmental support in the way of stimulus complexity. The subjects also had hallucinations, similar to drug-induced hallucinations, that ranged from simple objects to complex scenes, such as rows of yellow men with caps on or squirrels with packs on their backs marching purposively along. The hallucinations weren't totally visual but also often included specific voices or sounds, and specific feelings. This seems to be the same type of phenomenon as the hallucinations reported by aviators during long flights, by truck drivers during extended trips, and by radar screen watchers whose shifts are too long. The explanation is probably that when the environment does not provide enough complexity, the mind draws from other sources.

While some of the subjects were in sensory deprivation they heard a recording of a talk arguing in favor of the existence of ghosts and supernatural phenomena. For some reason the talk in this situation was particularly persuasive. Some of the subjects said that for days after they left the sensory deprivation they were afraid they would see ghosts. This finding suggests that sensory deprivation might be a powerful influence technique, but almost no one has seriously investigated it. Adams (1965) put a hospitalized mental patient in mild sensory deprivation and presented to him a taped message discussing his particular case and the aims, procedures, and rationale of psychotherapy. Adams reports that this message resulted in general improvement in the subject. Part of the effect of sensory deprivation is that it focuses the subject's attention on the message, minimizing most sources of distraction. Unfortunately Adams had only one subject in this report and the results are confounded with other parts of the treatment program.

Arousal Induction Theories. There are no true arousal induction theories — theories that argue that animals seek to experience the most arousal they can. Such a theory would be at variance with too much data. But several theories are almost arousal induction theories. Some theorists, such as Sheffield (see Chapter 6), argue that stimuli that elicit arousal have a greater determining effect on the animal's behavior. Thus the animal may often behave in ways that, at least temporarily, raise his arousal, for the stimuli that increase arousal have a greater effect on the behavior than other stimuli. This will be explained in more detail in Chapter 6.

Miller (1963) suggested that there are one or more *go-mechanisms* in the brain which intensify ongoing responses to cues and traces of immediately preceding activities. These go-mechanisms are activated by events such as rewards, drive reduction, and the removal of discrepancy between intention and achievement. Thus if a rat learns to press a bar when a light comes on in order to get food, the reward of the food activates a go-mechanism which intensifies the response of pressing the bar to the cue of the light. Miller also suggested that the go-mechanism can become conditioned to the occurrence of the response so that future occurrences of the stimulus will elicit both the response and the excitatory state. If one equates the excitatory state of Miller's go-mechanism with arousal, then Miller's theory comes close to being an arousal induction theory.

Optimal Arousal Theories. According to optimal arousal theories there is a level of arousal that is ideal for each animal. If its arousal is too low, the animal will seek stimuli to increase arousal, whereas if arousal is too high, due to fear or hunger, for example, the animal will try to do what is necessary (e.g., flee or find food) to reduce the arousal to its optimal point.

Walker (1964) suggested a theory stating that the more complex a stimulus is the more arousal it elicits. An organism seeks those stimuli that elicit optimal arousal. However, according to Walker, as an animal experiences a stimulus, there is a decrease in the complexity of the stimulus relative to the animal. Thus stimuli that may have maintained optimal arousal for a while lose complexity, and the animal seeks out other stimuli. (In pacer theory the complexity of stimuli stays the same, and it is the *animal's* complexity level that changes. In Walker's theory the animal's complexity-arousal level is constant while the complexity of stimuli changes.)

Walker equates the effects of rewards with arousal. This yields the following interesting prediction: "The rewarded event should undergo progessive and selective reduction in psychological complexity. Eventually it should reach a level of psychological complexity that is lower than that of the unrewarded alternative." That is, rewards affect behavior as they do because of their effects on arousal. But as the animal encounters the same reward for the same response over and over again, the reward reduces in complexity, thus reducing its effect on arousal. If this were continued long enough the animal should abandon the rewarded response in favor of another response — probably non-rewarded — that produces more arousal. Most experiments, however, are terminated long before this point would be reached and observed. Unfortunately, there is little research on this prediction of the theory, although Walker does give some suggestive data. Partial support of the prediction occurred in an experiment (Walter & Mikulas, 1969) in which rats were tested each day for over 5 months in an operant chamber where they pressed a bar for food. The rates of bar-pressing decreased over time, which would seem to indicate that the food had lost some of its rewarding value.

Berlyne (1967) has offered an optimal arousal theory in which variables such as novelty, complexity, and ambiguity produce conflict, which in turn produces arousal. For example, seeing a novel stimulus, such as a picture of a dog's body with a bird's head, produces some conflict which in turn increases arousal. The greater the conflict, the greater the arousal. According to Berlyne, moderate increases in arousal (or decrements if the animal is already highly aroused) activate a reward system. This system underlies learning based on approach responses and pleasant feelings (e.g., positive reinforcement, appetitive classical conditioning). Thus an animal will seek out and be rewarded by a stimulus which produces a moderate increase in its arousal. High increases in arousal activate an aversion system which underlies learning based on avoidance responses and displeasure (e.g., punishment, defensive classical conditioning). Too much conflict and too much arousal create aversion and will be avoided. Activation of the aversion system is assumed to inhibit the reward system.

On a practical level, complexity theory might be helpful in many disparate areas. For example, in education it might help us to match the complexity of material to be learned with the student's optimal complexity level. Or workers in a plant might be shifted among various positions in order to maintain sufficient complexity for optimal performance.

Having seen some possible ways in which learning and perception interact to affect information entering the system and how it is interpreted, we turn in the next chapter to a discussion of the possible stages the information goes through while being processed.

SUMMARY

Man does not passively perceive his environment. Rather he selects, filters, and interprets environmental stimuli, largely on the basis of his past learning. Thus man's subjective perception of everything from simple objects and visual illusions to complex social interactions is based on the interplay between his sensory-perceptual mechanisms and what he has already learned. Even what man attends to is partly determined by learning. On a broader level is the concept of *set*—a predisposition to perceive and respond to stimuli in specific ways. Set is influenced by a variety of factors, including past experiences, motives, context, rewards, and instructions.

An important and unresolved question is whether learning ever affects the actual initial perception of an object or if it affects only the responses made to the object. The *Whorfian hypothesis* suggests that the way a person perceives his environment is molded by the nature of the language he has learned. But do people with different languages actually see environmental objects differently or do they merely respond to the objects differently or process the information differently?

To a large extent people must learn how to perceive, which is called *perceptual learning*. There are basically two categories of theories of perceptual learning. The first category, which includes *Gibson's perceptual differentiation theory*, assumes that the environment supplies most of the needed information and that we must learn how to use this information. The second category, which includes *transactional theory*, assumes that the environment supplies inadequate information, and thus we must learn to make extrapolations from this information.

In verbal learning studies it has been shown that it is easier to learn associations to words that elicit a number of images than to words that elicit fewer images. Also, the way a person codes the stimuli he is perceiving affects the ease and nature of associations he learns to the stimuli.

Animals, including humans, strive for variety, novelty, and complexity in their environment, even though such striving does not necessarily satisfy any biological need. The complexity of stimuli is assumed to affect the animal's arousal—the amount of general excitation. Theorists differ on how much arousal they believe an animal will seek out. Minimum arousal theorists assume that the less arousal there is, the better. Arousal induction theorists, on the other hand, emphasize how stimuli that elicit arousal have a greater determining effect on the animal's behavior. Finally, there are the optimal arousal theorists, who assume that the animal tries to maintain some intermediate optimal amount of arousal.

SUGGESTED READINGS

Dember, W. N. *The Psychology of Perception.* New York: Holt, Rinehart & Winston, 1960.

Gibson, E. J. *Principles of Perceptual Learning and Development.* New York: Appleton-Century-Crofts, 1969.

Gregory, R. L. *Eye and Brain.* New York: McGraw-Hill, 1966.

Vanderplas, J. Perception and learning. In Marx, M. H. (ed.) *Learning: Interactions.* Toronto: Macmillan, 1970.

information holding mechanisms

Environmental stimuli generally pass by too quickly for us to select and interpret them satisfactorily. To slow things down we need some types of *holding mechanisms* — hypothesized storage processes that hold information long enough so that it can be properly processed. This chapter discusses some such holding mechanisms.

A complication in the learning process is that not everything we wish to associate together occurs together in time. Two stimuli to be associated might be separated by several seconds, or the reward for a behavior might come after the behavior has stopped. Learning such delayed associations may also involve some type of holding mechanism.

SENSORY STORAGE

Stimuli that affect the sense receptors produce neural activity in various parts of the central nervous system. It appears that only part of the information that reaches the sensory areas is later attended to and perceived. The rest dissipates in a short period of time, probably less than a second. The holding mechanism that holds all the sensory input for a short time is called *sensory storage* (also known as short term sensory storage, sensory memory, and pre-perceptual store).

In a classic experiment on sensory storage, Sperling (1960) presented to subjects an array of 12 letters, three rows of four letters each. This array was shown to the subjects for only 50 milliseconds. Immediately after the presentation of the array, the subjects heard one of three tones which told them which row of letters to try to remember. Since the tone came on *after* the letters were presented, the subjects could not know in advance which row they would have to remember. The subjects were good at this task, remembering a high percentage of the letters of the signaled row. However, once remembering one row they had great difficulty trying to remember either other row, for the image of the 12 letters quickly dies as the subject recites the letters of the required row. Similarly if the signal tone, instead of coming on immediately after the array of letters, is delayed by one second, memory of the signaled row drops to less than one half of what it is with no delay.

This suggests that sensory storage very briefly holds more information than can be perceived and processed. That part of the information that is quickly chosen (attended to?) continues in perceptual processing, while the rest of the information is lost from the system. Although not as well researched as vision, auditory perception seems to have similar storage phenomena (Massaro, 1972).

It is assumed that the information that is "chosen" from sensory storage goes into another holding mechanism, short term memory. Some of the information from short term memory is then assumed to enter long term memory. This trichotomy of sensory storage, short term memory, and long term memory, however, is an explanatory fiction. One can argue that there are fewer or more separate stages. Also, it is possible that none of the proposed stages may correspond to any real physiological processes, although we will suggest some. Finally, the following discussion is based on a linear model which shows information going from sensory storage to short term memory to long term memory. However, some theorists argue for a parallel model where information from sensory storage may go simultaneously into short term memory and long term memory.

SHORT TERM MEMORY

A person looks up a phone number and remembers it just long enough to dial it. If he gets a busy signal and decides to dial again, he might find he has forgotten the number already. This appears to be an example of *short term memory* (STM), or primary memory, a short duration memory-holding mechanism. STM is generally considered a store of limited capacity in which information dissipates with time and/or is easily displaced by newer information. It may be somewhat contradictory to describe this holding mechanism in terms of short term *memories,* since memories are usually defined as being relatively permanent (see Chapter 1). Broadbent (1963) suggests that forgetting in STM is due more to the deterioration of information with time than to actual stimulus properties of the information. That is, information that enters STM weakens over time, and this effect is largely independent of any interfering effects between different pieces of information in memory storage. Waugh and Norman (1965), on the other hand, suggest that information loss in STM (they call it primary memory) is not due to a dissipation with time but is due to the information being displaced by newer information. They suggest that primary memory has a limited capacity, and new information, if not redundant, will displace the old.

After looking up the phone number we can make sure we remember it until dialed by running it over and over again in our minds or by repeating it out loud. This process of *rehearsal* is a common way to keep information in STM. It is as if information keeps being taken out of STM and put back in to be sure it is never lost from STM. Rehearsal is a key part of many models of STM. For example, in the Waugh and Norman (1965) model rehearsal is seen as a way to keep information in primary memory as well as a way to facilitate the entry of the information into more permanent memory storage systems (i.e., secondary or long term memory).

Rehearsal often involves the subject's coding the stimulus into verbal symbols, such as words, which can then be rehearsed. If shown a string of letters to remember for a short time, a person probably won't rehearse a visual image of the letters as much as a verbal reading of the letters. However, rehearsal does not *have* to be verbal or even conscious.

If STM does have limited capacity, what is its storage capacity? Miller (1956) suggested that the answer is seven, plus or minus two, units of information. That is, STM usually holds between five and nine units of information, depending on some aspect of the person's intelligence and the nature of the material. Thus a person might be able to remember a string of nine random digits or a string of seven random letters. Miller uses the word *chunks* to refer to the units of information that can be remembered. He argues that although a person can remember only about 7 chunks of information, people differ in how much information they code into any one chunk. The process of *chunking*, then, is a coding procedure for converting environmental information into chunks of information.

The following example illustrates how Miller's theory works. If we read the following series of digits—011100101011001010101100—to a person and ask him to repeat back, in order, as many as he can, he might remember only the first eight digits, for each 0 or 1 is coded as a single chunk and he remembers 8 chunks. If, however, we teach the subject a simple binary code in which two digits are chunked together and coded as one digit (00=0, 01=1, 10=2, 11=3), then the first eight digits would be coded as follows: 1302. After learning well this binary chunking code, our subject might still remember only eight chunks, but this would now correspond to 16 digits. Miller reports examples of several engineers who learned to remember a string of 20 lights in terms of the specific sequence of on and off. They did this by grouping the lights in sets of three, chunking the on—off information for each group into a single chunk, and then remembering about seven chunks (on—off—on might be considered 101 and coded as the number 5). Chunking of more meaningful material often utilizes codes where considerable information can be carried by one meaningful word.

TWO STORAGES OR ONE?

A number of distinctions have been made between the nature and processes of STM and those of long term memory (LTM):

1. STM is generally considered to be of limited capacity whereas LTM, for all practical purposes, is unlimited.

2. Information in STM dissipates with time and/or is displaced by new information. Storage in LTM, on the other hand, is considered fairly permanent, and forgetting is explained in terms of interference from other learned material. (This will be covered in more detail in the next chapter.)

3. Less processing of information takes place in STM than in LTM.

4. STM is affected more by acoustic similarity of the material than by semantic similarity, while the opposite is true for LTM. That is, interference and confusion between material in STM primarily depends on how similar the different materials *sound* to each other, whereas in LTM the *meaning* of the material plays a greater role.

5. Some theories, such as Hebb's (discussed later), suggest that STM involves an active, ongoing physiological process, while LTM involves some structural change in the CNS.

Other theorists, such as Melton (1963), argue against the dichotomy between STM and LTM. They suggest that the characteristics of STM storage are basically the same as those of LTM. Current research is showing that many of the principles of forgetting that are known to be true in LTM also apply to STM. Apparent differences between STM and LTM, then, do not indicate different processes, but are artifacts of the amount of time the subject has to do his tasks and the type of task required of him. STM and LTM are just different points on the same continuum that differ quantitatively, but not qualitatively.

For example, consider the distinction that STM is primarily acoustic whereas LTM is primarily semantic. Shulman (1971), who was one of Melton's students, has argued that semantic encoding can be demonstrated in STM tasks if the task requires it or if the rate of incoming information is slow. However, in most STM tasks the subject does not have time, particularly if rehearsal is taking place, to encode stimuli semantically, and therefore the acoustic properties of the stimuli are more important. With more time, semantic encoding is possible, and becomes dominant. Thus the degree of semantic encoding is assumed to lie along a continuum of time available for the task, rather than to reflect distinct processes of STM and LTM. However, Baddeley (1972) argues that semantic coding, being more complex and slower than acoustic coding, results in a more durable memory trace. He suggests that if LTM is defined in terms of trace durability, then semantic coding takes place in only LTM, and not in STM. According to Baddeley, effects of apparent semantic coding in STM reflect semantically coded retrieval rules from *LTM* being used to interpret *acoustically* coded material in STM.

Even if many of the mechanisms of STM and LTM are the same, there might still be some qualitative differences. Although Peterson (1966) agrees that many mechanisms affect STM and LTM similarly, he suggests that there still is a recency factor in STM, the effectiveness of which decreases with time and which interacts with learning mechanisms.

Hebb (1961) did an experiment in which he disproved to his satisfaction his own assumption of the independence of STM and LTM. He gave his subjects the task of learning an unordered sequence of nine digits, presented at the rate of one per second. The subjects then had to immediately repeat them back. This was done for 24 trials. However, on every third trial the same sequence of digits was presented, while the other 16 sequences were all different. Now since the subject is asked only to remember a sequence long enough to repeat it back, the sequence of each trial should replace in STM the sequence of the previous trial. So, Hebb argued, if STM and LTM are distinct, recall of the repeated sequence should not be better than that for any other sequence. However, the experiment showed that recall of the repeated sequence improved over trials. Melton (1963) repeated and extended Hebb's experiment, and achieved similar results. Hebb and Melton interpreted these results as suggesting a continuum of STM and LTM. It could, however, also be argued that STM and LTM are distinct and parallel processes, and that the information during the Hebb experiment entered both STM and LTM simultaneously.

A general problem in memory experiments, except perhaps with those carried out in long time intervals, is that we often can't be sure whether the recall came from STM or LTM. Just because we choose a short recall interval and call our experiment a study of STM doesn't mean that the recall couldn't really have come from an LTM system which is qualitatively different than an STM system. Perhaps many of the similarities found between STM and LTM merely show that the experimenter was really measuring LTM in both cases. In this sense the terms "short term memory" and "long term memory" may be misleading since they imply a time distinction which may or may not exist. There is no reason why the processes of STM and LTM can't overlap in time. Thus the question of whether there are two storages or one remains unanswered.

LONG TERM MEMORY

With long recall intervals, theorists agree that the information comes from an LTM storage. What are the properties of this storage? How is information stored and how is it found again (retrieved) once stored? Underwood (1969) suggests that memories can be conceptualized as involving a collection of attributes. The attributes of a memory are a result of the process by which information is encoded into LTM. They are the distinguishing characteristics of the memories by which the encoding process separates one memory from another. Underwood gives a number of possible attributes, including the following:

1. A *spatial* attribute occurs when the memory can be associated with some spatial coordinates. In trying to remember a chemistry formula the student might remember that it was at the bottom of one of the pages in the text, and this spatial cue may then facilitate his remembering the formula.

2. A *temporal* attribute occurs when the memory can be placed in time relative to some other event. You remember that you went to Dunham's Flower Shop before you went to Dunn's Antique House.

3. A *modality* attribute is based on the sense mode of the incoming information. Information might be coded according to whether it was written or verbal, or there might even be different storage systems for visual and auditory memory.

Attributes, then, are the labels and hooks that serve to discriminate memories and facilitate later retrieval. In reviewing studies of animal memory, Spear (1973) argues that "the attributes of a memory represent those events that were noticed by the organism during learning." Spear suggests that events that trigger memory attributes may reactivate inactive memories and improve retrieval of these memories.

Norman and others (Bower, 1973; Norman, 1969, Chap. 6) have investigated the properties of LTM in terms of systems that people use to improve their memory. These memory devices are called *mnemonics*, after Mnemosyne, the Greek goddess of memory. Norman included in his studies the following mnemonic devices: rhymes, method of loci, and analytic substitutions.

Rhymes. "Thirty days hath September ... " is a common rhyme that people use to help remember the numbers of days in each month, for it is easier to remember the rhyme than to memorize the number of days for each month. Another common rhyme is the spelling rule "I before e except after c."

Method of Loci. Early Greek orators who had to remember long speeches from memory used a simple device now called the method of loci. They would memorize each part of the speech in association with a particular part of their home, i.e., by practicing that part while looking at or thinking about the corresponding part of the home. Then when giving the speech their minds would systematically move through their home in the same order, letting the images of the different loci facilitate the memory of the associated part of the speech.

Analytic Substitutions.   The method of analytic substitutions consists of translating the material to be remembered into a form that is easier to remember. This translation may involve numbers, sounds, words, and so forth. For example, to remember number values for the transcendental number pi (the ratio of the circumference of a circle to its diameter) many people have devised sentences where the number of letters in successive words give the sequence of digits for pi. One such sentence devised by Sir James Jeans goes, "How I want a drink, alcoholic of course, after the heavy chapters involving quantum mechanics."A common way of remembering numbers is by coding each digit into a specific word: one—bun, two—shoe, three—tree, four—door, five—hive, six—sticks, seven—heaven, eight—gate, nine—line, ten—hen. First the person learns the code well. Then when he wishes to remember a number he forms a bizarre image based on the words corresponding to the numbers. For example, to remember that a person was born in '52 you might imagine him walking over to a bee hive and putting his shoe in it.

Analytic substitution schemes can get quite complicated. It may take a long time to learn and to develop any skill at using some of the schemes, but when mastered they impressively improve memory. Without going into the systems it might be interesting to look at a complex example from Norman (p. 122). Consider having to learn the following sequence of digits: 001100001001100001101010001111111100000. This sequence could first be encoded into the octal digits 1411415217740, where each octal digit represents (chunking) three of the original digits. Using a number-consonant transformation on the octal digits results in the letters trttrtlntkkrs. These letters are then changed into the equivalent (by this system) sequence of trd drt ln tng grs which is put into the word-picture "tired dirty lion eating grass." Thus 39 original digits were translated into one easy to remember word-picture.

Norman suggests that mnemonic devices work simply by reducing long, unrelated strings of material into short, related lists according to a previously learned scheme. Norman also suggests that mnemonic devices are effective for retrieval rather than learning, as they usually add more to learn. Paivio (1969) suggested that some of these devices may work by increasing the amount of imagery associated with the material to be learned and recalled.

Norman (p. 123) offers the following maxim for improving memo-

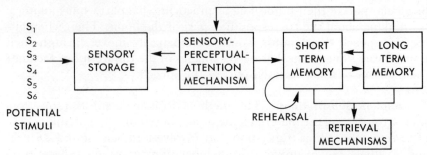

Figure 4–1   *A possible model of information processing and storage.*

ry: "If you wish to learn something, rather than plunge blindly ahead reciting the material endlessly, it would be best to first summarize briefly its overall meaning and structure, second, to decide how it relates to what you already know and, finally, to divide the material into a small set of logical subdivisions."

When forgetting does take place in LTM it appears to be a retrieval problem rather than a storage problem. Although some information may be lost from LTM storage, as with advanced age, forgetting is generally due to not being able to *retrieve* information that is in the storage. The major cause of this retrieval failure, as will be discussed in the next chapter, is interference resulting from other learned material. In trying to retrieve one piece of information you instead retrieve another piece of information.

Figure 4–1 (an extension of Figure 3–1 from the preceding chapter) shows a possible set of relationships between the processes discussed so far.

REVERBERATORY CIRCUITS

Lorente de No (1938) was one of the first to provide evidence for networks of neurons in the brain that close back on themselves and thus could be potentially self-exciting. Neural impulses that start in such a network, as the result of stimulation from neurons outside the network, might travel through the network, which closes back on itself, and thus restimulate the same neurons again. This neural activity might keep circling through the same network over and over many times. Such closed networks of neurons that can keep restimulating themselves are called *reverberatory circuits.* Physiological evidence related to the functioning of such circuits is still highly debatable. Some evidence was supplied by Burns (1954) working with cortical slabs isolated from the rest of the brain but with an intact blood supply. Burns found that electrical stimulation of parts of these slabs could result in bursts of electrical activity lasting for 30 minutes. Such activity may involve the activity of reverberatory circuits. However, there is some question as to how representative such a surgical preparation is of what goes on in the cortex of an intact animal.

Figure 4–2 shows a highly simplified schema of one reverberatory circuit. It should be remembered that the only criterion for a reverberatory circuit is that it close back on itself and re-excite the network. It might be composed of only two neurons or of hundreds of neurons. It could be in the form of a simple circle or it could be a complex network with many different routes and side-paths. The neural impulses might or might not utilize exactly the same neurons through the network each time. But to be a reverberatory circuit the network *must* close on itself and re-excite itself.

The reverberatory circuit is a possible candidate for a holding mechanism. Information could go into such a circuit and stay there during the duration of the reverberation. Many psychological theories have drawn on such a construct, the most influential theory being that of Hebb.

Hebb's original theory (1949) explained STM in terms of reverberatory circuits, meaning, for example, that remembering a phone number just long enough to dial it involves holding the information in reverberatory circuits. Continued activity of a neural network was assumed to produce structural changes in the neuron, probably at the synapse. (Hebb suggested the possibility of enlargement of the synaptic knobs.) This structural change was thought to be the basis for LTM. At first, then, Hebb had a sharp dichotomy: STM involved an activity trace, LTM involved structural change. More recently, as was discussed earlier in this chapter, Hebb has been questioning this distinction.

According to Hebb's model, continued use of a neural pathway results in facilitation of transmission in the involved synapses. This facili-

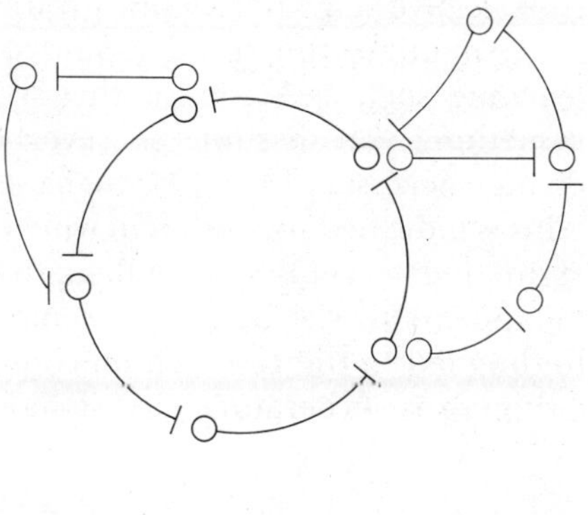

Figure 4–2 Simplified schema of a reverberatory circuit (impulses going counterclockwise).

tation makes it more probable that the next neural impulse will take the same path which then can lead to reverberatory activity of a given neural network. Hebb calls such a network a *cell-assembly*. With more complex learning, cell-assemblies become associated so that the firing of one cell-assembly tends to also fire related cell-assemblies. Hebb calls such a group of associated cell-assemblies a *phase sequence*.

There were a number of problems with the early Hebbian model, many of which were related to the predicted spread of excitatory effects from cell-assemblies and phase sequences: What keeps impulses from spreading to inappropriate pathways? What keeps too many neurons from being tied up with single memories? Why doesn't the whole brain eventually become one giant phase sequence? These problems arose because Hebb emphasized the excitatory effects of neurons on each other, but did not account for any checks on these excitatory effects. To deal with these problems Milner (1957) introduced the concept of inhibition into the Hebbian system. That is, in addition to excitatory effects, neurons also have inhibitory effects on other neurons, and thus input into a nerve network might be inhibitory or excitatory. Repeated activity of a neural network was assumed to inhibit neighboring neurons, thus restricting excitatory neural activity to the appropriate neurons. The activity of a cell-assembly might be stopped by inhibitory influences from outside the network. Now the Hebbian model, like almost all current psychological models of brain functioning, explains behavior and brain processes as being the result of a complex interplay of excitatory and inhibitory effects.

Using Hebb's theories, a tremendous number of psychological phenomena can be explained in terms of contructs such as cell-assemblies. For example, Hebb (1972, Chap. 5) uses cell-assemblies to explain the mediating processes between stimuli and responses in situations which involve a sequence of associations between stimulus and response as opposed to cases where the stimulus elicits a reflex or simple conditioned response. Simple holding of information for a period of time is accomplished by cell-assemblies. Thoughts are mediating processes involving one or more cell-assemblies, with thinking occurring when a number of such mediating processes stimulate each other. Attention and set involve the selective activation of one group of cell-assemblies over other groups.

An interesting prediction from reverberatory circuit models of learning such as Hebb's is that if immediately after an animal learns something you disrupt the reverberatory circuits, then the structural change necessary for LTM will be stopped, as well as the activity of STM. This is indicated by studies in which an animal is given a disruptive agent right after learning (e.g., a drug that produces convulsions), after which he appears to not be able to remember what he learned. This type of finding led to the research on consolidation discussed below. However, although reverberatory circuit models were a major factor leading to consolidation research and theories, current theories and explanations of consolidation do not depend on any particular assumptions about reverberatory circuits.

CONSOLIDATION

Whatever physiological change might underlie LTM, it is highly improbable that this change occurs simultaneously with learning. Rather, after a learning experience there is probably a period of time during which some process, called *consolidation*, converts the effects of the experience into LTM. The assumption of consolidation is only an assumption that there is such a non-instantaneous process, and not an explanation of what the process is or how long it will take. From this assumption has come a massive number of experiments and theories (Grossman, 1967, Chap. 14; Lewis, 1969; McGaugh, 1966; McGaugh & Herz, 1972; Spevack & Suboski, 1969). First we will consider some indirect evidence for consolidation — phenomena that are supportive of consolidation, but are equally well explained without appealing to consolidation processes.

In conditioning eyelid blinking in humans, Spence and Norris (1950) found that the percentage of conditioned responses increased as the mean inter-trial interval (ITI, the amount of time between successive conditioning trials) increased from 9 to 90 seconds. A possible interpretation of this is that with short ITI one trial impairs the consolidation of the previous trial, thus retarding learning. Similarly Kettlewell and Papsdorf (1967) conditioned an eyelid response in rabbits while the rabbits were in a darkened chamber. They found that 10 seconds of illumination during the ITI impaired learning. Although there are other possible explanations (see Ost, 1969), it may be that the ITI illumination impaired the consolidation of the previous trial.

Another phenomenon suggested as being supportive of consolidation is the *Kamin effect*. This refers to the observation that retention is often poorest at some intermediate time after learning. Kamin (1963) trained rats in a shuttle box, where they had to run from one side to the other on cue to escape or avoid shock, to a criterion of three correct avoidance responses. The rats were tested for retention 1 minute, 30 minutes, 1 hour, 6 hours, 24 hours, and 20 days after the last training trial. Kamin found little deficit in all but the 1-hour and 6-hour groups. The deficit at 1 and 6 hours might be because the learning is being consolidated and thus less available for retrieval, although other research suggests that consolidation is completed much sooner than this. A popular alternative explanation of the Kamin effect (see Barrett et al., 1971) is that the shocks during training induce some type of behavioral inhibition or suppression which impairs performance of the avoidance response during retention. This inhibition is assumed to have its maximum effect at intermediate retention intervals. Its effect gradually increases and then decreases.

If a person is in an accident in which he is hit on the head or receives some other type of traumatic brain injury, *retrograde amnesia* often occurs (Russell & Nathan, 1946). In retrograde amnesia the person cannot remember what happened during some period of time just prior to the accident. With time, many of the memories come back, the temporally most distant memories returning first. But there is often a period of time just prior to the accident that is never recovered in memory. (Similar results occur following cerebral anoxia, carbon monoxide poisoning, and Korsakoff psychosis.) Although these results can be interpreted as being due to the accident's disruption of consolidation of the memories just prior to the accident, we will need a somewhat different explanation for those memories that eventually recover.

To investigate this retrograde amnesia with animals in the laboratory researchers have utilized a variety of agents that are presumed to disrupt the consolidation process. The most frequently used disruptive agent is *electroconvulsive shock* (ECS). ECS is usually administered by attaching electrodes to both ears of the animal and inducing a strong enough current to produce convulsions, although some researchers (e.g., Jarvik & Kopp, 1967) have reported ESC-induced amnesia with stimulation below the level necessary for convulsions. The direct physiological effects of ECS are unknown, as it affects a number of variables such as amount of neural firing and neural metabolism. A human parallel of ECS is electroshock therapy, discussed later.

Other disruptive agents include drugs such as metrazol (pentylenetetrazol) which produce convulsions when given in sufficient dosage, carbon disulfide gas, anesthetics in some situations, spreading depression, microwave radiation, polarizing currents, anoxia, and some types of subconvulsive electrical brain stimulation. Almost anything that significantly alters the neural activity of the brain appears to be a potential disruptive agent. However, it may not be necessary to have gross changes in brain chemistry or electrical activity for memory disruption. Jacobs and Sorenson (1969) reported having been able to produce retrograde amnesia in mice by dunking them for 10 seconds in hot (48° C) or cold (1° C) water.

A typical consolidation experiment consists of training a group of animals in some learning task and then, immediately after learning, giving the disruptive agent to half of the animals (keeping the other half as a control group). Depending on the nature of the disruptive agent, the control animals are given some other treatment, such as shock to the tail, instead of the disruptive agent. If on later retention tests the control animals perform better than the experimental animals, then perhaps the disruptive agent did in fact impair consolidation. What makes the consolidation literature difficult is that there are many things other than impairing consolidation that the disruptive agent might do that could result in poor performance on the retention test. Lewis (1969) lists a few of the alternative effects of the disruptive agent: (1) it might affect some of the processes of the storage mechanisms, such as the way information is catalogued for later retrieval; (2) the memory itself may be unimpaired, but the animal cannot associate the memory with the appropriate cues; (3) the subject might lose the motivation to express the memory in its behavior; (4) the disruptive agent may produce various forms of suppression, competition, and inhibition. All of this highlights an earlier point: that many variables affect performance, of which learning is only one.

The type of learning task used is very important in consolidation research. Most of the experimental tasks are ones in which the animal can learn the task in one trial, because learning tasks requiring more than one trial have the following complications. If the animal is given several trials before the disruptive agent, then considerable consolidation may be going on between and/or during the trials. Thus the effects of the disruptive agent would be confounded with the number of trials, the inter-trial interval, the disrupting aspects of a trial on prior consolidation, and the varying times of consolidation. On the other hand, if the disruptive agent were given after each trial, the possible effects on consolidation would be confounded with artifacts of multiple treatments of the disruptive agent. For example, repeated ECS treatments in rats may result in a decrease in general activity, decreased heart rate, and weight loss. Although some of these effects may occur with a single ECS (Reuttenberg & Kay, 1965), the effects are less than with multiple ECS's.

The most common type of one-trial learning task with rats and mice is a variation of *passive avoidance*, a situation where the animal can avoid a shock by *not* making some specified response. The type of passive avoidance task used in consolidation research often involves the animal's receiving a shock when it first makes a fairly common response, such as jumping from a platform onto a grid floor or going from a large bright compartment into a smaller dark compartment. Usually one such shocked trial is enough for the animal to refrain from making the response again.

Theoretically, by applying the disruptive agent at various times after learning we should be able to determine how long consolidation takes. For at the point at which the disruptive agent no longer impairs retention, consolidation may be over. Using such an approach many investigators suggest that consolidation takes about an hour, but this is far from being commonly accepted. Other estimates vary between 10 seconds and a week. Probably consolidation time varies according to factors such as the difficulty of the learning task, the nature and duration of the disruptive agent, and the species of the animal.

When the animal in a passive avoidance task receives a shock, an emotional response is elicited and may become conditioned to stimuli of the test apparatus, so that later the test apparatus tends to elicit this *conditioned emotional response* (CER). The CER may cause a decrease in general locomotion by the animal, which would facilitate later performance in the passive avoidance task since it decreases the probability that the animal will make the punished response. If the disruptive agent, such as ECS, impairs the CER, the animal will make *more* incorrect responses, giving the appearance that the ECS disrupted memory of the punished response. Chorover and Schiller (1966) argued that when CER's are minimized, ECS has little effect when given more than 10 seconds after training. Apparent disruptive effects after 10 seconds are due to the ECS's interfering with the CER. Spevack and Suboski (1969) have made a similar argument, saying that the CER incubates (increases in strength) following the shock and that ECS after a minute does not disrupt consolidation but only the incubation of the CER. In a critique of the Spevack and Suboski theory Dawson (1971) included the following arguments: (1) there is no evidence that the retrograde amnesia gradient is short when no CER is produced; (2) there is no good evidence for ECS halting the incubation of a CER; and (3) Spevack and Suboski have not well specified how consolidation and CER incubation actually work and can be measured independently. Thus ECS may in fact disrupt consolidation, but considerably more research is necessary to separate out other possible effects of ECS, such as its effects on CER's.

Retrieval Explanations

As mentioned earlier, following traumatic amnesia, humans generally regain most of their lost memories. Similarly some animal experiments (Nielson, 1968; Zinkin & Miller, 1967) have reported recovery of memories that appeared to be disrupted by ECS. But if ECS disrupts the consolidation of memories, then the memories should never return. Unfortunately the experimental data on memory recovery following ECS is quite complex and contradictory (see McGaugh & Herz, 1972, p. 14). Possible recovery is confounded by factors such as the species of experimental animal, the experimental task and procedure, the strength of original learning, the amount of ECS-produced amnesia, dissipation or counterconditioning of ECS artifacts, opportunity for new learning, and cues prior to the retrieval test that remind the animal of his learning experience. McGaugh and Herz (1972, p. 20), however, point out that there are numerous studies showing amnesia to be stable over long periods of time and that, at least in some situations, the memory loss is permanent. They argue that this is "all that is required by the most general form of the consolidation hypothesis."

The recovery of memories has suggested to some theorists that the disruptive agent affects retrieval, not consolidation (see Nielson, 1968; Thompson & Neely, 1970; Weiskrantz, 1966). Most retrieval theories of the effects of ECS appeal to state-dependent learning effects. That is, the ECS produces a state different from the one under which the animal learned the response. This change in state then impairs retrieval of the information. With time the brain returns to "normal," and recall improves.

To test this hypothesis, Thompson and Neely (1970) gave rats ECS at varying times relative to learning and retention of a one-trial passive avoidance task. They found that rats given ECS 25 minutes before training showed no later retention under "normal" conditions. Similar results occurred with rats that had not been given ECS before training but had been given ECS before retrieval. However, there was no disruption if ECS was given before *both* training and retention. The best results were when the ECS was given the same amount of time before training as it was before retention. Thus the more similar the brain states are at training and retention, the better the retention is. In a second experiment, Thompson and Neely gave rats ECS 5 seconds after learning and found the best retention in those rats that were also given ECS before the retention trial. As in all the consolidation literature, there are experiments that appear to be contradictory to the data and theories just discussed (see McGaugh & Herz, 1972, p. 19).

Miller and Springer (1973) have pointed out problems in such state-dependent theories. First, such theories would generally predict recovery over time from experimental amnesia, which often does not occur. Secondly, memories which are recovered by giving the subject an ECS at the time of retrieval do not disappear again when the brain returns to "normal." Miller and Springer suggest a retrieval model in which the disruptive agent often impairs "the establishment or future functioning of the cataloging system necessary for retrieving the information from long-term storage at some later time." That is, ECS might not affect the memory itself, but rather it affects an associated system that catalogs information for future retrieval.

Facilitation of Consolidation

If consolidation can be disrupted, then perhaps it can also be facilitated or speeded up. There is some evidence that drugs, particularly central nervous system stimulants such as amphetamines, can, when given in proper dosages, facilitate performance, and perhaps consolidation (McGaugh & Herz, 1972, p. 48; McGaugh & Petrinovich, 1965). To show that the drug affects consolidation rather than original learning or motivation, it is necessary to give the subject the drug *after* the learning trial rather than before. Again, there are many reports contradictory to the studies supporting drug effects on consolidation. The effect seems to depend on variables such as the environment in which the subject was raised, the strain and age of the animal, the complexity of the learning task, the amount of time between learning and drug administration, the nature and dosage of the drug, and the animal's post-training environment. Finally we need to know a lot more about the exact physiological effects of the different drugs.

The assumption of consolidation seems reasonable, although experiments trying to pin it down have produced a complex and ambiguous set of data and a variety of different explanations. Future research will have to factor consolidation out of all the other effects. Also it will be necessary to tie together the research on consolidation with research on the physiological bases of memory.

ELECTROSHOCK THERAPY

From the observation that epileptics appeared to be less inclined to become schizophrenic than were "normals" came the following questionable inference: Perhaps many forms of mental illness can be improved by artificially inducing the equivalent of an epileptic seizure. This was the genesis of a therapeutic treatment called *electroshock therapy* or *electroconvulsive therapy* (ECT). ECT is essentially the application of ECS to humans. Surface electrodes are attached to the head (sometimes the current is applied directly to the brain) and a current is applied in a strength great enough to produce highly abnormal activity throughout the brain. The ECT first causes the person to go unconscious. Then there is a general convulsion throughout the body, often accompanied by overt motor seizures. Many practitioners minimize the motor effects of ECT by using muscle relaxants and anesthetics. In those cases where such drugs are not used—and many practitioners believe that they shouldn't be used—the patient could thrash around in a fashion similar to an epileptic suffering from a grand mal seizure. When the patient later regains consciousness, he is very confused and has general memory disturbances.

Although ECT has been given for almost all forms of mental illness, it now is primarily used for various forms of depression, for patients with very agitated mood changes, and for very acute catatonics. The number of treatments a patient receives varies according to the case and the institution, and might be as few as two or three or as many as 75, spread over time.

The exact physiological and psychological effects of ECT are basically unknown. As would be expected from our discussion of consolidation, ECT does produce forgetfulness of events immediately preceding the shock treatment and often of the shock itself. There is some evidence that multiple treatments of ECT may produce intracranial hemorrhaging. When such patients have their heads opened up their brains are found to be engorged with blood. ECT also often produces a general flattening of the EEG (Kimble, 1965, p. 250).

ECT has been reported to be successful in many cases and the question is why. Although no one really knows, there are scores of explanations, some of which border on the ridiculous. One theory is that ECT is a punishment by which the patient atones for his sins. Another is that the coma produced by ECT is a symbolic form of death. A third theory is that ECT helps suicidal patients by making them fight for their life. The most commonly accepted theory is that in the confused state following ECT many (although not all) patients are more suggestible and amenable to forms of therapy that they resisted before. Therefore ECT is best when immediately coupled with psychotherapy.

It may well be that most of the effects of ECT can be explained in terms of thinking about ECT as an extreme form of punishment. To vastly oversimplify: if every time you act depressed you are shocked unconscious, pretty soon you will stop acting depressed in the presence of other people. The evidence that ECT acts like a punishment is quite strong. Although patients receiving ECT do not at first report pain or fear of the treatment (probably because of the ECT-produced amnesia), they generally do develop an aversion to the ECT applications, and often dread having another treatment (Gallinek, 1956). With continued treatment this conditioned aversion generalizes to situations which are similar to situations where the patient received the ECT. The author worked with one patient who, following his release from a hospital where he received ECT, became very anxious whenever he saw someone in a white uniform because they reminded him of the attendants who forcibly took him down to the ECT room. To try to minimize such conditioned aversion many practitioners anesthetize the patient to the point of unconsciousness before taking him for ECT.

An example of the use of ECT as a punishment is provided by a report of an American psychiatrist working in a Vietnamese mental hospital (Cotter, 1967). The main object was to get the patients to work more. Patients who would not work were punished with three ECT treatments a week. This program significantly increased the number of people volunteering for work. (Some patients who wouldn't work in order to avoid ECT were made to work in order to eat.) Although Cotter says that part of the effect of the ECT may have been a reduction of mental illness, "with others it was simply a result of their dislike or fear of ECT." Cotter attempted to justify his program by saying that "The use of effective reinforcements should not be neglected due to a misguided idea of what constitutes kindness."

If ECT produces its major effect through punishment, then there are a number of problems. First, ECT is probably a much stronger form of punishment than should be necessary to cure mental illness. Second, the ECT-produced convulsions may disrupt the consolidation of some of the learned effects of the punishment, thus partially defeating the objective. Third, and most important, as will be seen later, punishment is generally an inefficient and often undesirable technique of behavioral change. There are many more powerful techniques that do not produce conditioned aversion or possible brain damage.

There is some biochemical evidence suggesting possible effects of ECT. For example, drugs such as reserpine, which produce depressive reactions in humans, also produce abnormal biogenic-amine content in the brains of animals. ECS has been reported to increase the turnover of these biogenic amines. This suggests that some forms of human depression might have a biochemical origin which can be offset by ECT. However, there are still many gaps in such research. For example, how similar biochemically are drug-induced depressions and other forms of depression? Of all the different behaviors lumped under the term "depression," which may be due to a biochemical imbalance? Is ECT the most effective way to alter the brain chemistry? Which comes first?—these changes in brain chemistry or changes in behavior?

The use of ECT as a treatment procedure has been on a gradual decline for a variety of reasons: the advent of tranquilizing drugs, more effective procedures for dealing with problems such as depression, questions about the effectiveness and morality of ECT, and the fact that the effects of ECT are often short lived. In many hospitals now it is extremely rare for anyone to receive ECT. Unfortunately, in some hospitals it is still used indiscriminately, perhaps many times a day, primarily by practitioners who do not know alternative treatment procedures and/or are enchanted by the speed with which ECT can be applied in comparison to the slowness of other forms of therapy. In this latter case it is clear that the disadvantages of ECT greatly offset any possible advantages. The important question is whether we will eventually be able to isolate a small specific class of people (perhaps with a biochemical imbalance) for which ECT is the most effective and desirable treatment procedure. Meanwhile studies of ECT should provide information about the nature of ECS, consolidation, and holding mechanisms.

SOME THEORETICAL EXTENSIONS OF HOLDING MECHANISMS

A number of theorists have developed psychological models, based on holding mechanisms, that make predictions that extend beyond the original conceptualization of the holding mechanism. One such theory of *action decrement* was proposed by Walker (1958). Action decrement refers to the lowered capacity for rearousal of the same event. That is, right after an animal makes a particular response in a stimulus situation, this situation has less of a chance of re-exciting the neural network necessary to produce the same response. This decreased probability, or action decrement, persists for some time and then dissipates. Action decrement is assumed to be a direct result of the process which produces consolidation. Thus, information is less accessible for retrieval during consolidation. Action decrement may have some biological utility in that it protects the consolidation process from interference.

Consider a rat which on its first trial in a T-maze chooses to go into the right arm. According to the action decrement theory, some of the neurons related to this choice become less easily fired. If during this decremental phase the rat is given a second trial in the T-maze, there is a tendency for the rat to go left because the neural networks involved in turning right are less easily excited. Rats do, in fact, often show this type of alternation of responses, called *spontaneous alternation*, during early stages of learning.

The more the consolidation that takes place, the greater the long term memory (LTM). At the same time, the more the consolidation, the more the action decrement. Thus the theory predicts that the amount of action decrement is highly correlated with the amount of learning. It is also assumed that the more arousal or excitement in the animal's nervous system during learning, the more consolidation will occur. Also, rewards are considered a powerful source of arousal. All of this produces the following logical sequence: The more rewarded the animal is for a behavior, the more aroused he is; the more the arousal, the more the consolidation, and thus the more the LTM and action decrement. This leads to the prediction that if we rewarded our rat for turning right on the first trial in the T-maze, it would be even more probable that it would turn left on the next trial. Walker (1956) showed that thirsty rats rewarded with water have a greater tendency to alternate than non-rewarded rats. This simple experiment gave great support to the action decrement theory, since many other theories of learning would probably have predicted that rewarding the animal would make alternation less probable.

Later Walker (1967, p. 226) expanded on the relationship between consolidation and action decrement by suggesting that the end of the perseverative consolidation process might be signalled not only by the end of ECS effectiveness in disturbing permanent memory but also by the duration of action decrement and the time between trials required to minimize intertrial interference.

Another prediction from the action decrement theory is that the more arousal is associated with some information, the poorer it can be recalled at first, because of action decrement, but the better it will be recalled later, as the result of greater consolidation and better LTM. This then is a situation where motivation (arousal) is assumed to affect learning and not just performance.

This prediction was examined by Kleinsmith and Kaplan (1963). They had college students learn paired associates in which eight words were each paired with a different single digit. The words (e.g., kiss, vomit, swim) were chosen to differ in the amount of arousal they elicited. (Remember that arousal refers just to general neural excitement regardless of whether the subjective experience is pleasant or unpleasant.) The amount of arousal elicited by each word for each subject was determined by the *Galvanic skin response* (GSR) — changes in the electrical conductivity of the skin. For each subject, then, it was possible to select the three words of highest arousal and those of lowest arousal. After learning, different groups of subjects were tested for recall of the paired associates at a recall interval of 2 minutes, 20 minutes, 45 minutes, 1 day, or 1 week. At 2 minutes the low arousal material was remembered five times better than the high arousal material. At 20 minutes they were recalled about the same. By 45 minutes the high arousal material was recalled significantly better.

The explanation suggested by Kleinsmith and Kaplan is that at 2 minutes there is more reverberatory activity associated with the high arousal material and so the information is not as available for STM (short term memory). However, this increased reverberation produces better LTM, which is reflected by the fact that the high arousal material is better remembered at 45 minutes. (The reader can verify the effects of arousal on LTM by recalling memories from his distant past and observing that most of them were associated with states of arousal, i.e., the event was particularly pleasurable or painful. This is not proof, of course, of the above theory.) Later Kaplan altered his theory somewhat, suggesting that the relative unavailability of high arousal material at first is the result of reverberation-generated neural fatigue, rather than of the reverberation per se (Kaplan, 1972, personal communication; Pomerantz et al., 1969). The later improved recall with high arousal material thus is a joint effect of the dissipation of fatigue and the time required for the biochemical changes underlying LTM.

Butter (1970) replicated the results of Kleinsmith and Kaplan with some procedural changes (e.g., controls for serial position and GSR habituation effects). In addition, Butter also used nouns that differed in noun-imagery, the ability of the word to elicit images (cf. Paivio's research, discussed in Chapter 3). Butter found that nouns low in this imagery elicited high arousal; nouns high in imagery elicited low arousal; and recall associated with the material agreed with the expected crossover of low and high arousal material.

A number of experiments report approximately the same types of effects of arousal on learning or recall. However, interpretations become too complex and often confused when one tries to interrelate these results with the subtleties of verbal learning and other responses (such as the orienting response), which are also tied in with arousal states (Maltzman et al., 1966; discussion in Walker, 1967). This does not devaluate the phenomenon, but suggests the need for considerably more research.

The concepts discussed in this chapter, such as reverberatory circuits, short term memory, consolidation, and action decrement, seem as if they could all be reduced to a few basic constructs that could account for a wealth of disparate phenomena. Although such a synthesis can be fairly easily made at a general theoretical level, any proposed model readily falls apart when we investigate the specific parameters of the various phenomena. For example, the time courses of STM, consolidation, and action decrement appear to be substantially different depending on a wide range of experimental variables. However, hopefully such a synthesis of constructs will eventually be possible.

SUMMARY

Many events happen so quickly that the related information would pass us by unless we had some storage procedures — *information holding mechanisms* — to temporarily hold the information until it can be adequately processed. Such holding mechanisms also permit us to associate events which do not occur together in time. The existence, number, and nature of holding mechanisms are debatable. One possible sequence is as follows: (1) perceived information goes into the temporary holding mechanism of sensory storage; (2) some of the information then goes from sensory storage into the temporary holding mechanism of short term memory; and (3) some of the information from short term memory goes into the permanent storage of long term memory.

Sensory storage holds all information picked up by the sense receptors. This information is held only a fraction of a second, after which time part of the information is processed further and the rest is dissipated away. *Short term memory* is usually conceived of as a storage with a limited capacity; in short term memory, information dissipates out with time and/or is readily displaced by newer information entering short term memory. *Long term memory*, on the other hand, is generally conceived of as a permanent storage with practically unlimited capacity. Information stored in long term memory may never be lost, even though there may be problems in retrieving the information from storage, as in forgetting. Many differences have been proposed between short and long term memory, although some theorists suggest that they are not really different storages at all but simply different points on a continuum of storage. Apparent differences between short and long term memory, according to these theorists, are due to the amount of time the subject has to perform his learning task.

Memories may be stored in long term memory according to their attributes—distinguishing characteristics that help separate memories during initial storage and later retrieval. One way of studying the processes of long term memory is by investigating memory devices and systems, known as *mnemonics*.

One candidate for a physiological network that may function as a holding mechanism is the *reverberatory circuit*. Reverberatory circuits are closed loops of neurons that circle back on themselves and thus restimulate the circuit. In this way information might be held for the duration of activity within the reverberatory circuit. The exact functions of such circuits are still highly speculative.

Information cannot be instantly stored in long term memory. Rather the information is held until a process of consolidation results in the physiological changes necessary for long term memory. Evidence for a consolidation process comes from many sources, the primary one being the apparent disruption of consolidation resulting in a failure to remember events that occurred just prior to the disruption. This disruption occurs in accidents, as when a person is hit on the head, and in experiments where electroconvulsive shock is applied to the brains of test animals. Other evidence for consolidation comes from studies that apparently facilitate consolidation through the use of drugs.

Noted in the literature are many confounding effects of *consolidation* that allow for various interpretations. For example, in addition to producing brain seizures, electroconvulsive shock also acts as a punishment, which suppresses some responses and alters the brain in ways that may impair retrieval. Some theorists argue that consolidation of memories is seldom disrupted, and that only retrieval is impaired.

Related to consolidation is the theory of *action decrement*, which postulates that after an animal makes a response the underlying neural network has a lowered capacity to be rearoused, probably because it is involved in consolidation. This unavailability of the neural network makes it less probable that the animal will repeat the same response to the same stimulus situation. It is also assumed that the more aroused the animal, the greater the action decrement, the greater the consolidation, and hence the better the long term memory. This leads to experiments suggesting that high arousal material, as opposed to low arousal material, will not be remembered as well immediately after learning, but will be remembered better later when action decrement and consolidation are more completed.

SUGGESTED READINGS

Hebb, D.O. *Organization of Behavior.* New York: Wiley, 1949.
Kintsch, W. *Learning, Memory, and Conceptual Processes.* New York: Wiley, 1970. Chapter 4.
McGaugh, J. L., & Herz, M. J. *Memory Consolidation.* San Francisco: Albion, 1972.
Norman, D. A. *Memory and Attention.* New York: Wiley, 1969.

stimulus contiguity

For centuries philosophers, and later psychologists, proposed many laws and principles to account for how we develop relationships between different events and ideas. Why do we associate some things together, and exclude others that do not "fit"? In the mass of proposed laws is one that is the most basic, most common, and one of the simplest. This "law," the *law of contiguity*, states that *events that occur close together in space or time tend to become associated.* Explanations of the complexity of human and animal behavior involve understanding the role of contiguity, given the functional organization of the organism. In other words, given the way an organism is wired up (e.g., its neuroanatomy), what types of environmental events will be processed as being contiguous? For a particular organism and particular events, what constitutes occurring "close together in space or time?" What functional changes occur within the organism as a result of contiguity? What are the effects of such functional changes?

Theorists differ on the sufficiency of contiguity to explain different learning phenomena, but no-one questions that it is basically necessary, although often complex and disguised.

One of the simplest situations used to investigate contiguity in learning was employed in experiments by Kandel and others on the sea-snail Aplysia (Kandel, 1970; Kandel & Spencer, 1968; Kandel & Tauc, 1965). In this sea-snail there are two connectives, or nerve trunks, that enter the abdominal ganglion, a mass of nerve cells. The experiments involved electrically stimulating the two connectives and recording the effects from different cells in the ganglion. The "test stimulus" consisted of stimulating one connective sufficiently to have an excitatory effect on the ganglion cell, but not enough to fire the cell, whereas the "primary stimulus" involved stimulating the other connective sufficiently to fire the ganglion cell. Continued presentation of a high intensity priming stimulus sensitized the ganglion cell to the point where a later presentation of the test stimulus now fired the cell. With a lower intensity of the priming stimulus it was often necessary to pair the test stimulus and priming stimulus (contiguity) a number of times before the test stimulus by itself could cause the cell to fire. It is important to note that when the stimuli were paired it often did not make any difference in which order they were presented, that is, which came on first.

The changes that occur in the Aplysia in these experiments are short-lived, and some people question whether they are related to learning. On the other hand this may be what learning is like in one of its simplest forms. Kandel and Tauc referred to their observed results as *heterosynaptic facilitation.*

When a stimulus is perceived by an organism it elicits some response. The response might be readily observable, such as a rat jumping to the stimulus of a foot-shock; or it might be more subtle, such as a person shifting his attention toward the stimulus of a strange sound. Now what happens when we systematically pair two stimuli (contiguity), both of which elicit responses? There are basically two possible outcomes: (1) the responses are compatible (it is possible for both to occur at the same time) and both stimuli come to elicit both general responses; or (2) the responses are incompatible and/or one is dominant and both stimuli come to elicit just one of the general responses.

In either case a stimulus comes to elicit a response it did not elicit before the stimulus pairing. This form of learning is called *respondent conditioning* (also known as *classical conditioning, Pavlovian conditioning,* and *Type S conditioning*). Respondent conditioning, then, is the learning paradigm in which one stimulus, as the result of being paired with a second stimulus, comes to elicit a response it did not elicit just previously. Often this new response is similar to the one previously elicited only by the second stimulus. In this paradigm the first stimulus is called the *conditioned stimulus* (CS) and the response it comes to elicit is called the *conditioned response* (CR), whereas the second stimulus is called the *unconditioned stimulus* (UCS or US) and the response it already elicited is called the *unconditioned response* (UCR or UR). The word "unconditioned" does not mean that the UCS innately elicits the UCR. It only means that at the time of the pairing of the CS and UCS, the UCS was already eliciting the UCR, either because it is innate or because of previous learning.

In the classic example, Pavlov, while studying digestive processes in dogs, paired the tone from a tuning fork with dry food which caused the dog to salivate. After a number of such tone–food pairings, the tone by itself was capable of eliciting salivation. Here the tone (CS) at first did not elicit salivation, but elicited responses such as orienting toward the tone.

Food (UCS), however, did elicit salivation (UCR). After the tone and food had been paired a while, the tone (CS) came to elicit salivation (CR) even when the tone was presented by itself without food. (Later critics such as Hebb (1956) have questioned whether the dry food that Pavlov used actually elicits salivation or whether dry food is aversive and the dog learns to salivate to convert the dry food into a desirable wet mash.)

Other examples of respondent conditioning might include the following:

1. When Timmy was in his school classroom (CS) he was ridiculed (UCS) by the teacher for making the wrong answer and so he felt bad (UCR). After this happened a few times (CS–UCS pairings), Timmy learned to dislike (CR) even being in a classroom (CS), and developed a school phobia.

2. Bruce and Jan were enjoying themselves at the beach while listening to a particular song. Now when Bruce hears the song he experiences some of the same emotions he had at the beach, and specific memories and images of the beach and Jan are elicited.

The CR is not identical with the UCR. It is often very similar, but may differ in magnitude. Thus some theorists speak of the CR as being a fractional part of the UCR. For example, a tone paired with food may come to elicit salivation, but perhaps not as much salivation as that elicited by the food. In some situations the relationship between CR and UCR is often unclear. A rat exposed to electric shock (UCS) generally becomes quite active (e.g., tries to flee or attack objects). Yet if a tone is paired with the shock, the tone may not elicit increased activity, but rather the opposite: freezing and immobility (Gray, 1971, p. 26). To understand situations such as the latter, we will have to determine (a) the different types of responses elicited by the UCS, (b) which responses come to be elicited by the CS and why, and (c) how this learning might relate to innate behaviors.

If the CS is presented time and again without being paired with the UCS, eventually the CS will no longer elicit the CR. The decrease in CR probability due to presenting the CS without the UCS is called *extinction*. Respondent conditioning then is due to establishing a contingency between the CS and the UCS, while respondent extinction is due to removing this contingency. Note that in both conditioning and extinction the procedures are described in terms of stimulus relationships, independent of what responses the organism makes. Following extinction the CR may gain somewhat in strength over a period of time without further conditioning. This gain is called *spontaneous recovery*.

An unfortunate bias in most American research on respondent conditioning is that the UCR is generally a much stronger or more dominant response than that elicited by the CS before conditioning. The bias is so pervasive that researchers often don't even mention any responses originally elicited by the CS. This is unfortunate in that it may be that the relative dominance of the responses determines which responses become conditioned to which stimuli. Consider the following situation: A person with a fear of heights is conditioned to relax to the word "relax." Now we put him on a balcony 10 floors above street level, tell him to look over the edge, and present the cue "relax." What will happen? We have the stimulus situation of the balcony eliciting anxiety, the stimulus "relax" that elicits relaxation, and we are pairing the stimuli. Since anxiety and relaxation are incompatible, both stimuli cannot come to elicit both responses. But does the person become conditioned away from anxiety toward relaxation or away from relaxation toward anxiety, or is the net result a combination of both these processes?

The answer to such questions usually hinges on the dominance of the responses. It is assumed, by people using respondent conditioning with applied problems, that in situations where the responses are incompatible, the more dominant response will be elicited (Mikulas, 1972a, p. 31). Thus if the anxiety is dominant to the relaxation, the word "relax" will be the CS, whereas if relaxation is dominant to the anxiety, the balcony will be the CS.

This assumption of the effects of response dominance is an implicit assumption underlying many powerful behavior change techniques; however, the basic nature and truth of the assumption has not been adequately investigated (some relevant Russian research is mentioned later). In fact it is not even possible to specify exactly what constitutes dominance. Perhaps it is not even the dominance of the responses, but rather some form of dominance between the stimuli, of which the responses are just a measure.

A second variable is the order in which the two stimuli are presented, in those cases in which one stimulus comes on before the other. The general rule in respondent conditioning is that you get good conditioning when the CS comes on before the UCS (*forward conditioning*) and little or no conditioning if the UCS comes on before the CS (*backward conditioning*).

This finding of the great superiority of forward conditioning over backward conditioning, however, may be an artifact of not manipulating the variable of dominance. The Russian researchers I. S. Beritov and E. A. Asratyan (see Cole & Maltzman, 1969, p. 769) have studied two-way connections, the simultaneous development of forward and backward connections. They report that if the CS and UCS are of approximately equal physiological strength (something similar to the idea of dominance), then you will get conditioned connections between both stimuli and the opposite responses. And if the CS is much stronger than the UCS, then backward conditioning may be more effective than forward conditioning. The relative weights of the two variables, dominance and order of the stimuli, is not clear from the small amount of relevant data. Asratyan believes that the sequence of the stimuli is more critical than the relative strengths of the stimuli. It may be that simply being presented first gives one stimulus, and its associated response, some degree of dominance over the other stimulus and its associated response.

It may also be that at the most basic level of learning the order of the stimuli is unimportant—only contiguity is important. Remember that in the sea-snail studies stimulus order was unimportant. Perhaps the reason that the order of the stimuli is important in respondent conditioning is that stimulus order affects such things as how the information is processed through the system and what events are perceived as separate and contiguous, whereas learning might require only contiguity, with the stimuli in any order.

A third variable is how much time there is between the onset of the CS and the onset of the UCS. This is referred to as the *interstimulus interval* or *ISI*. In much of human respondent conditioning the optimal ISI is about 0.5 second. If it is less than a half second, the CS and UCS may not be perceived as separate events. On the other hand we wouldn't want learning to occur with ISIs of much more than a half second, because this might result in irrelevant learning. To take an extreme example, consider what it would be like if humans were wired up to associate most events that occurred within a 15-minute period and what it would be like if all of these events were associated with each other. In such a case, one of this multitude of stimuli would elicit all the rest—a highly undesirable condition. Associations between more distant events, then, require a chain of conditioned responses and stimuli tying the events together or the specialized use of holding mechanisms to allow neural effects of a previous event to occur contiguously with later events. Forward conditioning is sometimes discussed as involving a positive ISI, while backward conditioning involves negative ISIs.

An important exception to this discussion of optimal ISI occurs when the CS is a specific taste and the UCS is some event that elicits nausea (Rozin & Kalat, 1971). For rats the UCS might be x-rays or nausea-inducing drugs. In this paradigm it is possible to condition an aversion to specific tastes with an ISI of several hours. The reason for this special case of long ISIs may be illustrated by the following example. Imagine two sets of animals that are possible evolutionary antecedents to rats. Say they both eat some poison food—not enough to kill them but enough to make them sick several hours later. Let us assume that one set of the animals, because of the way they are wired, does not associate the sickness with the taste of the food several hours previously. These animals will probably go back, eat more of the poisoned food, and die. If the other set of animals are capable of forming long ISI associations between taste and illness, they will avoid the poisoned food and live. And live animals generally produce more offspring than dead animals. Of course, evolutionary processes are certainly not as simple as this. But we can see, in this special case of poison avoidance, the survival value for long ISIs. The mechanisms for how such learning takes place are still unknown.

THEORIES OF RESPONDENT CONDITIONING

Although respondent conditioning is defined operationally in terms of the pairing of the CS and UCS, many theories have been offered to explain the mechanisms that underlie this type of learning. Figure 5–1 shows three of the possible relationships that have been the basis of some of these theories. In looking at the figure, remember that in traditional respondent conditioning the CS comes on first and the UCS later. The UCS, of course, is followed by the UCR. As learning progresses, the CR begins to occur. Where the CR occurs relative to the UCS depends on factors such as the latency of the CR (how fast the response can occur after the CS) and the interstimulus interval (the time between the onset of the CS and the onset of the UCS). However, in most situations the CR usually ends up occurring between the CS and UCS.

Contiguity theorists generally emphasize the pairing of the two stimuli, the CS and the UCS (S-S contiguity). For these theorists, respondent conditioning can be explained completely in terms of associations between these two stimuli. Thus the necessary and sufficient conditions for respondent conditioning is pairing of stimuli.

A problem with contiguity theories is that they predict conditioning in situations where conditioning may not occur. Studies of pupillary responses are such a case (see Goldwater, 1972). Experiments involving trying to condition pupillary constriction with a UCS of a light in the eye and a CS such as a tone have generally been unsuccessful. However, conditioning of pupillary dilation with shock as the UCS has been successful. This led Goldwater to suggest "that some type of motivational component is a necessary requirement for classical conditioning."

Also it appears (again, probably for evolutionary reasons) that some

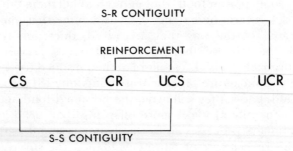

Figure 5–1 *Some relationships in respondent conditioning.*

responses are more easily conditioned to some classes of stimuli than to others. Garcia and Koelling (1966), using the UCS of x-rays or lithium chloride to induce nausea and gastric upset in rats, were able to condition avoidance responses to gustatory (taste) stimuli, but not to audio-visual stimuli. By contrast, avoidance reactions produced by electric shock to the paws of the rats were easily conditioned to audio-visual stimuli, but not to gustatory stimuli. Natural selection appears to have produced rats that associate tastes with gastric upset, and sights and sounds with external pain.

Rescorla (1967) has argued that in respondent conditioning the relevant dimension is not simply the number of times that the CS and UCS have been paired, but rather the contingency between the CS and the UCS. When the CS comes on, what is the probability (contingency) that the UCS will come on? This orientation emphasizes not only what is paired with the CS, but also what is *not* paired. According to Rescorla, there is a continuum of contingency that runs from maximum excitation where the CS and UCS are always paired to maximum inhibition where the CS and UCS are never paired.

At the excitation end of the continuum the CS provides information that the UCS is coming, and the CS comes to elicit the CR *(conditioned excitation);* whereas at the inhibition end of the continuum the CS provides information that the UCS is *not* coming, and the CS comes to elicit a tendency opposite to that of the CR *(conditioned inhibition)* (Rescorla, 1969). Since conditioned inhibition is a negative tendency, it can't be measured by itself, but can only be measured as it interacts with excitatory tendencies. For example, if we believed that a stimulus elicited conditioned inhibition, we might try to condition the stimulus to elicit the excitatory CR. If such conditioning took longer than simple conditioning to a neutral stimulus, this might suggest conditioned inhibition.

Near the middle of the continuum the CS does not provide any information at all about the UCS. The CS and UCS occur completely random to each other, sometimes paired, sometimes not. Rescorla (1967) suggests that this point is a good control procedure for the two ends of the continuum. He calls such a procedure where the CS and UCS are random to each other the truly random control procedure.

The S-R contiguity relationship in Figure 5-1 may be the key relationship in *higher-order conditioning,* where the UCS was just previously a conditioned stimulus to which the current UCR was conditioned (Rescorla, 1973).

Reinforcement theorists such as Spence emphasize the CR-UCS relationship. According to this position, the UCS reinforces the subject for making the CR. If the UCS is pleasant, the *onset* of the UCS is reinforcing, whereas if the UCS is aversive, the *offset* is reinforcing. A general problem for reinforcement theories of respondent conditioning is to explain how the CR first appears before it can be reinforced.

Some theorists emphasize more than one of the relationships shown in Figure 5–1. For example, Jones (Damianopoulos, 1967; Jones, 1962) proposed a theory for defensive conditioning (respondent conditioning with an aversive UCS). According to her model, the CS-UCR, S-R contiguity relationship is important in the early stages of learning. After the CR emerges, the critical variable is the CR-UCS reinforcement relationship. (Jones emphasized the onset of the UCS as reinforcing when it might be better to emphasize the offset.) An interesting prediction of Jones' model is that backward conditioning should yield the best results in the early stages of conditioning. Empirical support for this prediction, however, is small and questionable.

Using just the three relationships shown in Figure 5–1, a wide variety of theories can be evolved by answering questions such as the following: Which of the relationships are important at which times during conditioning? How do the different relationships interact with each other? How do these interactions vary with the amount of time and the nature of the task? How does the model differ if the UCS is pleasant or aversive?

EXAMPLES OF RESPONDENT CONDITIONING

To a newborn baby there are only a few classes of events which are pleasing, such as food when hungry and being held at certain times, and a few classes of events that are aversive, such as pain and discomfort. From this child will develop an adult in which a wide and varied number of classes of events will elicit complex feelings, emotions, and related physiological changes. Respondent conditioning is the major factor accounting for the learning of the more complex set of conditioned responses.

For example, consider eating habits and tastes. As Bates (1958, p. 21) points out, "there is no human society that deals rationally with the food in its environment; that eats according to the availability, edibility and nutritional value of the possible food materials within its reach." Rather there are strong cultural controls and conditioning which affect what we eat. Bates (1958) has catalogued many of the cultural differences: For example, in the United States the majority of the people have an aversion to eating dogs, horses, iguanas and insects, yet these foods are considered delicacies by other cultures. Iguanas are a highly prized food in much of tropical Central America, and grasshoppers are in the diet of some African, Middle Eastern, and American Indian cultures. Similarly some of the things people in the United States eat, such as cows, chickens, and frogs' legs, are objectionable to other cultures. People in the United States may eat invertebrates from the water, such as clams and snails, but curiously avoid invertebrates from the land. (For example, people in Florida will eat crabs from the sea but not land crabs, whereas Puerto Ricans prize the eating of land crabs.)

In New Guinea there was a group of mountain people who practiced cannibalism. After their friends had died from disease or accident, they would eat them. Often they would bury the corpse for a few days first. The resulting decayed flesh and accompanying maggots made the feast even more delicious. Bates suggests that this practice goes against the strongest food taboo in our culture. It is what we find the most disgusting. But why is this? Bates argues there is no evidence that the decaying flesh is a health hazard. And if you like insects, the maggots may add a nice taste. Finally, since there are no large native mammals in New Guinea, humans provide a good source of meat, the only other source being their few pigs. Among the Cocomas Indians of the Amazon there is a saying about cannibalism: "It is better to be inside a friend than to be swallowed up by the cold earth." (Bates, 1958, p. 91).

Clearly many variables affect individual food taboos and preferences, such as family influences, cultural taboos, and religious doctrine. But when even the thought of a food source that is nutritious and not naturally bad tasting causes us to feel somewhat nauseous, respondent conditioning is strongly implied. The food source is associated with stimuli that produce negative or aversive states in us: "Aren't lizards ugly creatures?" "The crunching sound of stepping on a grasshopper (let alone eating one) sends chills through my body." "Eating a dog is like eating a pet." Through such subtle, or not so subtle, conditioning, the culture perpetuates its food taboos. Respondent conditioning accounts for the emotional and physiological responses elicited by the item as a food source. As Bates (1958, p. 91) concluded about the New Guinea cannibals: "They liked the taste, their mothers had not taught them that rotten meat and worms were bad, their culture had no taboo on eating people."

A similar argument applies to sexual behavior. People are wired so that tactile stimulation of certain parts of their body produces sexual arousal. But different people are sexually aroused by a wide range of stimuli: heterosexual stimuli, homosexual stimuli, large breasts, leather boots, specific kinds of music, and so forth. To a large extent the ability of these stimuli to elicit a sexual response is the result of respondent conditioning. In the past these stimuli (perhaps imagined images) were paired with other stimuli, perhaps from masturbation, that elicited the sexual response. Now the culture and personality of the person may partially determine what stimuli become paired with sexually arousing stimuli, but it is the *pairing* which produces the learning.

For example, in the United States most people find it somewhat sexually arousing to put their mouths and lips against the mouth and lips of an appropriate sexual object. This curious sexual ritual, called a "kiss," would be unthinkable in cultures such as Micronesia (Bates, 1958, p. 23).

Why should a kiss be pleasurable and sexually arousing? The answer must depend, to a large degree, on respondent conditioning. In the past the kiss was paired with pleasurable stimuli such as social approval and sexual stimulation.

Rachman and Hodgson (1968) in a demonstration experiment were able to condition a sexual fetishism into their male subjects. The CS was a slide of a pair of knee-length, fur-lined boots. The UCS's were colored slides of nude or scantily dressed women. In the conditioning the CS was projected on the screen for 30 seconds, and followed by 10 seconds of one of the UCS's. Eventually the CS alone was capable of eliciting sexual arousal. Such conditioning is easily extinguished unless the subject perpetuates it in his sexual practices.

Staats (1968), among others, has shown how the meanings of words depend to a large extent on respondent conditioning. Words like "joy" and "happy" are paired with pleasant stimulus situations and come to elicit positive effects, whereas the opposite is true for words like "hurt" and "awful." Words often acquire meaning through respondent conditioning by being paired with other words. Repeatedly hearing that "adultery is a sin" may cause some of the meaning of "sin" to become conditioned to "adultery." Thus words, via respondent conditioning, come to elicit specific meanings, combinations of emotions, images, and verbal associations. (Some theorists define "meaning" differently, but this is simply a distinction in terminology.) Staats (1968, p. 34) provides the following illustration: In the past the word "hurt" to a child was paired with painful situations so that the word "hurt" elicits a negative emotional meaning. If later the child is told, "That is dangerous, you will get hurt," the emotional response to "hurt" may become conditioned to "dangerous." Still later the child might be told that "Motorcyles are dangerous." Then the negative emotional response becomes conditioned to "motorcycle." The result is that when the child now sees a motorcycle and makes the naming response "motorcycle," he experiences the negative emotion. Such an example is, of course, grossly oversimplified, but one can see how the logic would apply to more complex situations.

Expanding on this type of analysis of word meaning, we can see how attitudes are partially determined by the meanings conditioned to words such as "communist," "Negro," "redneck," and "abortion." Political propaganda often involves pairing the opponent's name or position with emotionally laden words. Advertising consists, to a large extent, of pairing a product name or image, or both, with pleasant stimuli such as attractive women or a country scene. One mistake that advertisers often make is that they design an ad to attract the public's attention without realizing that the responses elicited by the ad might not be the responses they wish to be associated with their product.

A number of experiments have demonstrated the respondent conditioning of emotions. In a classic study, Watson and Rayner (1920) conditioned fear in an 11-month-old infant named Albert. Before the conditioning Albert had no fear of furry objects such as white rats. During conditioning every time little Albert reached out to touch a white rat, the experimenters scared Albert with a loud noise caused by the striking of a steel bar. Soon the white rat elicited fear in Albert, and the fear generalized to other furry objects such as a rabbit and cotton.

Campbell, Sanderson, and Laverty (1964) presented to their subjects a 600 cps tone as the CS. Following the subjects' habituation to the tone, the tone was paired with a drug-induced respiratory paralysis as the UCS. The respiratory paralysis, which lasted 90 to 130 seconds, was a horrible experience for the subjects. They were not able to breathe or move, and some subjects thought they were going to die. One such ethically questionable conditioning trial produced a strong emotional response to the tone that did not extinguish over a three-week period which included 100 unpaired presentations of the tone. One can compare this with the acquisitions of some phobias, such as one case of the author's in which a woman watched her mother get run over by a car and the mutilated body dragged down the street. Following this accident, the mere sight of a car made the woman hysterical and she had to be hospitalized.

CONDITIONED DRIVES AND CONDITIONED REINFORCEMENT

In the first chapter we discussed drives, such as the hunger drive, which provide a source of motivation. Will stimuli that are paired with such drive states come to elicit the drive? Possibly, and if so these drives acquired via respondent conditioning are called *conditioned drives*. Most of the research has been based on fear as an acquired drive with an aversive UCS such as electric shock. A common demonstration involves rats in a shuttle-box. For example, the rat is put in a two-compartment box with a grid floor. A buzzer is sounded and 10 seconds later electric shock is applied to the floor of the compartment the rat is in. After a while the rat learns to jump into the other compartment as soon as the shock comes on (*escape conditioning*). With more learning trials the rat learns to avoid the shock by jumping as soon as the buzzer comes on (*avoidance conditioning*). Now the rat will keep jumping to the buzzer for many trials after it has stopped being shocked. But what is the source of motivation for these continued avoidance responses? A common explanation (see Mowrer, 1947) is that the buzzer, by being paired with the shock, comes to elicit fear as a conditioned drive. The rat is then motivated by the fear elicited by the buzzer. In addition, the offset of the shock or the offset of the buzzer, or both, may function as a reinforcement for the escape or avoidance response, "reinforcement" here being an event which strengthens the learned response.

In order for the conditioned fear to be extinguished, the rat would have to stay in the presence of the buzzer without being shocked. To anthropomorphize, we can say that the rat must learn that the shock is off and he doesn't have to avoid it any more. But the rat keeps avoiding and not extinguishing, demonstrating that avoidance behavior is one of the hardest behaviors to extinguish.

However, not everyone accepts this conditioned drive interpretation of the avoidance behavior (see Seligman & Johnston, 1973). Herrnstein (1969) suggests that the buzzer does not elicit a conditioned drive but rather merely provides an informative event which signals the rat to make the avoidance response. (In the terminology of the next chapter the buzzer is a discriminative stimulus to which the rat learns to make the discriminative operant of the avoidance response.) Herrnstein offers several arguments in favor of this thesis, including evidence that physiological measures of fear decrease as the avoidance response is learned. He also argues that it is difficult to use the CS from one avoidance task as the basis for other avoidance learning.

Little research has been done on conditioned appetitive drives such as a conditioned hunger drive. The reason for this is that most appetitive drives have too slow an onset and offset to provide the kind of temporal control ideal for respondent conditioning. In a general review of the research, Cravens and Renner (1970) concluded that there was no good evidence for conditioned appetitive drives. This does not mean that conditioned appetitive drives are not possible (e.g., Seligman et al., 1970), only that there is a need for well controlled supporting evidence.

In the next chapter we will discuss the concept of *reinforcement*. But for our purposes now we can roughly think of reinforcement as reward—something the organism will work to attain, such as food. If a neutral stimulus is paired with a reinforcement, it often acquires reinforcing properties. If a light comes on every time just before a thirsty rat is given some water, the light will eventually acquire reinforcing properties. The rat will do things simply in order to see the light.

A few years ago theorists used the term *primary reinforcement* to describe an event which innately functioned as a reinforcement, such as food and water. *Secondary reinforcement* referred to stimuli which acquired reinforcing properties by being paired with a primary reinforcement. Such distinctions soon became unwieldy. Events thought to be primary reinforcements often turned out to be secondary reinforcements based on an even *more* basic source of reinforcement. Stimuli acquiring reinforcing properties by being paired with secondary reinforcements were sometimes called tertiary reinforcements. Now the term *conditioned reinforcement* is generally used for all stimuli with acquired reinforcing properties. The phenomenon of conditioned reinforcement has been well supported by a large amount of literature and a number of theoretical interpretations (see Hendry, 1969).

There are basically two ways to demonstrate the existence of a conditioned reinforcement: resistance to extinction, and new learning. In the first method it is shown that the animals with the conditioned reinforcement take longer to extinguish than animals without the conditioned reinforcement. For example, consider two groups of rats pressing a bar to receive food pellets. For both of these groups a click is sounded with each bar-press. This click, by being paired with the food pellet, will become a conditioned reinforcement. When the rats are put on extinction, with food no longer following the bar-press, we leave the click on for the one set of rats and see how long it will take for all the rats to stop bar-pressing. The rats hearing the click during extinction take longer to stop bar-pressing because the conditioned reinforcement of the click maintains the bar-pressing somewhat longer.

In the new learning method, a stimulus established as a conditioned reinforcement in one situation is used to reinforce a new response in a different situation. We might use the conditioned reinforcement of the click, established in the bar-press situation, to reward the rat to make an entirely different response.

LoLordo (1969) argued that the following two criteria must be met to demonstrate that a stimulus with a particular history is a conditioned reinforcement: (1) the stimulus must be shown to function as a reinforcement, such as by one of the two demonstration methods above; (2) it must be demonstrated that the reinforcing power of the stimulus depends upon a conditioning operation, such as the pairing with an established reinforcer.

Until the early 1960's there were basically two theories of conditioned reinforcement: the *discriminative stimulus hypothesis* and the *S-S hypothesis* (Hendry, 1969, p. 12). According to the discriminative stimulus hypothesis, as suggested by theorists such as Skinner, only discriminative stimuli become conditioned reinforcements. That is, for a stimulus to become a conditioned reinforcement it must be a cue to which the animal has learned to make a response that is reinforced. If a monkey learns to slide open a window for a piece of banana only when a tone comes on, the tone will become a conditioned reinforcer. The discriminative stimulus hypothesis has not been supported by the data (Hendry, 1969, p. 14). Rather, simple pairing of a stimulus with a reinforcement is often sufficient to establish the stimulus as a conditioned reinforcement.

The S-S hypothesis, as advocated by theorists such as Hull (1943), simply states that stimuli which occur in close temporal contiguity with a reinforcing state of affairs become conditioned reinforcers. For our purposes we can think of the S-S hypothesis as an example of respondent conditioning. That is, the neutral stimulus (CS) is paired with a stimulus situation (UCS) that elicits a reinforcing effect (UCR). After a number of such pairings the neutral stimulus becomes a conditioned reinforcer capable of producing a reinforcing effect (CR). If the conditioned reinforcer is presented enough times without being paired with another reinforcer, the conditioned reinforcer may extinguish.

In 1962 Egger and Miller argued that an important variable in conditioned reinforcement is the amount of information a stimulus provides about the onset of the reinforcement. They suggested that a necessary condition for establishing any stimulus as a conditioned reinforcer is that the stimulus provide information about the occurrence of the reinforcement. In their experiment they had two stimuli (S_1 and S_2) which, when presented together, ended just prior to the rats' receiving food. For Group A, S_1 always came on, followed by S_2, and then the food. Here S_2 was redundant, since S_1 already provided the information that food was to come. On the other hand, in Group B, S_1 sometimes came on by itself, not followed by either S_2 or food. Sometimes S_1 was followed by S_2 and then food. Thus in Group B, S_2 was the only reliable predictor of food. S_2 became a stronger conditioned reinforcer when it was informative (Group B) than when it was redundant (Group A). Similarly S_1 became a stronger conditioned reinforcer when it was informative (Group A) than when not (Group B). And S_1 became a more powerful conditioned reinforcer than S_2 when S_2 was redundant (Group A).

Egger and Miller's study cast doubt on the simple S-S hypothesis, which would probably predict that S_2 in both cases should be the more powerful conditioned reinforcer because the onset of S_2 occurred closer to the onset of the food. However, we still might be able to interpret the establishment of conditioned reinforcement as a case of respondent conditioning. To do so our respondent conditioning model must include how much information the CS provides about the onset of the UCS. This is the position that Rescorla, as described earlier, has been advocating for respondent conditioning.

The discussion so far has centered on stimuli which become conditioned reinforcers by being paired with the onset of a reinforcing event. There is also evidence (LoLordo, 1969) that stimuli can become conditioned reinforcers by being paired with the offset of an aversive event, such as the offset of an electric shock. Similarly, there is a little evidence that stimuli paired with the onset of an aversive event may become conditioned punishments (Hake & Azrin, 1965). There are, however, a number of problems to be worked out in these two sets of theories. For example, if a tone comes on for N seconds and then is followed by the onset of electric shock, does the tone become a conditioned punishment because of its association with the shock or does it become a conditioned reinforcer because it signals N seconds of freedom from shock? What are the effects of how long N seconds is? What are the effects of other experiences with shock during this learning? What are the relative roles of the information value of the tone in predicting shock onset and the simple pairing of the tone and shock? Questions like these are being answered, but much more experimentation is needed for any final solutions.

Although adult humans do work for primary reinforcers such as food and sex, most of their behavior can be interpreted as seeking to maximize positive conditioned reinforcers (e.g., attention, approval, money) and to minimize conditioned punishments (e.g., ostracism, criticism). Why does a person work hard simply for professional recognition? Why do people have such different preferences in music? Why does a person who lives in Las Vegas enjoy trying to grow a lawn in the desert? Why do people enjoy forms of competition that mean success at the expense of other people? Complete answers to such questions are quite complex, but probably the major variable is that the different events (recognition, specific type of music, lawn, success in competition) are conditioned reinforcers to the people.

TWO-PROCESS THEORY

We have seen how respondent conditioning may be the basis of conditioned drives and conditioned reinforcers. In the next chapter we will discuss operant conditioning, which includes behaviors that the animal learns to do in the presence of conditioned drives and in order to receive conditioned reinforcers. Thus the final overall explanation for many behaviors will have two components: respondent variables, such as conditioned drives and conditioned reinforcements, and operant variables. Such an analysis can also be expanded to include related variables such as conditioned punishment. Breaking down behavior into these two general classes of variables is the basis of *two-process theory* or *two-factor theory* (Mowrer, 1947; Rescorla & Solomon, 1967).

Two-process theory assumes that respondent conditioned variables function as mediators of operant behavior, serving as instigators or reinforcers, or both. An organism is always in some state of motivation, part or all of which is due to respondent variables such as conditioned drives. In the presence of this motivation, and the current stimuli, the animal, drawing on past learning, makes some response called an operant. Following the operant the animal may receive some form of reinforcement or punishment, which again may be based on respondent variables such as conditioned reinforcement. These respondent variables need not be related to peripheral responses (in fact, it appears they seldom are), but may be central responses, ones not readily observed from external behavior. An experiment by Solomon and Turner (1962) will illustrate this theory. First they trained dogs to press a panel in order to avoid being shocked when a visual stimulus came on. Then they gave the dogs a drug to paralyze them. While paralyzed the dogs were presented with two tones, one paired with a shock (CS+) and one not (CS−). Later, unparalyzed, the dogs were returned to the panel press apparatus and were presented the two tones. The dogs pressed the panel to CS+, but pressed little or not at all to the CS−. That is, the respondently conditioned CS+ instigated the operant response of panel-pressing even though the dogs had never before pressed the panel to the CS+.

Consider the hypothetical case of Timmy, who because of unpleasant experiences in school develops a school phobia. Through respondent conditioning the classroom has come to elicit anxiety. One day the anxiety becomes too unpleasant and Timmy leaves school early. Leaving the school causes a reduction in the anxiety, which rewards his leaving. Later on the way to school one day he begins to feel anxious, goes somewhere else for the day, and is rewarded for avoiding school by the reduction of anxiety and omission of the high anxiety he would have felt in school. Through such conditioning Timmy may learn to avoid going to school and might develop a school phobia. According to two-process theory the respondently conditioned anxiety was a mediator for the operant behavior of avoiding school.

Thus stimulus contiguity may underlie the acquisition of drives and reinforcements. Below we will see how this same principle of contiguity may be the basis for the processes that produce forgetting.

ASSOCIATIVE INTERFERENCE THEORY

Why do we forget things we once learned? Has the memory trace weakened with time? Probably not. Most psychologists currently believe that once information is in long term memory it will not weaken simply as the result of the passage of time. Rather the assumption is that forgetting is due to problems in retrieving the information. Potentially then, anything that was ever learned can be recalled with appropriate retrieval procedures. Practitioners of hypnosis and psychoanalysis appear to have techniques for the recovery of at least some forgotten memories.

A major problem in retrieving information from memory storage appears to be interference resulting from other stored information. For example, when trying to remember a person's name, retrieval may be impaired by other names that come to mind—competing responses. This type of reasoning underlies the *associative interference theory*, which postulates that retention loss is due to competition from alternative responses at the time of recall (see Keppel, 1968; Slamecka & Ceraso, 1960). The sources of the alternative, competing responses are stimuli, present at the time of recall, which because of past learning now elicit these alternative responses. How the stimuli come to elicit the responses is probably explained by the processes of contiguity learning.

The two main sources of interfering responses are retroactive inhibition and proactive inhibition. *Retroactive inhibition* (RI) is the retention deficit resulting from new learning that takes place between the learning of the material being tested and the retention test (McGeoch, 1942). In the paradigm "learn A, learn B, test for A," RI refers to the deficit in the test for A resulting from the learning of B. If a person in a paired associate learning test learns to say specific digits to color names (e.g., RED−8), he might later learn to say nonsense syllables to the color names (e.g., RED−GEX). Now when presented with the stimulus "RED" and asked to remember the number first learned to it, the subject might be somewhat impaired in his remembering of "8" owing to the interference of the elicited response "GEX." If such impairment does occur it is called retroactive inhibition.

The more similar two different sets of material to be learned, the greater the RI. If in the second learning the subject simply learned to say different digits to the colors (e.g., RED−5), rather than nonsense syllables, we should get even more RI. For now the stimulus "RED" elicits the responses "8" and "5" which, because of their similarity, interfere with each other. A parallel case can be made that if the stimuli of the two sets of learning are quite similar there might be considerable RI.

Melton and Irwin (1940) added the factor of *unlearning* to the area of RI. Here it is assumed that during the learning of the second set of material, responses from the first set are unlearned as the result of their unreinforced elicitation or punishment. The effects of unlearning are considered transitory and recover over time, although the exact nature of the recovery and time to recovery are still debatable. RI thus has two components or factors: (1) competition between responses, and (2) unlearning. (It may be useful to think of unlearning as extinction plus resulting spontaneous recovery, but many theorists believe unlearning to be different than extinction.)

For a while most forgetting was explained purely in terms of RI, but this explanation seemed somewhat strained. Eventually Underwood (1957) emphasized the idea of proactive inhibition. *Proactive inhibition* (PI) is the retention deficit resulting from learning that took place prior to the learning of the material being tested. In the paradigm "learn A, learn B, test for B," PI is said to occur when the responses of A compete with those of B on the recall test for B. As with RI, the degree of similarity between A and B is a major determinant of the degree of PI.

Thus when trying to remember something learned about a week ago, retrieval may be impaired by interfering responses elicited from current stimuli. Some of these responses were learned over a week ago (PI) and some were learned less than a week ago (RI). The combined competition effects of RI and PI are called *specific competition*.

Currently the terms "retroactive interference" and "proactive interference" are often used synonymously with "retroactive inhibition" and "proactive inhibition" respectively. However, earlier the term "interference" sometimes described the phenomenon, whereas "inhibition" implied specific theoretical explanations for the phenomenon.

Although RI and PI compose the main part of associative interference theory, many other variables have been added over the years. These include contextual associations, generalized competition, and list differentiation, to be discussed below.

Whenever specific learning takes place, it must be in some setting, and thus the stimuli of the setting will come to elicit the responses learned in the setting. This learning results in *contextual associations.* The responses elicited by the context may facilitate or interfere with responses to be recalled. For example, a student might do better on an exam if he studies for the exam in the same room where he will take the exam, because the stimuli of the room help elicit the desired learned responses. Contextual associations help to explain phenomena such as a reduction in RI with contextual change and a subject in a paired associate task being able to simply recall a list of the responses without being presented with any of the specific stimuli used in the task. Little research has been done on the nature or properties of contextual associations.

Independent of specific associations, subjects appear to have a response bias toward responding with the *last learned* material. This tendency is called *generalized competition.* Generalized competition, like RI, favors the recall of the more recently learned material. It appears that generalized competition decreases in effect with time. Thus, in a "learn A, then learn B" situation, right after learning B, generalized competition favors the recall of B material over A material. But as the amount of time since B was learned increases, the generalized competition decreases.

List differentiation is the ability of the subject to isolate the particular set of material that a response came from. When given the stimulus "RED" and asked for the first response he learned to it, the subject might remember the responses "5" and "8," but might not be able to remember from which set of material each response came. If he can, however, remember that 8 came from material A and 5 from B, then we say that he can "differentiate" the lists. The merging of two or more sets of material as the result of lack of differentiation is sometimes called *crowding.*

Contiguity is probably the best explanation for the learning of the various associations involved in associative interference theory. Nodine (1969) investigated the role of temporal contiguity in paired associate learning. He found that those items whose pairs occurred the closest together in time were the best learned and remembered. He also found that the subject's rehearsal of the material often compensated for lack of contiguity.

Saltz (1971) has proposed a learning model in which an association achieves near maximum strength during the first trial in which the subject attends to the two elements to be associated, or at least early in training if not the first trial. Changes over time with additional learning trials, then, do not primarily increase the strength of an association. Rather, over time, what develops is resistance to interference from other material. Saltz uses the term *boundary strength* to refer to the source of resistance to interference.

Most of the research in associative interference has used human subjects learning verbal material that is relatively meaningless, such as paired associates of nonsense syllables. When meaningful material is used, the results become more complex. RI and PI are often not found when meaningful prose is used, particularly if the subject is asked to recall only content, as opposed to verbatim recall. In one study (Ausubel et al., 1968) high school students first learned about Zen Buddhism and then learned about more standard Buddhism. These two kinds of Buddhism were chosen because they differed in many basic concepts, but were similar enough so that interference effects could be expected. Learning about standard Buddhism not only did not produce RI for the concepts of Zen Buddhism, but in fact facilitated retention of the Zen information. The authors suggested that the second learning produced recall *and* rehearsal of the first material, as well as systematic contrasting of the two sets of material.

When we talk about people learning material in a natural setting, it implies more than simply that the material is meaningful. In addition, people often have already acquired definite attitudes toward the material, or the material elicits specific emotions. Thus a complete understanding of verbal learning involves, among other things, a synthesis between learning variables such as associative interference theory and variables investigated in social psychology, such as attitude change (see Hoppe, 1969; Mikulas, 1970 b).

In the other direction there have been a few studies attempting to apply associative interference theory to non-human learning. In one study (Spear et al., 1972) rats were first trained in a *passive avoidance* task which required them to refrain from making a response to avoid shock. Then they were trained on an *active avoidance* task in which they had to make a specific response to avoid being shocked. They found that the prior learning of the passive avoidance interfered with later retention of the active avoidance. The more times the rats had to practice the passive avoidance, the greater the deficit. These results seem very similar to proactive inhibition.

COUNTERCONDITIONING

Occasionally the response elicited by a stimulus situation is undesirable, as in the case of a student becoming anxious when speaking before a class or a child being afraid of dogs. Other examples of undesirable responses are the immediate pleasurable effects of alcohol resulting in a man becoming a problem drinker, and a sexual deviation in which a man is aroused only by women in leather boots.

Using respondent conditioning there are two ways to change such undesirable responses: respondent extinction, to be discussed in the next section, and counterconditioning. *Counterconditioning* is the use of respondent conditioning to condition a desirable response to a stimulus situation in place of an undesirable response. Of course, what makes a response "desirable" or "undesirable" is an arbitrary decision based on some ethical or value system. For example, the child with a fear of dogs might be conditioned to feel relaxed rather than anxious in the presence of dogs. Here relaxation is used to countercondition anxiety and is considered more desirable than anxiety. Within counterconditioning, many specific treatment procedures are being evolved in the area of *behavior modification*—the application of experimentally derived principles of behavior (primarily learning) to problems of human behavior (Eysenck & Beech, 1971; Mikulas, 1972a; Salter, 1949).

The general approach in all behavior modification counterconditioning procedures is about the same (see Fig. 5–2). First we identify those stimuli or combinations of stimuli (S_1) that are eliciting the undesirable response (R_1). (For example, examination settings may cause a person to feel anxious [test anxiety].) Second, we choose a response (R_2) that is incompatible with R_1 and preferable to it (as relaxation is incompatible with test anxiety). Third, we find a stimulus (S_2) that elicits R_2, or we train or condition the person to emit R_2 to S_2. Finally we systematically pair the two stimuli in such a way that S_1 comes to elicit R_2 in place of R_1. In our example we might train our test-anxious subject how to relax himself in the examination settings until these settings no longer elicit anxiety.

To accomplish our counterconditioning, either we have S_1 and S_2 presented simultaneously or we have the onset of S_1 occur just prior to the onset of S_2. A general problem in counterconditioning involves the relative dominance of the two responses. It is generally implicitly assumed, although far from adequately tested, that in counterconditioning there is a tendency for both stimuli to come to elicit the dominant response. If R_1 is dominant to R_2, the counterconditioning will go in the direction opposite to what we wish. To insure against this we choose a very strong R_2 and/or use a hierarchy.

$S_1 \longrightarrow R_1$ (UNDESIRABLE)

$S_2 \longrightarrow R_2$ (DESIRABLE)

Figure 5–2 The start of counterconditioning.

Let us say that R_1 is more dominant than R_2. To handle this we might construct a hierarchy of stimulus situations that gradually approximate S_1, the items on the top of the hierarchy being most like S_1 and the items on the bottom the least like S_1. For example, with a person who has a fear of heights, an item high on the hierarchy might be standing on a fire-escape 10 floors up, whereas an item low on the hierarchy might be looking out of a closed window on the second floor. If we have chosen an adequate hierarchy, our response R_2 should be dominant to the responses (similar to R_1, but weaker) that are elicited by the items on the bottom of the hierarchy. Thus we can countercondition R_2 to these items. The assumption is that the effects of this counterconditioning generalize as one goes up the hierarchy, so that the responses elicited by the next lowest items on the hierarchy can be counterconditioned with R_2. The general strategy is to slowly move up through the hierarchy, never moving to the next item until we are sure that R_2 will be dominant to the response elicited by that item. Eventually S_1 will be reached, and R_2 counterconditioned to it. In practice, this counterconditioning procedure works very well; however, much more research is needed to determine if it really works for the precise reasons described above.

In applied human situations, counterconditioning never consists simply of replacing R_1 with R_2. Rather, during counterconditioning, the response elicited by S_1 slowly moves along a continuum from R_1 to R_2 (Mikulas, 1972b, p. 87). If only a small degree of counterconditioning is employed, you will still get R_1, although it will be a weakened version of it. You may wish to stop the counterconditioning at some neutral point between R_1 and R_2, or you can continue counterconditioning until S_1 elicits R_2. In the following paragraphs we will consider a few counterconditioning procedures.

Perhaps the most common problems that may be dealt with by counterconditioning are unadaptive fears and anxiety. Some fears, such as test anxiety, fear of flying, and fear of heights, are relatively common, while others are more unusual and often exceptionally debilitating, as in the case of a mental patient with an exceptionally irrational fear or *phobia* about being touched by anyone. Many responses have been used to countercondition anxiety, such as relaxation, meditation, laughter, anger, eating responses, the conjuring up of pleasant scenes, and sexual activities. The most common such behavior modification procedure, developed by Wolpe (1958), is desensitization.

Desensitization has been defined in different ways, but basically it refers to the counterconditioning of relaxation to stimuli that previously elicited anxiety. There are basically three stages of desensitization (see Wolpe, 1969). First the subject is taught how to relax himself on cue so that relaxation can be used as the incompatible response. (If the subject cannot be taught to relax, relaxation is elicited by other means, such as hypnosis or drugs). The second part involves identifying those stimulus situations that elicit anxiety and constructing appropriate hierarchies. Finally, the anxiety is gradually counterconditioned out as progress is made through the hierarchy. Counterconditioning is usually taken only to the point of neutrality. For example, desensitization of a snake phobia is stopped at the neutral point at which the subject no longer feels anxious about snakes, rather than continued until the snakes elicit relaxation.

Desensitization is an exceptionally powerful technique. Phobias that have impaired a person's life for many years are often eliminated in a few weeks. Desensitization can be used by people on themselves, done with large groups at a time, and carried out totally by tape-recordings. Subjects can learn how to use relaxation procedures for self-control of a wide range of problems. As desensitization is a relatively new procedure, there are still theoretical debates about how it actually produces its effects. For example, some theorists (e.g., Wilson & Davison, 1971) suggest that desensitization is really respondent extinction rather than counterconditioning.

Desensitization has primarily been applied to situations which elicit responses of anxiety. However, there is no reason why desensitization-like procedures could not be applied to *any* state of arousal—anxiety, anger, frustration—or associated phenomena such as racial prejudice. Schachter and Singer (1962) have suggested that the arousal components of various emotions are similar, but that, based on cognitive factors, emotions are labeled differently depending on the situation. Hearn and Evans (1972) have reported results suggesting that anger can be treated by a desensitization type of approach.

Masters and Johnson (1970) have devised an important treatment program to deal with sexual inadequacies. Much of their program can be interpreted in terms of counterconditioning, although Masters and Johnson do not conceptualize it this way. A common part of several different treatments consists in first eliciting the desired sexual response in a non-coitus situation. Then, while maintaining this response, the subject is gradually phased into situations that more and more approximate coitus. This could be interpreted as moving up a hierarchy of items related to coitus and gradually counterconditioning a sexual response in place of whatever responses were impairing sexual functioning. There is, of course, much more to Masters and Johnson's program than this, but counterconditioning does seem to play a major role.

In some situations the stimulus elicits a positive or approach response that is considered undesirable; for instance, the calming effects of smoking a cigarette may cause a person to smoke excessively. In such a situation an aversive or unpleasant response is counterconditioned in place of the undesired approach response. Hence the procedure is called *aversive counterconditioning* or *aversion therapy*, although there is some ambiguity in the last term since it often includes both aversive counterconditioning (respondent conditioning) and punishment (operant conditioning, as discussed in the next chapter).

Aversive counterconditioning is primarily used with undesirable, self-reinforcing behaviors that often are difficult to treat by other means (see Rachman & Teasdale, 1969). The counterconditioning is usually not continued past the point of neutrality. A person who no longer wishes to be aroused by homosexual stimuli might be subjected to watching homosexual slides projected on a screen while the slides are paired with electric shock. This counterconditioning could be continued until the person felt aversion to the slides, but usually treatment is stopped when the slides simply cease to elicit sexual arousal.

The most commonly used sources of the incompatible aversion response are electric shock and drug-induced nausea. Other sources are social disapproval, slides of unpleasant scenes, and imagined unpleasant scenes. Often in aversive counterconditioning the aversion response is clearly dominant to the other response, so that no hierarchy is necessary. However, there are still situations in which hierarchy is valuable.

Although not as powerful as other counterconditioning procedures, aversive counterconditioning is useful in treating some of the most difficult cases, the ones that are self-reinforcing. Also some of the newer variations, based on the subject's imagining unpleasant scenes, are very useful to a person in general self-control procedures, such as control of smoking and overeating.

It should be noted that the counterconditioning procedures mentioned above are not necessarily full treatment programs by themselves. Rather a particular case may or may not require a combination of different approaches, of which counterconditioning is just one. The practitioner might also use operant techniques, modeling, or other techniques in combination with counterconditioning.

RESPONDENT EXTINCTION AND FLOODING

Respondent conditioning results from the systematic pairing of the CS and UCS until the CS elicits the CR. If the CS is presented time and again without its being paired with the UCS, eventually the CS will extinguish and will no longer elicit the CR.

Although the procedure for producing respondent extinction is clear, the mechanisms by which it works are not so clear (see Kimble, 1961, Chap. 10). It may be that respondent extinction is a subset of counterconditioning; i.e., the CR does not extinguish until another response is conditioned in its place. On the practical level the difference is that in counterconditioning one specifically provides the alternative response, whereas in respondent extinction one does *not* specifically control the source of the alternative response. If this is true, counterconditioning should be potentially more efficient and effective than simple extinction.

Many theorists conceptualize extinction as the learning of a new response, based on simple contiguity (e.g., Guthrie) or on reinforcement (e.g., Hull, Amsel), or both. In an early consolidation study (Gellhorn et al., 1942), rats were trained to make an active avoidance response and then were given complete extinction. Rats given electroconvulsive shock (ECS) following extinction showed a greater recurrence of avoidance responses than control animals not given the ECS. One interpretation of these results is that extinction involves the learning of new responses, and that the consolidation of this learning was disrupted by the ECS. However, there are other interpretations and much more research is needed in this area.

The following examples illustrate how respondent extinction works. Leo, a high school student, felt very anxious about taking a foreign language, as this was a new experience for him. However, after a few weeks in Frau Boehm's German class with no bad experiences, he no longer felt anxious. Whenever Jack thought about a particular childhood experience it made him angry, so he tried not to think about it. During psychotherapy Jack talked a lot about this incident and soon found it no longer made him angry. Little Penelope was a problem because she would occasionally tear up magazines or newspapers. One day her father gave her a stack of magazines and newspapers to tear up as she wanted. She tore quite happily for a while, eventually stopped, and never again did any tearing.

Consider a rat that has learned to make an avoidance response to a buzzer. That is, it has learned that five seconds after the buzzer (CS) comes on, an electric shock (UCS) will be applied to the grid floor that the rat is standing on. By jumping to the other side of the apparatus when the buzzer first comes on, the rat can avoid the shock. Respondent extinction would consist of presenting the buzzer *not* paired with the shock. However, in a case like this, the rat will make the avoidance response *before* the time of the shock onset; it will not stay around long enough for extinction.

One way to extinguish this avoidance behavior is to force the rat to stay in the presence of the buzzer so that it is unable to make the avoidance response. This is called *flooding* or *response prevention* (Baum, 1970). This is a very effective way to eliminate avoidance responses in rats, although the avoidance response often drops out before extinction of the fear to the buzzer.

Flooding is the basis of a treatment procedure called *implosive therapy*, developed by Stampfl (Stampfl & Levis, 1967) to deal with human anxieties and phobias. The general approach is to flood the subject with imagined scenes of the feared object until the anxiety extinguishes. For example, if a girl had an excessive fear of spiders she would be told to imagine increasingly horrible scenes relating to spiders, such as spiders crawling all over her. Such scenes will elicit considerable anxiety in her, but the scenes are continued until she no longer responds with anxiety. It is not yet clear exactly how effective implosive therapy is. In some cases it seems to be beneficial, while in others it conditions even more anxiety in the patient (see Morganstern, 1973). There is also some question as to whether implosive therapy really produces its results by respondent extinction, or whether some other explanation is needed.

Much of this chapter has revolved around contingencies between stimuli, i.e., if one stimulus occurs, what is the probability of another specific stimulus occurring? The next chapter is partially concerned with contingencies between responses of the animal and subsequent events. If the animal makes a particular response, what will happen?

SUMMARY

Perhaps the most basic principle of psychology is the *law of contiguity*, a principle of association that states that events that occur close together in space or time tend to become associated. A learning paradigm that derives from contiguity of stimuli is *respondent conditioning*, in which one stimulus (CS), as the result of being paired with a second stimulus (UCS), comes to elicit a response (CR) similar to the response (UCR) previously elicited only by the UCS. Generally the best respondent conditioning occurs if the CS comes on about one-half second before the UCS and if the UCR is compatible with or dominant to the response originally elicited by the CS.

If the CS is presented time after time without being paired with the UCS, the tendency for the CS to elicit the CR will decrease, a process called *extinction*. *Flooding* is an accelerated approach to respondent extinction in which the subject is bombarded by one CS after another in quick succession in such a way that the subject cannot keep making CR's. *Implosive therapy* is a form of flooding in which a human subject is flooded with CS's that elicit anxiety.

There are many theories of respondent conditioning, most of which are forms of contiguity theories or reinforcement theories. *Contiguity theories* emphasize the pairing of the CS and UCS (S-S contiguity). Unfortunately such theories predict conditioning in situations where it often does not occur. Also, some theorists are moving away from explanations in terms of the simple pairing of the CS and UCS and toward the idea of the contingency between the CS and UCS, i.e., how well the onset of the CS predicts the onset of the UCS. The contingency approach leads to the following continuum: At one end of the continuum the onset of the CS indicates that the UCS is sure to soon come on, so that as a result of learning the CS elicits conditioned excitation—the CR. At the other end of the continuum the CS indicates that the UCS will not come on for some period of time, and thus the CS comes to elicit conditioned inhibition, a tendency opposite to that of the CR. *Reinforcement theories* of respondent conditioning emphasize the CR being reinforced either by the onset of a pleasant UCS or by the offset of an aversive UCS. Other theories combine both contiguity and reinforcement principles.

Sources of motivation (conditioned drives) and sources of reinforcement (conditioned reinforcements) may be acquired via respondent conditioning. This is the basis for the *two-process theory*, which asserts that respondent variables provide much of the motivation and/or reinforcement for many behaviors. The two processes or factors, then, are respondent factors (conditioned drives and conditioned reinforcements) and operant factors (the actual response made, as discussed in the next chapter).

Associative interference theory, based on contiguity learning, suggests that forgetting is due to problems in retrieving information from storage because of interference from other stored information. Retention loss thus results from some stimuli, at the time of recall, eliciting alternative responses which interfere with the desired response. The source of the interfering responses may be material learned before the material to be recalled *(proactive interference)* or material learned after the material to be recalled *(retroactive interference)*, or both. Associative interference theory involves a number of other factors, including contextual associations, generalized competition, and list differentiation. The theory, based primarily on studies of learning nonsense material, needs to be much expanded to account for the learning and forgetting of meaningful affective material.

In clinical situations a powerful application of respondent conditioning is *counterconditioning*—respondently conditioning a desired response to a stimulus situation in place of an undesired response. Two examples of counterconditioning are *desensitization*, the counterconditioning of relaxation to stimuli that previously elicited anxiety, and *aversive counterconditioning*, the counterconditioning of aversive responses to stimuli that previously elicited a positive or approach response.

SUGGESTED READINGS

Beecroft, R. S. *Classical Conditioning.* Goleta, Calif.: Psychonomic Press, 1966.

Black, A. H., & Prokasy, W. F. (eds.) *Classical Conditioning II: Current Research and Theory.* New York: Appleton-Century-Crofts, 1972.

Eysenck, H. J., & Beech, R. Counterconditioning and related methods. In Bergin, A. E., & Garfield, S. L. (eds.) *Handbook of Psychotherapy and Behavior Change: An Empirical Analysis.* New York: Wiley, 1971.

Gormezano, I., & Moore, J. W. Classical conditioning. In Marx, M. H. (ed.) *Learning: Processes.* New York: Macmillan, 1969.

Hall, J. F. *Verbal Learning and Retention.* Philadelphia: Lippincott, 1971.

Kimble, G. A. *Hilgard and Marquis' Conditioning and Learning.* New York: Appleton-Century-Crofts, 1961.

Razran, G. *Mind in Evolution.* Boston: Houghton-Mifflin, 1971.

feedback

When turning a corner in a car, a driver will adjust how far he turns the wheel based on visual information about the position of the car to the road and what effect the last turning of the wheel made. When talking to a group, a good lecturer or teacher will adjust the pace, content, and style of his presentation to fit the group, according to cues, such as facial expressions, that he picks up from the group. Both the driver and the lecturer are altering their behavior based on *feedback*, information fed back into the system about the effects of an output of the system. Feedback provides people with information about the effects of their behavior on the environment.

A thermostat is a mechanism that utilizes feedback. When the temperature goes below some value, the thermostat turns on the furnace. The furnace then stays on until the thermostat receives feedback that the temperature has reached the desired point. Without such a feedback device you would have to manually turn the furnace on and off. In 1948 Wiener argued that the logic of feedback theory, as it had been developed with machines such as the thermostat, could be applied to other areas, such as biology, neurophysiology, and psychology. Wiener used the term *cybernetics* for the application of such an approach to machines and animals. Feedback is now a key psychological concept from the level of simple muscle control to complex group interactions.

One important type of feedback, called *proprioception*, comes from the muscles. Simple walking involves a complex set of muscle movements that require feedback about where different muscles are and what they are currently doing. With your eyes shut you should be able to touch your index fingers together, regardless of where your hands start from. This requires proprioceptive feedback. The disease *tabes dorsalis* blocks proprioceptive feedback from the limbs. A person with this disease may have poor control over voluntary movement of the limbs and might not be able to do the above finger touching with his eyes closed.

Human speech utilizes a large number of different feedback mechanisms. During speech there is constant feedback about the spatial position, direction of movement, and velocity of movement of the various structures involved in speech, particularly the tongue (Sussman, 1972). As Sussman points out, "any attempt to explain how the tongue signals the higher brain centers concerning its highly complex positional adjustments during speech activity must necessarily incorporate a rapidly acting, highly discriminative, and comprehensively informative neurosystem." The complexity of such a feedback system is mentioned by Sussman in the case of a man speaking with a pipe clenched between his teeth. Here the entire muscular movement patterns of the tongue and lips must compensate for non-moving jaws.

Hearing your own voice is another source of feedback for normal speech. One way of demonstrating this is with *delayed auditory feedback* (Yates, 1963). Here the subject hears his voice while talking, but instead of hearing it immediately, it is electronically delayed a fraction of a second. For example, while counting from one to ten you might hear "two" while saying "three." Talking during delayed auditory feedback is quite difficult. While counting you might repeat the same number several times, and speech is generally slower, and contains many more errors. A similar phenomenon occurs with people giving speeches in a large hall. Sometimes a speaker in such a situation will hear his own speech slightly delayed, as from his amplified voice bouncing back to him from a far wall, and this effect may severely impair his speech. Rock musicians will often have small speakers on the stage with them for immediate feedback of their sound. Otherwise their timing might be disrupted from hearing their music delayed as it rebounds off walls. On the other hand deaf people often show peculiar inflections and intonations in their speech because they lack auditory feedback.

Smith (1972) has shown similar disruption in performance with delayed visual feedback. Subjects had to track a moving geometrical figure with a wand. However, they could not directly see their hands or the objects. Rather they saw what they were doing on a television monitor which could delay the visual feedback. As the delay increased (from 17 to 820 msec.), performance decreased. With the intermediate delay times, about 250 msec., the subjects often reported that their arm and hand movements had a peculiarly "rubbery" appearance and feeling.

Adams (1968) has summarized some of the ways in which feedback is incorporated with learning as follows. S-R learning theorists conceptualize the learning process as associations formed between stimuli (S) and responses (R), whereas S-S theorists view learning in terms of associations between stimuli, such as stimulus relationships in the environment (see discussion of S-R and S-S theories in Chapter 1).

For the S-R theorist, feedback, such as proprioception, is a source of stimuli. New responses can be learned to these feedback stimuli and/or the stimuli may become conditioned reinforcers. This feedback provides the basis for *chaining,* a sequence of responses in which the occurrence of one response provides part of the cues for the following response. One rat named S. R. Rodent was taught the following chain of behaviors. Rodent first had to climb a spiral staircase, then run across a drawbridge, climb a ladder, get into a cable car and pull himself across a gap, climb another stairway, play a toy piano, run through a tunnel, climb into an elevator and pull a chain to start it, ride to the bottom floor, and then press a bar to receive pellets (Bachrach, 1964). This chain of behaviors was conditioned into the rat by starting at the end (pressing the bar) and moving backward. In the final chain each component of the chain occurs to two sets of stimuli, the stimuli of the apparatus and feedback stimuli from the previous behavior. Thus Rodent's behavior of climbing the ladder provides feedback stimuli which help lead to the next response of getting into the cable car. The feedback stimuli might also become conditioned reinforcers that then reinforce that member of the chain. Similarly in learning to say a long poem from memory, the feedback from saying one line may facilitate remembering and saying the next line.

For S-S theorists, according to Adams, feedback provides information about the proper conditions for the behavior. Feedback stimuli feed into the whole stimulus complex to which the animal makes some responses. These approaches are often cognitive in nature, and one may interpret learning as being primarily perceptual. Feedback cues are often thought of as information about which behaviors are appropriate, rather than stimuli that elicit responses.

Adams favors a *closed-loop theory* of behavior in which "the consequences of a response with sufficient habit strength to occur are fed back and compared with a reference which is the desired value for the system. Any difference between a reference and its response feedback is error, and the detection of errors results in a response sequence that can lead to error nulling." In other words the animal has a certain goal to attain, and makes responses in that direction. Feedback following the responses provides information about whether the goal has been reached or what responses might now be appropriate toward reaching the goal.

Miller, Galanter, and Pribram (1960) proposed a closed-loop analysis of behavior based on TOTE units, as opposed to S-R units. A *TOTE unit* stands for Test-Operate-Test-Exit. The "test" is an analysis of information, mostly sensory data, about any incongruities between the current state of affairs and some goal. If there is some incongruity, the animal responds, or "operates." After it operates, the animal again tests. If there is still an incongruity, it operates again, and then tests again.

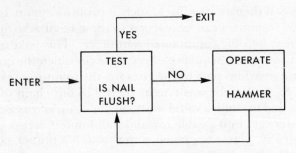

Figure 6-1 A simple TOTE unit.

When the test finally shows no incongruity, the animal exits and stops this one type of behavior.

Figure 6-1 shows a basic TOTE unit related to hammering a nail until it is flush with the surface. During the test the person inspects whether the nail is flush. If the nail is not flush, then he hammers (operate). If the nail is flush, he no longer hammers this nail (exit).

A TOTE unit is an example of a closed-loop mechanism since the organism tests the outcome of its behavior against a reference until there is no error. Complex human behavior, of course, can seldom be explained in terms of a simple TOTE unit. Rather, Miller, Galanter, and Pribram showed how behavior might be explained in terms of a number of interrelated TOTE units. They called such a set of TOTE units a *plan*. A plan may involve several TOTE units functioning simultaneously, as well as TOTE units that work sequentially.

Another type of feedback theory is *ideo-motor theory*, originally proposed by William James in 1890 and propounded more recently by Greenwald (1970). According to ideo-motor theory, a response is selected on the basis of its own *anticipated* sensory feedback. In this theory a perceptual image or idea of an action initiates the performance. William James argued that the mere thought of a movement "awakens in some degree" the actual movement. (Think about swinging a golf club or riding a bicycle and note tendencies in the related muscles toward movement.) The only thing that stops the actual movement is inhibitory influences from other sources, such as other thoughts. Thus the simple thought of an action results in anticipation of its own sensory feedback which in turn helps to determine which behavior will finally occur.

SENSITIVITY TRAINING GROUPS

Feedback is the key ingredient in *sensitivity training groups*, also called *T-groups* (see Aronson, 1972, Chap. 8). In a T-group a number of people get together with a trainer to learn more about how their behavior affects other people. The discussions of the group center on a current analysis of the social dynamics of the group itself. Each member learns how to provide feedback to other members of the group about how he feels and is affected by their specific behaviors. Through such feedback each member can find out what other people really think and feel about different behaviors. Feedback of this nature is useful to some people who do not ordinarily receive it, either because of selective perception on their part or because people are not giving them this feedback. It can be a useful source of information which may or may not provide cues and consequences that will affect later performance.

For feedback in a T-group to be most useful it should usually meet the following requirements. It should describe the speaker's feelings and reactions, not simply make evaluations. It should provide specific examples, rather than generalities. It should not just be dumped on the person, but should be presented to him in a time and a way that is most useful to the receiver.

T-groups, of course, include much more than feedback, but feedback is probably the major objective. The research on T-groups is currently grossly inadequate. For example, it would be interesting to analyze T-groups in terms of modeling and reinforcement.

The types of skills and behaviors a person learns in interacting with members of a T-group may or may not be useful behaviors in dealing with people outside of the T-group, particularly if there is not a good transition between the T-group and the rest of the world. Too many T-groups merely provide the person with another reference group manipulating his behaviors, while denying any such manipulation. A second problem is that feedback is not always a very powerful change mechanism. The feedback may convince the person that he wishes to act differently (more assertively, for example), but he might not have the desired skills in his behavioral repertoire. Other change procedures (e.g., assertive training) then might be useful.

OPERANT CONDITIONING

Occasionally the consequence of some response or behavior will make it more or less probable that the response will occur again in similar situations. If a hungry rat presses a bar and receives food, the consequence of the food will usually make it more probable that the rat will press the bar again. If, however, the bar-press yields electric shock to the rat's feet, the consequence of the shock will make it less probable that the rat will bar-press again.

Operant conditioning, also called *instrumental conditioning* and *type R learning,* is the study of the effects of *contingent* (contiguous) events on the behaviors they follow. A contingent event is a *dependent* event when it occurs if and only if a specified behavior occurred first. In the case of the rat bar-pressing for food, the food appears if and only if the rat presses the bar. If the contingent event makes it more probable that the response will be repeated, then the event is called a *reinforcement.* If the contingent event makes the behavior less probable, the event is called a *punishment.* It should be noted that the concept of "contingency" has been defined in various ways by operant conditioners. Some theorists (e.g., Schoenfeld & Farmer, 1970) argue that "contingency" should imply more than simple contiguity, perhaps some form of causal relationship between the distribution of responses and the distribution of contingent events.

Figure 6–2 shows the temporal sequence in operant conditioning. In the presence of certain antecedent stimuli the animal makes some response. Contingent on this response is some event. Following this event there may be a change in the probability of the response re-occurring in the presence of the antecedent stimuli. Such contingent events then are clearly a form of feedback, for they inform the animal about the consequences of his behavior.

The contingent event may increase or come on (positive) following the response, or it may decrease or go off (negative). Also, the contingent event may increase the probability of the response (reinforcement) or decrease the probability (punishment). This yields the following four combinations: positive reinforcement, negative reinforcement, positive punishment, and negative punishment.

Positive reinforcement is an event whose increase results in an increase in the probability of the response it is contingent on. The rat *increases* his probability of bar-pressing because each bar-press *increases* the amount of food present. A child cries at bedtime if this ensures that his parents will read him a story.

Negative reinforcement is an event whose decrease results in an increase in the probability of the response it is contingent on. A rat will *increase* his probability of bar-pressing if each bar-press *decreases* the electric shock in the grid floor. A person begins taking a different route home because he learns it decreases the traffic he encounters. Note that a very common error is for people to confuse negative reinforcement with punishment. Remember that negative reinforcement *increases* response probability, while punishment decreases it.

Positive punishment is an event whose increase results in a decrease in the probability of the response it is contingent on. The rat *decreases* his probability of bar-pressing if each bar-press *increases* the amount of electric shock in the grid floor. A student stops answering questions in class if his answers are met with derision.

Negative punishment is an event whose decrease results in a decrease

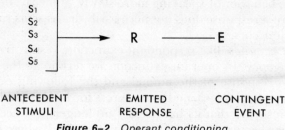

ANTECEDENT   EMITTED   CONTINGENT
STIMULI   RESPONSE   EVENT

Figure 6-2   *Operant conditioning.*

in the probability of the response it is contingent on. A rat might *decrease* his probability of bar-pressing if each bar press *decreases* the supply of something it likes, such as the amount of available food. A child stops yelling if each time he yells his television program is turned off for 10 seconds.

Figure 6–3 shows the relationships between these four types of contingent events. Note that the onset and offset of the same event may function differently depending on what behaviors they are contingent on. Thus if the onset of a pleasant event can be a positive reinforcement, the offset of the event can usually be a negative punishment. Similarly, if the onset of an aversive event can be a positive punishment, the offset can be a negative reinforcement. These relationships correspond to the diagonals of Figure 6–3. It should also be noted that increasing the *probability* of a response does not necessarily increase the *rate* or *magnitude* of the response when it occurs; it merely increases the probability of it occurring. For example, a person might receive positive reinforcement for talking more slowly. Here the positive reinforcement increases the prob-

Figure 6-3   *Types of contingent events.*

CHANGES IN CONTINGENT EVENT

		INCREASE	DECREASE
EFFECTS ON PROBABILITY OF RESPONSE	INCREASE	POSITIVE REINFORCEMENT	NEGATIVE REINFORCEMENT
	DECREASE	POSITIVE PUNISHMENT	NEGATIVE PUNISHMENT

ability of the behavior of speaking more slowly. Similarly, decreasing the probability of a response does not necessarily decrease its rate or magnitude when it occurs.

Operant extinction, like respondent extinction, results from terminating a contingency. In operant extinction we terminate the contingency between the response of the animal and the following event. For example, the rat that had learned to bar-press for food could be put on extinction by insuring that its bar-presses no longer produced food. The rat's behavior would be considered extinguished when it no longer pressed the bar at higher than baseline level, the rate it was pressing the bar before food was made contingent on bar-pressing. Or a child in a classroom might kneel in his chair to get the teacher's attention, but stop doing it after the teacher no longer responded to this behavior. An extinguished operant response may show *spontaneous recovery,* an increase in the probability of the extinguished response following a period of time.

In respondent conditioning we speak of the CS as *eliciting* the CR. The CS forces the animal to make the CR. In operant conditioning the animal is said to *emit* the response in the presence of the antecedent stimuli. That is, these stimuli do not elicit the response. The rat does not immediately press the bar the instant he is put in the operant chamber. Rather the antecedent stimuli "set the occasion" for the operant response. Some people equate "elicited" with "involuntary" and "emitted" with "voluntary," but this is not necessarily true. B. F. Skinner, dean of current operant conditioners, would argue that an operant response is as determined and involuntary as any respondent response. For any operant response there is a sequence of stimuli that causes the response to occur, as the CS causes the CR to occur. But the operant stimuli are not as easy to identify as the CS. Nor, for most practical purposes, is it important to be able to identify them. In operant conditioning we often have satisfactory prediction and control merely through manipulation of the contingent events.

Occasionally some of the antecedent stimuli, through learning, develop a particularly strong control over the operant behavior. These stimuli are then called *discriminative stimuli,* and the behavior they control is called a *discriminative operant.* For example, a rat might be trained that when the left light is on, bar-pressing yields food, whereas when the right light is on, a bar-press produces no food. If the left light is on for only a short time, we will probably find our hungry rat will learn to hurry to the bar when the left light is on and generally avoid the bar when the right light is on. Here we would say that the discriminative stimulus of the left light sets the occasion for the discriminative operant of pressing the bar. The discriminative stimulus is often abbreviated S^D while the other stimuli, such as the right light, are abbreviated S^Δ.

An operant conditioner might decide to reinforce a particular be-

havior that he wishes to occur more often. But what happens if the behavior never occurs the first time? Or what if the behavior occurs, but
only very infrequently? In these situations, it is desirable to find some
way to get the behavior to occur for operant conditioning. There are
many ways to do this, the three most popular of which are known by the
terms shaping, modeling, and fading.

Shaping, also called *successive approximation,* consists of reinforcing
behaviors that gradually approximate the desired behavior. If you want
a rat to press a bar, you don't wait until it presses the bar to reward it.
Rather you shape it to press the bar by first reinforcing it just for being
in that half of the apparatus where the bar is. Next it has to be within a
certain area of the bar to be reinforced, then it has to touch the bar, then
put its paw on the bar, and finally it has to press the bar. In practice,
shaping is more fluid and less discrete than this description, but the
approach is the same. It is not unusual for a skilled shaper to have a
naive rat bar-pressing within 15 minutes of the time the rat is put in the
test apparatus.

Similarly, if you were working with a chronic catatonic who has not
talked in ten years, it would be a poor operant program to wait until he
said a sentence to reinforce him. Rather you must gradually shape him
to talk. Perhaps you would first reward him just for blowing a little air
out of his mouth, and from there slowly move on to getting him to
produce simple sounds.

As a further illustration, take the case of a secretary who is always 15
minutes late for work. If you decide to reward her with praise on the day
when she does come in on time, you might have a long wait. Rather you
should use shaping; i.e., reward her closer approximations to being on
time.

Modeling, as mentioned in the first chapter, is often a quick way of
first getting a response to occur for operant conditioning; this method
often works much faster than shaping. A rat that watched another rat
press a bar may imitate or model the other rat and have a tendency to
press the bar itself. With humans it is often easy to demonstrate the behavior we wish and reward the modeling.

Fading is keeping the behavior the same while gradually changing
the stimuli. Thus fading consists of approximations on the stimulus side,
whereas shaping consists of approximations on the response side. As an
example of fading, a pigeon might be trained to peck a disc to the stimulus of a blue square. If it is now shown a red circle, the pigeon might not
peck the disc, as the red circle is too different from the blue square. But
if we keep rewarding the disc-pecking as we gradually change, or fade,
the blue square stimulus into a red circle stimulus, we can eventually
have the pigeon pecking to the red circle without ever having lost the
original disc-pecking.

Principles of fading become important when we wish to transfer learning from one situation (e.g., school room, clinic) into a new situation (e.g., home). Here it is often useful to provide some transitions between the different settings.

REINFORCEMENT DELAY AND SCHEDULE

As a general rule reinforcements are most effective when they occur immediately after the behavior (see Renner, 1964). The time between the response and the reinforcement is called the *delay of reinforcement*, and short delays usually produce better learning than long delays. As the delay of reinforcement increases, the animal often must find ways of mediating the time. A rat may learn some behavior, such as chewing on the food dish, which mediates the time. Humans often use language, both out loud and internalized as thoughts, as mediating behavior. Also, the presence of conditioned reinforcers during the delay period may help to support mediating behaviors. A problem with long delays of reinforcment is that they generally allow for many intervening events to become associated with either the response or the reinforcement, and such associations may interfere with the response-reinforcement learning. Experiments designed to minimize such interfering associations permit learning with longer delays of reinforcement. For example, rats in a simple two-choice learning task learned the correct response with reinforcement delays of up to 8 minutes if they were removed from the test apparatus during the delay period (Lett, 1973).

In practical settings we often find behaviors more affected by sources of immediate reinforcement than by events that are temporally distant. The alcoholic's drinking behavior (which may involve physiological addiction) is often more affected by the immediate reinforcing effects of drinking (e.g., reduction in anxiety, social approval, good feelings) than by the longer term punishing effects of having been drunk (e.g., hangovers). Similarly, a graduate student who only has to complete his thesis may often find that the more immediate rewards associated with play affect his daily life more powerfully than the long range rewards associated with the completion of his thesis. The long range rewards may be substantially stronger than the immediate rewards, but this is often more than offset by the delay of reinforcement and the person's experience of working under long delays.

Thus, many programs geared toward altering human behavior involve providing reinforcements with short delays and/or taking existing reinforcers with long delays and building in mediating behaviors and conditioned reinforcers. This cutting down on long delays will be seen later when we discuss contingency contracting.

We have been discussing reinforcement as if it occurred after every correct response, but this is not necessarily the case. For example, we could arrange to reinforce only every third response. The pattern by which reinforcements are related to responses is called the *schedule of reinforcement* (see Ferster & Skinner, 1957; Schoenfeld, 1970; Thompson & Grabowski, 1972). There are two general types of schedules: (1) *continuous reinforcement (CRF)*, in which every correct response is reinforced; and (2) *intermittent reinforcement*, in which only some of the correct responses are reinforced. Generally, original learning is faster with continuous reinforcement, but the number of trials before extinction occurs is larger under intermittent reinforcement. This longer time to extinction with intermittent schedules is called the *partial reinforcement effect*. There are basically four types of intermittent schedules: fixed ratio, variable ratio, fixed interval, and variable interval.

A *fixed ratio* schedule means that the animal must make a fixed number of responses before being reinforced. Thus a rat on an FR-5 schedule must make 5 bar-presses before being reinforced. By gradually increasing the ratio, an animal can be trained to make an enormous number of responses for a single reinforcement. Fixed ratio schedules correspond to piecework pay. A laborer payed for every 3 items he produces is on an FR-3 schedule.

A *variable ratio* schedule is the same as the fixed ratio except that the number of responses required each time varies around some average. Thus a rat on a VR-9 schedule must press, on the average, about 9 times before being reinforced. However, one time he might press only twice and another time might require 12 presses. VR schedules often result in very long times to extinction. Consider a man playing roulette in Las Vegas and only betting one number each time. He is on a VR-38 schedule since 38 different numbers come up randomly. Thus on the average he wins once for each 38 bets (and is paid only 35 to 1 odds), but he might win twice in a row or go 200 times without a win. However, with no-one influencing the wheel, the long term average will be about 1 in 38. A behavior maintained under such a schedule is, of course, difficult to extinguish, and this is one of the variables feeding into gambling fever.

A *fixed interval* schedule is one where the animal is reinforced for the first correct response it makes after some period of time has passed. Thus a rat on an FI-1-minute schedule will be reinforced for the first response he makes after one minute has passed. Responses made before this time is up will have no effect.

A *variable interval* schedule is the same as the fixed interval except that the amount of time varies from trial to trial around some average. A rat on a VI-1-minute schedule is reinforced for the first response he makes after some period of time. This period may be different each time, but will average out to about one minute. VI schedules often produce some of the stablest responding, since the animal can't "figure out" when to respond and when not to respond. VI schedules often produce very long times to extinction. Thus people who want to build in a strong behavior often start their animal or human subject on CRF and gradually phase them onto a VI schedule.

These four intermittent schedules can be combined in various ways, such as requiring the animal to respond first on VR-5, then FI-2 (minutes), then VR-5, and so forth. There are also many other schedules, too numerous to be fully discussed here.

THE NATURE OF REINFORCEMENT

The simplest approach to reinforcement is to define it operationally: An event which when contingent on a response increases the probability of the response is a reinforcement. This has a touch of circularity to it in that an event is identified as a reinforcement after it functions as a reinforcement. This circularity can be overcome by showing that the reinforcement is *trans-situational*. That is, it is possible to demonstrate that the event which functions as a reinforcement in one situation also functions as a reinforcement in quite different situations. (One problem is what constitutes a "different" situation.) At the empirical, operational level there is fairly good consensus about the *properties* of reinforcement. However, at the theoretical level there is little consensus about the *nature* of reinforcement.

A major theoretical issue is whether reinforcement affects learning or only performance. Theorists who hold that reinforcement affects learning (e.g., Thorndike and Hull) argue that the reinforcing event somehow facilitates the learning process or strengthens the learned association. For example, Landauer (1969) assumes that learning is by contiguity and that reinforcement facilitates the consolidation of the learning. To Landauer, a reinforcement is any event that strengthens learning, such as contingent food or CS-UCS pairings.

On the other hand some theorists (e.g., early Tolman) hold that reinforcement affects only performance, and not learning. Such theorists often think of the reinforcement event as being an *incentive*, an event that the animal is motivated to try to acquire, rather than an event which strengthens learning. Bolles (1972) argues that contingent reinforcement is neither a necessary nor a sufficient condition for operant learning. Bolles' expectancy theory of learning states the following primary law of learning: "What is learned is that certain events, cues, (S), predict certain other, biologically important events, consequences, (S*). An animal may incidentally show new responses, but what it learns is an expectancy that represents and corresponds to the S-S* contingency." According to Bolles, when an animal learns a relationship between its behavior (R) and some consequence of this behavior (S*), the animal learns an R-S* expectancy. These two expectancies, S-S* and R-S*, are all that is usually learned in operant conditioning. These expectancies then become "synthesized" so that in the presence of S the animal makes the response R. Thus if "an animal is placed in a situation where there are cues predicting food, and food is made contingent upon some response, the animal will learn first that these cues predict food, and second, that its behavior produces food. If the animal is hungry, then it is likely to make that response." In Bolles' theory, operant and respondent conditioning both involve learning S-S* expectancies, and in operant conditioning the subject may also learn an R-S* expectancy.

THEORIES OF REINFORCEMENT

Let us now turn to a few of the many theories of reinforcement, most of which were proposed by theorists who believed that reinforcement affects learning. Hull (1943) suggested that all basic drives, such as hunger or the sexual drive, feed into one non-specific drive. This non-specific drive then energizes whatever behaviors the animal makes in the particular stimulus situation. According to Hull, reinforcement is any event which produces a reduction in this non-specific drive. Hull's theory is thus referred to as a *drive-reduction* theory of reinforcement.

Sheffield (1966a, 1966b), on the other hand, has suggested a *drive-induction* theory of reinforcement. Sheffield argues that animals learn those responses which arouse motivation. If a rat receives food for turning right in a T-maze, as opposed to turning left, the consummatory response of eating becomes conditioned to the stimuli of the right side as well as to response-produced stimuli of the instrumental behavior. When the rat now approaches the choice point, these stimuli elicit, to some degree, the consummatory response. But since the rat can't consume the food until he gets to it, the consummatory stimulation without consummation is drive induction, which motivates the rat to make the response (turning right) which in the past preceded the consummatory response. Thus Sheffield's rat is forced to make the response because of the drive induction. Although originally more general, Sheffield's theory now is basically only applied to consummatory situations, as opposed, for example, to punishment situations. The consummatory response may also be a central response without overt behaviors.

Gibson's theory of perceptual learning, discussed in Chapter 2, suggests that reduction of uncertainty is the reinforcement for much of perceptual learning (Gibson, 1969, p. 120). The complexity-arousal theories in Chapter 3 also deal with reinforcement effects.

Premack (1965) has proposed a theory of reinforcement in which responses reinforce responses. To determine which responses will act as reinforcers we must first measure the independent rates of the different responses. This is done by putting the animal in a situation where it can freely do either of two responses with no contingencies between the responses. From this, Premack predicts that the higher probability response will reinforce the lower probability response if a contingency is established between the two. For example, if a hungry rat is put in a situation where it can eat food or press a bar (where the bar-press does not yield anything), the independent rate of eating food will be higher than the independent rate of pressing the bar. So if the response of eating food is made contingent on the response of pressing the bar, the rate of bar-pressing will increase, being reinforced by the opportunity to eat food.

Premack's theory has two major strengths. First, it allows us to incorporate into reinforcement theory well-known examples of activities reinforcing activities, such as when the mother tells her son that he must first eat his vegetables (low-probability behavior) before he may go out and play (high-probability behavior). Although there are other explanations for such conditions, they fit so well into Premack's theory that Premack's principle of reinforcement is sometimes called "Grandma's rule." The idea that the opportunity to engage in some activity is a reinforcement underlies much of contingency contracting, discussed later.

The second strength of Premack's theory is its suggestion of reinforcement relationships that are not as obvious from other theoretical positions. For example, in some situations Premack showed that humans' pinball playing was reinforced by eating, while in other situations eating was reinforced by pinball playing. Premack was also able to reinforce a rat's drinking with giving it the opportunity to run in an activity wheel.

So far we have discussed only positive reinforcement in Premack's theory. The same logic applies to negative reinforcement as well, except that now we are talking about the probability of the offset of an activity or response. Altogether, then, Premack's principle of reinforcement is as follows: If the onset or offset of one response is more probable than the onset or offset of another, the former will reinforce the latter positively if the superiority is for "on" probability, and negatively if it is for the "off" probability.

The next set of reinforcement theories are based on possible physiological bases of reinforcement. More specifically they center on observations that electrical stimulation to certain parts of the brain produces strong reinforcing effects.

REINFORCING BRAIN STIMULATION

In the early 1950's, Olds and Milner (1954) were doing experiments which involved putting small electrodes into the brains of rats so that they could electrically stimulate specific areas of the brain. Since brain functioning is at least partially electrical in nature, electrically stimulating an area of the brain, and thus forcing that area to be activated, is one way of testing approximately what that area does in natural functioning. In the course of one experiment, while Olds and Milner were aiming their electrodes at one area of the brain (reticular formation), one electrode, by mistake, ended up much further forward in the brain. It was observed that stimulation through this electrode seemed to be "pleasant" to the rat in that the rat would go to specific places on a table or run a maze to receive this stimulation. Thus began the massive research on reinforcing electrical stimulation of the brain (ESB). (Similar effects can be produced by chemical stimulation, but this literature will not be discussed here.)

The effects of ESB are usually defined in an operant paradigm. If the animal will make some response, such as pressing a bar, to turn the stimulation on, the ESB is considered positively reinforcing, whereas if he will respond to turn it off, the ESB is negatively reinforcing. The results, however, are often not this simple. In some situations the ESB is reinforcing at first, but becomes aversive if continued (Bower & Miller, 1958). This may be because the electrical current spreads from reward areas into aversive areas or it may be the result of an actual functional change in the stimulated site.

By putting electrodes in various parts of the brain, it is possible to map out the "reward" areas of the brain. It appears that most of the brain, particularly the cortex, is motivationally inert, with ESB producing neither positive nor negative reinforcement. The positive reinforcement areas are mostly in subcortical areas and seem to outnumber the subcortical negative reinforcement areas.

The reinforcing effect of ESB varies according to the exact placement of the electrode, the species of the animal, the duration and intensity of the stimulation, and a number of other variables. But at its best, reinforcing ESB is one of the most powerful reinforcements that man has discovered. In the extreme, rats will bar-press for reinforcing ESB to the point of physical exhaustion, often not taking out sufficient time to eat or drink. The strength of the reinforcing effect of the ESB is often measured in terms of rate of response, such as how fast the animal will press a bar. But there are problems with the use of response rate as a measure (see Valenstein, 1964). For example, the ESB may also elicit a motor response or seizure which *decreases* the rate at which the animal is capable of responding. Or the animal might be reinforced for responding at a specific rate, as in micromolar theory (Logan, 1956). Thus, to determine which of two brain areas produces the strongest reinforcing effect, it might be better to give the animal a choice between ESB to the different areas rather than to merely compare the response rates of the different areas.

What is the relationship between reinforcing ESB and other more conventional reinforcements? One thing that stands out is that many of the areas of the brain where reinforcing ESB is found are also areas concerned with other sources of reinforcement, such as from eating. For example, the hypothalamus — perhaps the most popular site for reinforcing ESB — is a critical brain structure for the control of a wide range of consummatory behaviors, including eating, drinking, and sex. This has suggested to several theorists, including Olds (1962), that reinforcing ESB stimulates the actual physiological substrates of conventional reinforcements.

Miller (1961) showed correlations between drive reduction theories of reinforcement and reinforcing ESB, suggesting that the ESB might be stimulating a reward mechanism usually triggered by drive reduction. For example, it is known that electrical stimulation of a part of the hypothalamus reduces the amount of food that an animal will eat. This, then, might be the area stimulated by the drive reduction from eating. Thus we would expect that ESB in this area would be reinforcing, which Miller showed was true. (Although Miller reported that continued stimulation quickly became aversive.) Miller also defended his position by showing how manipulations of drives often affected how reinforcing the ESB was. Later Grossman (1967, p. 591) summarized these findings, saying, "The available evidence indicates that the rate of self-stimulation at a specific electrode site correlates positively with only one particular drive, suggesting a close functional relation between specific drives and the reward effect." However, there are many reports of conflicting and confusing results in trying to correlate sites of reinforcing ESB with neural sites related to conventional reinforcements.

Others have pointed out a number of apparent differences between reinforcing ESB and more conventional reinforcements. These differences include the following: (a) extinction of a response which had ESB as the reward is often more rapid than extinction of responses based on other rewards; (b) satiation to reinforcing ESB often takes much longer; and (c) it is often difficult to maintain responding under an intermittent schedule of ESB.

Deutsch (Deutsch & Howarth, 1963) proposed a theory that accounts for some of these differences. According to Deutsch, in reinforcing ESB the electrical current stimulates both a reinforcement system and a motivation system. Stimulation of the motivation system motivates the animal to make the response which results in reinforcement *plus* motivation to repeat the response. Hence the effect is self-perpetuating, resulting in less satiation with some ESB than with other rewards. Faster extinction and difficulty in maintaining response with intermittent schedules of ESB thus occur because the motivation is eliminated or greatly reduced. (This contrasts with the hungry rat bar-pressing for food that stays hungry even though the bar-press no longer yields food.)

Although there are many clever experiments supporting Deutsch's theory (e.g., Deutsch & Howarth, 1963; Gallistel, 1966), there are also many that refute it. For example, Cantor (1971) used a situation in which the reinforcing ESB was made predictable by preceding it with a brief warning signal. In this case rats would bar-press for a variety of different intermittent schedules of ESB, including FR-2000 and VI-2 minutes. After reviewing a number of studies critical of Deutsch's theory, Trowill, Panksepp, and Gandleman (1969) concluded that many of the apparent differences between reinforcing ESB and other rewards are due to the specific conditions of deprivation and training used by researchers such as Deutsch, and that the results do not hold up in more general testing situations. They prefer to conceptualize the motivating effects of ESB in terms of incentives rather than as the stimulation of a motivational energizing system such as Deutsch's.

The issues are, of course, far from resolved. For example, Lenzer (1972) has offered a model which argues again that there are differences between behavior maintained by reinforcing ESB and behavior reinforced by more conventional rewards. According to Lenzer, in CRF situations or where the ESB's follow each other closely, the controlling stimuli (those stimuli leading to the operant response) are internal stimuli produced by the ESB, whereas in similar situations with conventional rewards, the stimuli produced by the reward do not have a major role in controlling the response. Lenzer assumed that those ESB-produced controlling stimuli decay rapidly with time, yielding Deutsch's type of results. In other situations, such as widely spaced ESB's, the subject receiving reinforcing ESB learns to respond to stimuli similar to those controlling the behavior under conventional rewards. So in these situations little difference will be found between the effects of reinforcing ESB and other reinforcements.

Glickman and Schiff (1967) noted that there was an overlap between those brain areas mediating positive or negative reinforcement and those areas related to species-typical behaviors — behaviors that occur in almost all members of a species. Since these species-typical behaviors are generally important to the animal, as in survival value, it is useful for them to become linked with a reinforcement mechanism that will maintain them in the animal's behavior. According to Glickman and Schiff, reinforcement evolved as a mechanism to insure some species-typical behaviors to appropriate stimuli. Thus reinforcing ESB is the stimulation and facilitation of a neural system underlying species-typical behavior. Aversive effects of ESB are due to the stimulation of areas related to withdrawal behaviors.

Consider a domestic cat growling and attacking objects. It may appear to the observer that the cat is experiencing something unpleasant. But, as Glickman and Schiff point out, such behavior may have had survival value in the history of the cat and thus became associated with reinforcement mechanisms. So our growling cat may actually be experiencing pleasure.

Reinforcing ESB has also been investigated in humans by a number of investigators, including Heath and his associates (e.g., Bishop et al., 1963; Heath, 1963). Heath uses ESB primarily in a therapeutic setting with mental patients. The "pleasurable" effects of reinforcing ESB can be used to disrupt undesirable behaviors that are incapacitating the subjects. In one case (Moan & Heath, 1972) the investigators took advantage of the fact that stimulation of the septal area of the brain may produce both pleasure and sexual arousal. The patient was a 24 year old homosexual male who was repeatedly hospitalized for chronic suicidal depression. When shown a stag movie of sexual intercourse he showed no interest. However, after a series of septal stimulations, the subject, while still feeling "high" from the ESB, was again shown the movie, which now caused considerable sexual arousal. With the help of more septal stimulations and a prostitute the experimenters were able to quickly build in the subject heterosexual behavior which lasted well after treatment. Heath's emphasis, then, has been to use ESB more for eliciting responses and emotional states than for reinforcing specific behaviors, although the two effects are often confounded.

Delgado (1969) has developed ESB technology to an impressive stage. Delgado's subjects (usually monkeys, although humans were used on occasion) are equipped with a unit in their skull that simultaneously records brain activity and stimulates specific areas. This unit can be monitored and controlled via radio communication so that the subject is not restricted in movement by wires coming out of his head. Through such a set-up the observer, which may be a computer, can monitor the subject's brain activity and stimulate different areas of the brain when specific reactions are desired. By stimulating different areas, the subject can be made sleepy, hungry, aggressive, afraid, or sexually aroused; almost any basic emotion, motivation, or simple physical movement can be elicited. And the stimulation may be used as a reinforcement.

People who have received reinforcing ESB say that it is pleasurable; they often describe the sensation in terms of one or more other types of rewarding sensations, such as sexual orgasm or the pleasure experienced from having something good to eat. At present we don't know just how powerful a reinforcing effect can be produced by ESB in humans. Is there an area or combination of areas in the human brain which when stimulated will produce so powerful a pleasurable sensation that the subject will choose this ESB over all other sensations or activities? We don't know, but there is no reason to believe that there isn't. The work done on ESB in humans by researchers such as Heath and Delgado has not really emphasized the reinforcing effects of some ESB; that is, they have not experimented with requiring the subject to make some response in order to receive reinforcing ESB. Such experimentation, however, has its dangers. An example of a misuse of reinforcement would be giving a mental patient a reinforcing ESB every time we recorded some specific aberrant activity in his brain. Although we may have intended the ESB to disrupt the aberrant activity and associated behaviors, we might actually be reinforcing this particular brain activity to occur more often.

The possibility of ESB's having powerful reinforcement effects in man raises a host of philosophical, ethical, and science-fiction issues. Under what conditions would we have the right to apply such a technology to someone else? If we find areas where ESB is pleasurable, should we then give it to everyone? If I had someone work around my house for me in order to receive reinforcing ESB each night and he told you he was doing the work voluntarily because he liked ESB so much, would you object to my coercing work out of him? If the ESB is so rewarding to my worker that he would do anything to receive it, where does the concept of "will" enter in? Or is man so complex that he can never be controlled through such a simple procedure?

PUNISHMENT

When used by itself the term "punishment" usually refers to *positive punishment*—a contingent event whose increase results in a decrease in the probability of the response it is contingent on. It is less probable that a child will touch the burner on the stove if he is burned when he first makes the touching response. Although it is easy to define punishment in terms of its effect on behavior, the mechanisms by which it produces these effects are highly debated (Campbell & Church, 1969; Church, 1963; Dunham, 1971; Johnston, 1972; Solomon, 1964). We will consider a few of the possibilities.

A punishment probably elicits emotional responses in the subject, such as fear and anxiety. These emotional responses then may become respondently conditioned to the situation in which the punishment occurred. To the extent that these emotions are incompatible with the punished response, the probability of the response may decrease. Or these emotional responses may lead to some other incompatible response which becomes conditioned to the situation.

The punishment may elicit some response, other than an emotional response, which becomes respondently conditioned to the situation. Again, to the extent that this response is incompatible with the punished response, there will be a decrease in the probability of the punished response.

Since the onset of the aversive stimulus is positive punishment, the offset of the stimulus is negative reinforcement. Thus whatever response the subject is making when the stimulus goes off, such as an escape response, will be reinforced. If this reinforced response is incompatible with the punished response, there will be a decrease in the probability of the punished response. Of course, punishment need not produce just one of the effects mentioned above, but may produce different combinations of the effects in different situations.

Dunham (1971) has summarized the effects of punishment due to electric shock into two basic rules: (1) That particular response in the organism's repertoire which is most frequently associated with shock onset, or which predicts the onset of shock within a shorter time than other responses, will decrease in probability and remain below its operant baseline; (2) That particular response in the organism's repertoire which is most frequently associated with the *absence* of shock onset, or which predicts the absence of shock onset for a longer period of time than other responses, will increase in probability and remain above its operant baseline.

Premack expanded his response-probability approach to reinforcement to include punishment as well (Terhune & Premack, 1970). That is, in reinforcement, response A will reinforce response B if A is more probable (has a higher independent rate) than B, whereas in punishment, response A will suppress response B if A is less probable than B.

In applied situations the practitioner should generally avoid the use of punishment as a change procedure for reasons such as the following:

1. Punishment by itself does not necessarily produce desirable behavior. Punishing a child for impolite behavior does not guarantee that he will then show polite behavior, as the desired behavior may not even be in his repertoire.

2. The punishment may condition in fear, anxiety, or other perhaps undesired emotions. A worker may develop a dislike for his job and show little commitment to his work because his supervisor keeps criticizing his mistakes.

3. The punished person may develop escape or avoidance behaviors. The author had a case of a boy with a school phobia so severe that the boy would no longer even enter the school building. The primary factor that led to this phobia was that the school emphasized corporal punishment which caused the boy to learn an avoidance response to school.

4. Attempted punishment of an escape or avoidance response in some situations increases the strength of the avoidance. The author watched a father at the beach trying to overcome his son's fear of the water. The father would take his son to the edge of the water and then retreat a short distance. As soon as a medium sized wave came in, the child became afraid and ran away from the water. The father punished the child's running away, verbally or physically, which only made the boy more anxious, and made him run from the water faster and sooner.

5. Punishment may result in masochism. If the only time that a child

really gets much attention from his parents is when they punish him, he may be willing to receive the punishment in order to receive the attention. In such cases the assumed punishment may become a conditioned reinforcement as the result of its pairing with the reinforcement of attention (see Chapter 7).

6. The punishing agent may provide a model for aggressive behavior. Children often model or imitate their parents. If they see their parents handle conflict situations by being aggressive, they too will learn to be aggressive.

7. The punished person often becomes less flexible or adaptable in his behaviors. On the wards of many mental hospitals there is much that the patient can do and be punished for, but little that he is rewarded for. In such situations the patient's best "strategy" is to do as little as possible.

Because of such possible effects of punishment as these, it is usually better to try to reinforce and shape in the desired behaviors, rather than punish the undesired behaviors. This, of course, is not always practical, as sometimes the behavior is so detrimental (e.g., the child who keeps running into the street or the autistic child who claws up his face) that it is necessary to use punishment to suppress the undesired behavior long enough to build in desired behavior. Also, a number of cases have been reported in which punishment was a useful change procedure (Baer, 1971).

If punishment does have many bad effects and is not one of the most effective change procedures, why is it so prevalent in our society? There are, of course, a myriad of reasons, such as moral and legal philosophies (e.g., "an eye for an eye") and the fact that the punishing agent often uses punishment to release his own anger or uncertainty about how to handle a situation. But a major variable is delay of reinforcement. The immediate effects of punishment are reinforcing to the punisher, the punished behavior is quickly suppressed, and the punisher releases some of his emotions. It is in the more long range effects that the disadvantages of punishment usually arise, but because behavior is so easily controlled by the short delay effects, people are reinforced to use punishment.

The United States generally puts more emphasis on punishment than on rehabilitation. This is particularly evident in the prison systems, but can be seen at all levels of society. In behavior change situations people tend to think in terms of punishing or stopping undesired behavior, rather than building in desired behavior. The teacher asks "How can I stop the children from running in the halls?" rather than "How can I get the children to walk in the halls?" The manager asks "How can I stop my workers from taking extra time during lunch?" rather than "How can I get the workers to take only one hour for lunch?" Although these differences may sound semantical, they generally lead to significantly different approaches to behavior change. A point that Skinner (see Skinner, 1971) continually makes is the importance to our society of switching from punishment to reinforcement. For, Skinner argues, reinforcement procedures are generally more effective than punishment procedures in changing behavior and maintaining desirable behaviors. Also, behavior control by pleasant consequences seems preferable to control by aversive consequences.

The second type of punishment is *negative punishment,* a contingent event whose decrease results in a decrease in the probability of the response it is contingent on. A mental patient may decrease his delusional talk if every time he talks this way the social worker walks away from him for five minutes. Significantly less research has been done on negative punishment than positive punishment (see Coughlin, 1972). Since negative punishment essentially consists of withdrawing a positive reinforcement, there are many possible explanations for the resulting effects. To a certain extent negative punishment is an operant extinction procedure since behaviors can now occur and not be reinforced, because the reinforcement is withdrawn. The act of removing the source of positive reinforcement may also function as a positive punishment.

A common form of negative punishment in schools is a *time-out procedure.* Here the student to be punished is sent to a room or section of a room in which he just sits for a short time. If the regular classroom is a source of reinforcement for the student, then the time-out procedure will be negative punishment. In an ideal classroom operating on reinforcement principles, time-out may be the most reasonable form of punishment.

EXAMPLES OF OPERANT CONDITIONING

Operant conditioning has been applied in an amazingly large number of different situations. Here we will mention only a few examples.

Verhave (1967) trained pigeons to inspect pills for a drug company. The pigeon would sit in a cage with two rounded discs before it; one was a translucent window, the other opaque. A conveyor belt moved pill capsules by the translucent window. If the pill was acceptable the pigeon pecked the opaque disc; if defective, it pecked the translucent disc. Within a week of training the pigeons were working at 99 per cent accuracy. The pigeons were rewarded with food for making the right discriminations.

During the second World War, Skinner (1960) trained pigeons to fly missiles. The pigeons worked as a homing device in an air-to-ground missile called the Pelican. In the training the pigeons' behavior was reinforced for pecking the appropriate keys controlling the direction of the missile toward the chosen target. Although Skinner's project worked quite well, it was not well received by the appropriate government officials, who caused the project to be terminated.

Pryor (1969) has shown how to operantly condition "creativity" in porpoises. Her method was to reward the porpoise only for behaviors that had not been rewarded before. Thus, after running through its usual repertoire of behaviors, it had to generate entirely new or creative behaviors. Many of these new behaviors (aerial flips, gliding with tail out of water) had never been observed in a porpoise by the staff at the Sea Life Park.

Skinner (MacCorquodale, 1969; Skinner, 1957) has suggested an analysis of speech as essentially a form of verbal behavior whose acquisition and maintenance is due to operant conditioning. For example, a small child's behavior might be reinforced by fondling for making the operant response "da-da" to the discriminative stimulus of the father (S^D = father; an S^Δ = milkman). It is also easy to imagine how the parents gradually shaped the response "da-da" by reinforcing approximations to this response. Parents' "ability" to hear "words" in the seemingly random sounds of their child often facilitates verbal shaping. The person gradually acquires a very complex set of verbal behaviors which have been learned because of how useful they are in maximizing reinforcements in the social environments. Critics of Skinner (e.g., Chomsky, 1959) argue that Skinner's analysis cannot account for all the complexities of language learning and speech. Perhaps there are other variables, such as a predisposition to acquiring certain grammatical styles, that have to be added. But this is a question that does not yet seem to have been adequately resolved, although some critics believe that it has.

An operant analysis of speech suggests the possibility that thoughts may, totally or to some degree, be considered covert internalized verbal behaviors that are under the control of operant variables. This has led to a procedure called *coverant control* in which thoughts are manipulated by operant conditioning (Homme, 1965; Mahoney, 1970). For example, the author had a case of a college student who in certain social situations kept having thoughts about his social inadequacies. The student was convinced that his thoughts were irrational and not well founded, but they kept occurring and bothering him. Through coverant control it was possible to operantly condition other thoughts to occur in place of the undesired thoughts, and in two weeks the problem was gone. This was accomplished by the student's writing the desired thoughts on small cards, which he then inserted in his cigarette pack. When in the social situation that elicited the undesired responses, he would occasionally read to himself one of the desired responses and reinforce himself, as with a cigarette or by thinking about something particularly pleasant. This was continued until the desired thoughts replaced the undesired thoughts.

Much of children's behavior can be thought of as operant behavior maintained by the reinforcement of attention, as in the following examples. When put to bed little Jeffrey will cry and refuse to sleep until his parents return to his room and read him a story. Although capable of working by himself, Stevie keeps coming up to the teacher's desk for help. When Susie's parents are engrossed in adult conversation with some visitors, Susie may do something "cute" to bring the group attention to her. Ideally parents and teachers should use their attention to reinforce desirable behaviors and not to reinforce undesirable ones. There is a natural tendency, however, to do just the opposite. That is, when the child is doing all right (emitting desirable behavior), the parent or teacher relaxes and probably leaves the child alone, whereas when the behavior becomes somewhat troublesome (child emitting undesirable behaviors), the parent or teacher decides that it is now time to attend to what the child is doing.

A good operant conditioner learns to ask the question "What is the function of this behavior?" That is, what are the operant contingencies maintaining this behavior? Rather than explaining problem behavior in terms of intra-psychic disturbances or in terms of the historical development of the problem, the operant conditioner looks for the contingencies currently maintaining the problem behaviors and how these contingencies or alternative behaviors might be manipulated. (This is not to suggest, however, that all behavior can be reduced to the operant paradigm.) Manipulation of operant contingencies, particularly with humans, necessarily raises ethical issues about what constitutes "desirable" behaviors and who has the right to alter another person's behavior, either intentionally or not.

Madsen and associates (1968) investigated the effects of rules, ignoring inappropriate behavior, and showing approval for appropriate behavior exhibited by students in an elementary classroom. They concluded that (a) rules alone had little effect on classroom behavior, (b) the combination of ignoring inappropriate behavior and showing approval for appropriate behavior was very effective in achieving better classroom behavior, and (c) approval for desirable behavior is "probably the key to effective classroom management."

Emery Air Freight Corporation had a goal for their customer service department of responding to customer queries within 90 minutes. The employees felt they met this goal about nine times out of ten, but in fact it was only three times out of ten. An operant feedback system was established in which the employees marked off on their sheets whether each call was answered within 90 minutes. The supervisor then gave praise and recognition for improvement in performance. Within one day performance went from the 30 per cent to 90 per cent and stayed between 90 and 95 per cent for at least three years (Business Week, Dec. 18, 1971).

Sabatasso and Jacobson (1970) worked with a 58 year old man who had spent five years in a ward for chronic schizophrenics. His diagnosis was "chronic brain syndrome, resulting from brain trauma, with psychotic reaction." The head injury resulted from being hit over the head with a board during a fight. The subject was considered a mute psychotic as he had only said one word, "yes," during his five years in the hospital. Through modeling and reinforcement with praise and candy the subject was gradually shaped to speak. Within ten hours of therapy the subject verbalized 307 words, 56 different words, and several simple sentences. At one point the subject shouted excitedly, "I'm talkin' to you."

A popular behavior modification procedure in applied operant situations is *contingency contracting*, a formal agreement about reinforcement contingencies and required behaviors. A parent specifies exactly what behaviors he expects from his children (e.g., being home for dinner by 5:30, maintaining a C average in school) and what reinforcements (e.g., allowance, being permitted to go to a movie) the child will receive contingent on these behaviors. A teacher posts the rules for the classroom (e.g., having specified supplies each day, staying in seat during self-work time) and each student who fulfills this contract may choose one reinforcement from a list (e.g., 10 minutes at the end of the class period to read whatever he wants, permission to leave class 2 minutes early). A person who wants to lose weight gives his favorite records to a friend and then must earn the records back by specified weight loss. A husband and wife undergoing marriage counseling learn to do contingency contracting with each other as a first step toward building give-and-take into their marriage (e.g., the husband agrees to be home by 2 A. M. on his poker night if the wife fixes one of a number of specified dinners at least twice a week.)

Various forms of contingency contracting have been applied to many different types of behaviors in a wide range of situations. Contingency contracting has many positive points:

1. It guarantees the systematic use of operant conditioning.

2. All required behaviors should be well specified so that there is no question about actually what is expected or arguments about whether the behavior occurred or not. Many arguments between parents and their children center on whether or not the child did what he was supposed to do.

3. It forces all participants to be consistent. The student in the classroom or the child at home enjoys contingency contracting since he knows that he will receive a specified reward for a specified behavior and that this is independent of the parent's or teacher's current mood or whether or not the teacher likes him.

4. It provides an easy way to guarantee reinforcement for behaviors that ordinarily are not reinforced or which are reinforced but with too long a delay of reinforcement. One of the author's graduate students who had trouble motivating himself to work on his thesis (too long a

delay of reinforcement for thesis completion) gave the author a number of things that were highly reinforcing to the student (e.g., guitar, records, books, clothes, and things to consume). The student gradually earned these back by completing portions of his thesis within specified time limits.

5. Contracts can be individualized to deal with the needs of each person. Classes can be set up for truly individualized instruction. A program in a mental hospital can take into account each patient's particular needs and problems.

A variation of contingency contracting is a *token economy,* in which the immediate reinforcement is tokens which can later be exchanged for other reinforcements. The tokens, such as poker chips or marks on a chart, are just the medium for exchange. A token system in a mental hospital might involve the patient's earning tokens for behaviors such as dressing himself, acting in specified ways, and attending vocational rehabilitation programs. These tokens can later be exchanged for rewards such as magazines, an opportunity to see a movie, or a trip to town, with the number of required tokens varying from item to item. The main advantage of tokens is that they can be administered almost anywhere with little delay of reinforcement. If there is a big enough selection of things to buy with the tokens, the tokens should always be reinforcing.

Token economies have revolutionized mental hospitals (Ayllon & Azrin, 1968), establishing programs that help large numbers of patients without necessarily increasing the staff. Token economies in classrooms (O'Leary & Drabman, 1971) provide settings in which both students and teachers work more effectively and with more enjoyment. Token systems have also been successfully used in homes, prisons, and half-way houses (see Kazdin & Bootzin, 1972).

CONDITIONING VISCERAL RESPONSES

The *somatic nervous system* is that set of nerves which controls "voluntary" actions of the skeletal-muscular system, such as moving an arm. The responses of this system are usually conditioned operantly, but many can also be conditioned respondently (e.g., human eyelid response or the pattellar reflex). The *autonomic nervous system* is that set of nerves that controls visceral responses, including circulation, digestion, and activity of glands. Historically this nervous system was considered inferior or more primitive than the somatic nervous system. It appeared to function fairly autonomously, outside of "voluntary" control. Until fairly recently it was almost universally held by learning theorists that the visceral responses of the autonomic nervous system could be conditioned respondently, but not operantly. This suggested that there are at least two different types of learning: operant conditioning affecting the somatic nervous system but not the autonomic nervous system, and respondent conditioning affecting the autonomic nervous system and *some* of the somatic nervous system. Today there is impressive data that visceral responses can be operantly conditioned (DiCara, 1970; Katkin, 1971; Miller, 1969) as well as brought under voluntary control (see next section on Biofeedback). On the basis of these experiments Miller (1969) has argued that there may be just one type of learning, based on reinforcement.

A problem in demonstrating operant conditioning of visceral responses is that any apparent effects may be an artifact of the conditioning of a skeletal response. That is, in trying to operantly condition the visceral response, the experimenter may actually be operantly conditioning a skeletal response which in turn produces changes in the visceral response. To avoid this problem, Miller and his associates (Miller, 1969) gave their rats the drug curare, which produces paralysis of the skeletal muscles. This drug also facilitated the conditioning of the visceral responses, perhaps because it removed some of the variability and distraction from the somatic nervous system.

Miller used reinforcing brain stimulation as a reinforcement for conditioning his curarized rats. Miller showed that he could shape the rats' heart rate either up or down by reinforcing changes in the desired direction. For example, if he wanted heart rate to go up he would wait until the natural fluctuations of the heart rate increased and then reinforce this increase with the reinforcing brain stimulation. Through shaping, larger and larger changes were required and generated. Miller also showed that these heart rate changes could be brought under discriminative control. For example, a rat could be conditioned so that his heart rate would go down when a light and tone came on. Miller and his associates then demonstrated the operant conditioning of a variety of other visceral responses, including intestinal contractions, urine formation by the kidney, and amount of blood flow in the tail. In one experiment they were even able to condition the rat so that more blood would flow into one ear than another. To show that such conditioning effects · are not specific to the use of reinforcing brain stimulation, Miller also conditioned heart rate changes, intestinal contractions, and changes in blood pressure where the reward was that the rat avoided shock to his tail.

However, visceral responses do seem resistant to relatively simple operant conditioning procedures. It may be that it would be evolutionarily disadvantageous if visceral responses were readily manipulated by operant contingencies. For health and survival, an animal's visceral responses must stay relatively stable despite drastic changes in environmental contingencies. Otherwise chance reinforcements might produce an animal with high blood pressure and inadequate responses by the kidney. On the other hand, it might also be evolutionarily undesirable if the visceral responses did not respond at all to operant variables. For in extreme situations such as malfunction, disease, or extreme constant environmental changes it may be desirable to have visceral learning.

These animal experiments suggest that many human psychosomatic illnesses might be due to operant conditioning of visceral responses. For example, blood flow to specific body organs has been shown to be conditioned operantly, so this could result in specific psychosomatic symptoms related to that organ. Perhaps reinforcers such as a mother's attention or avoidance of unpleasant situations might be sufficient to shape in psychosomatic illnesses. This is an open area of research.

BIOFEEDBACK

Feedback has been shown to be a powerful determinant of behavior. However, many response systems, such as visceral responses, provide little or no feedback regarding their functioning. For example, the reader might try to tune in to the activity of his liver or try to feel slight changes in blood pressure. Extreme activity of such systems may be perceived, particularly as they affect other parts of the body, but the normal fluctuations of activity in these systems are usually imperceptible owing to inadequate feedback. This is probably just as well, for if early man had feedback and control of visceral responses, he probably would have messed himself up more than helped himself.

Earlier we saw how visceral responses could be manipulated by operant conditioning, a form of feedback. This suggests that if people were provided feedback from systems that they don't usually receive feedback from, such as those controlling blood pressure, they might be able to learn to control these systems. This leads to the investigations with *biofeedback*, utilizing mechanical devices that provide knowledge of the activity of a body function for which the person usually has inadequate feedback (see Lang, 1970; Shapiro & Schwartz, 1972).

Say, for example, that we wished to teach a person how to lower his blood pressure. We could hook him up to a mechanical device that would measure blood pressure and turn on a green light when the blood pressure went below a specified level. At first this level might not be very low, but it could be gradually lowered, as in shaping. After the subject is hooked up to such a device, he is given the simple instruction to try to get the green light to come on. (He might also be given other instructions, such as how to relax, but this is not necessary.) Although he may not know how he is doing it, after a short time the subject can get the green light to come on "at will." With a little more training and shaping the subject is soon able to significantly lower his blood pressure when he wishes. Shapiro and his colleagues (1969) have shown how subjects can learn control of blood pressure through such biofeedback procedures. Schwartz (1972) demonstrated biofeedback control of heart rate and blood pressure. In fact, Schwartz's subjects could control heart rate and blood pressure independently, raising one and simultaneously lowering the other.

Because of the apparent absence of internal feedback, subjects learning to control response systems such as those involved with blood pressure often have no subjective feeling about what they are doing when they change these responses. They just "know" how to do it, but they don't feel any different. Some subjects develop superstitious behaviors, such as learning to tense or relax some muscle that is irrelevant to the effect. It remains to be seen whether some subjects will actually learn to respond to very subtle feedback cues that are actually correlated with the response system to be changed.

The potential implications of such studies are enormous. Researchers are currently investigating whether people with high blood pressure can learn to keep their blood pressure down by voluntary control. One wonders how many autonomic responses people can learn to control. Will people in the near future be able to learn control of their bodies so that a person might be able to voluntarily quiet an upset stomach or relax by lowering his heart rate? Will a person with a defective gland learn voluntary control over this gland? Will many medical problems fall under the domain of the biofeedback trainer? Under what circumstances is such control over autonomic responses undesirable or dangerous?

There are also a host of practical problems. For example, in the animal studies on operant conditioning of visceral responses, Miller found that the animals were much easier to condition while on the drug curare. Miller suggested that this might be because without curare the skeletal responses and autonomic responses elicited by these skeletal responses may interfere with the autonomic responses that the experimenter wishes to condition. This raises the question of how effective biofeedback training of autonomic responses in humans can be without control such as that produced by curare. Another practical problem is how long a person can maintain autonomic control after he is no longer hooked up to a biofeedback device. We know that control lasts for a little while, but we don't know exactly how long. Perhaps the subject would need occasional booster training sessions with a biofeedback device in a clinic or with a small unit at home.

Currently there is ongoing research on the role of biofeedback procedures in the treatment of headaches. One group (Budzynski et al., 1970) is reporting success in treating tension headaches by giving the subjects biofeedback about the muscle tension in his head and neck. Learning to relax these muscles through feedback reduces the headaches. Another group (Sargent et al., 1972) has been investigating migraine headaches by combining biofeedback techniques with autogenic training. (Autogenic training is a program to learn simultaneous regulation of mental and somatic functions. Control of somatic responses is accomplished by concentrating on specific phrases such as "My feet feel heavy and relaxed.") The biofeedback training consists of training the subject to voluntarily increase the blood flow into his hands and thus also increase hand temperature. This training seems to be an effective way of dealing with migraine headaches by decreasing the relative blood flow to the head, although the exact reasons why it works are not clear at the time of this writing.

The area of biofeedback training which has attracted the most publicity has been control of specific brain waves. Electrodes on the human skull record a variety of brain waves of different frequencies (EEG). Different ranges of the frequencies have been assigned different names: delta waves are in the range of 0 to 4 cycles per second; theta designates 4 to 8; alpha, 8 to 13; and beta, more than 13. Although the brain generally emits a complex combination of different waves, the waves are often predominantly of one type which correlates with various aspects of behavior. For example, delta waves are primarily seen during sleep, whereas beta waves are seen when the person is awake and looking at things or actively thinking something through.

Biofeedback devices can let the subject know when his brain waves are primarily within a certain range. One device might be a tone which sounds in proportion to the amount of alpha waves the subject is generating. Through such devices a person can learn to produce specific types of brain waves. The practical applications of such brain wave control have not been adequately researched yet, but the following are some possibilities: People who have trouble relaxing might learn to generate alpha waves as part of a procedure for calming down. Insomniacs might be partially helped by learning to produce delta waves. Epileptics might be able to control their seizures to some degree by generating specific brain patterns. Chapter 8 contains a discussion of some research that is trying to increase creativity with procedures that include learning to generate theta waves. Parapsychologists speculate that it may be possible to train a person to get his mind in that specific state which lends itself best for receiving extrasensory perception.

The most popular wave in such experimentation has been the alpha wave—the type of wave a person would probably be generating if he sat back in a chair with his eyes closed, relaxed, and tried not to think about anything specific. This is the wave that people often generate while in meditation. Many machines (most being of inadequate quality) are being sold to people to learn how to generate alpha waves. Societies and occult groups have formed around the idea of alpha wave conditioning. Varied and often preposterous claims are being made for alpha wave conditioning; for example, that it is a short cut to deep meditation states, and that it can produce various forms of extrasensory perception, faster learning, better memory, and better physical and mental health. It is possible that alpha wave conditioning may facilitate a variety of phenomena and may even be a necessary condition for some phenomena, but it is probably not a sufficient condition for most of the phenomena attributed to it. For example, it seems improbable that alpha wave conditioning can produce the "deeper" stages of meditation that come with considerable practice in controlling concentration and training the mind. Lynch and Paskewitz (1971) have suggested that much of "alpha wave conditioning" may not be the actual conditioning of brain waves so much as learning to ignore stimuli and to stop responses which block alpha waves.

KNOWLEDGE OF RESULTS

A common form of feedback, particularly useful in education, is *knowledge of results,* feedback about whether the person's response was correct or not (see Annett, 1969). Knowledge of results (KR) may or may not also contain information about what the correct response is.

The effects of KR on behavior have been explained in terms of simple reinforcement: On those trials in which a person was right, he is reinforced by finding out he was right; on those trials in which he was wrong, the wrong response is partially extinguished, or punished, or both. If this explanation is correct, then from our information about delay of reinforcement we would expect the KR to be most effective when given immediately after the behavior. However, this does not seem to be true, particularly when KR includes information about the correct response.

For example, Sassenrath and Yonge (1969) gave college students multiple-choice tests on material they had learned. One group received KR immediately after the test, while another group received KR 24 hours after the test. There was no difference between the groups on a retention test right after the feedback, but on a retention test 5 days later there was a small but significant difference favoring the delayed KR group. Sturges (1972) found a similar superiority for a 24-hour delay KR group, and presented evidence that the difference between the groups was due to factors operating at and/or following the feedback, rather than factors operating during the delay interval. Sturges suggests that with delayed feedback the subjects respond differently to the same feedback. For example, with immediate KR the subjects may be concerned only with that part of the KR which tells them whether or not they were right, whereas with delayed KR the subject reads through more of the KR information and hence learns more.

An important, yet unanswered, question for education is: What is the optimal amount of time to delay the KR? The answer probably depends on a number of variables, such as type of subjects used, the nature of the material to be learned, and the nature of the KR. In one study,

More (1969) investigated the effects of four different delays of KR (knowledge of how subjects did on a retention test plus what the correct responses to each item were) on the learning of eighth-grade students. In terms of later retention he found that KR was more effective when given either 2.5 hours or one day after the first retention test than if given immediately after or four days after the first test.

KR may also have a motivational effect, as when the subject decides to work harder. If a student finds out that his performance on the first exam earned him a C, he may decide to study harder for the second exam. After having all her house plants die, a woman may decide to water the next plants more than once a month. After reviewing the studies done on motivational KR, Locke and associates (1968) concluded that the main effect was on the goals that the subject set for himself. They concluded that motivational KR is most effective when specific goals are set and when the goals set are difficult ones.

One powerful application of KR is in the area of *programmed instruction,* a technology originally investigated by S. L. Pressey in the 1920's, but which got its main push from Skinner and his colleagues (Holland, 1960; Skinner, 1958). In programmed instruction, the material to be learned (the program) is presented to the student in a series of logical units (frames). The student is required to make a response to each frame, after which he is immediately told the correct answer. By this procedure the student is gradually shaped to the desired terminal behavior. The mechanical device which presents the program is called a *teaching machine*

In programmed instruction, a student is given a small amount of material to learn and then is asked a question on the material. The student might be asked to respond in one of a number of different ways, such as writing his answer or pushing a button to indicate his choice of answers from a number of alternatives. After he has answered, the student is told the correct response (KR). The student then moves to the next frame. If his answer was wrong, he might be diverted to some other part of the program to review the material he missed.

Many theorists interpret the effects of KR in programmed instruction as being reinforcement. However, we have already seen that this is an oversimplification of the effects of KR, for the KR also provides for additional learning and motivational changes.

Programmed instruction has a number of desirable characteristics:

1. Because he is required to answer questions, the student is more active in his learning than he is in other learning situations, such as listening to a teacher.

2. The student receives continual and immediate feedback as he progresses. This procedure catches errors early, before the student can go too far in the wrong direction. Also, to the extent that KR is reinforcing, it provides a short delay of reinforcement.

3. The student must usually learn some material before being permitted to continue. This is often critical to later learning that presupposes some previous knowledge.

4. The student can work at his own pace. This allows for individual differences in learning rate and style and lends itself nicely to individualized instruction.

5. The programmer receives feedback about how the student is doing on various parts of the program, and can thus adjust and improve the program accordingly.

On the negative side, for some people, such as many college students, the format of existing programmed instruction is too constricting for the type of freewheeling, conceptual, integrative learning they prefer and learn best with. Also, it seems that some types of skills, such as problem solving, are better learned by other teaching procedures. But these criticisms may be applicable only to the types of programs that currently exist, rather than to the logic of programmed instruction itself.

There are basically two types of programs: linear and branching. In a *linear program* all students progress through the same sequence of frames. In a *branching program* students are routed through different sequences of frames depending on how well they do at specific points in the program. Thus if a student misses a question, he may be routed through a number of different frames that cover the same material in a slightly different way, while students who didn't miss the question continue on to new material. Or, based on an assessment question, one student may be permitted to skip over a number of frames that cover material that he already knows.

Programmed instruction can be made even more flexible by the use of computers (Atkinson, 1968). This *computer-assisted instruction* (CAI) can handle very complex branching programs, almost instantly presenting to the student the next frame he needs based on his performance on the last frame. The computer can also record useful data pertaining to each student, such as areas of particular difficulty that a teacher might wish to attend to. The computer can keep data about the effectiveness of the program, such as which frames the students are making more mistakes on. In CAI the computer can do a host of other things as well, such as presenting visual displays on a screen, turning on slides and movies, and presenting audio messages through headphones to the student.

Throughout this chapter we have discussed a wide range of effects that feedback can have. Feedback may produce one or more of the following effects:

1. The feedback can be a reinforcement or a punishment.

2. The feedback can produce changes in motivation, such as changes in the goals a person sets for himself.

3. Feedback may provide informative cues that guide learning and performance, such as discriminative cues.

4. Feedback may provide a new learning experience or a rehearsal of previous learning.

SUMMARY

Feedback is the input to an organism resulting from a response of the organism. It includes both the sensory input from the muscles involved in making the response and information about how the environment was changed as a result of the response. Basic behaviors, such as walking and simple muscular control, require proprioception — feedback from the muscles. Normal speech depends on auditory feedback — the person's hearing his own voice — plus feedback from speech structures, including the tongue. Visual feedback is involved in tasks such as driving, writing, and drawing. T-groups involve social feedback in which the participants provide information about the way they perceive and feel about each other.

S-R theorists often describe feedback as a source of stimuli to which new responses can be conditioned. An example of this is *chaining*, a sequence of responses in which each response provides part of the stimulus cues (feedback) for following responses. Chaining is the process by which a rat learns a complex sequence of behaviors and a person learns a poem by rote. For many S-S theorists feedback provides information about which behavior is appropriate. TOTE units are an example of this approach. According to the ideo-motor theory, responses are chosen on the basis of their anticipated feedback. Overall feedback may be a reinforcement or a punishment; it may produce changes in motivation, provide discriminative cues, or provide a new learning experience or rehearsal of previous learning.

Operant conditioning is the study of the effects of events that are contiguous on responses. Perceiving these events, then, is feedback about the effects of the behavior. If the contiguous event makes it more probable that the response will occur again in a similar situation, the event is called a *reinforcement*. If the event makes the response less probable, the event is a *punishment*. Terminating the relationship between the contiguous event and the behavior results in *extinction*. There are many ways to originally get a response to occur for operant conditioning, three of the more popular ways being *shaping*, *modeling*, and *fading*.

For optimal learning, the *delay of reinforcement* — the time between the behavior and the reinforcement — should generally be as short as possible. *Continuous reinforcement* means that every correct response is reinforced, whereas with *intermittent reinforcement* only some of the responses are reinforced. Generally original learning is faster under continuous reinforcement than under intermittent, and extinction takes longer with intermittent reinforcement.

There is no consensus on exactly how reinforcement functions. For example, does reinforcement affect learning or only performance? *Drive reduction theories* of reinforcement suggest that animals learn those responses which reduce drives, such as a hunger drive. *Drive induction theories* stress that animals learn those responses which arouse motivation. The *Premack theory* is based on the idea that high probability responses can reinforce low probability responses. On the physiological level it has been shown that electrical stimulation of certain brain areas in man and other animals produces reinforcement. These reinforcement areas are often brain areas related to biological needs such as hunger and to species-typical behaviors. Some theorists thus argue that these are the same brain areas that underlie the effects of more conventional forms of reinforcement, such as food and water. However, other theorists have suggested a number of differences between reinforcing brain stimulation and the effects of the other types of reinforcement. These differences may exist because the reinforcing brain stimulation activates both a reward system and a motivation system, or because it results in internal stimuli having more control over the response than would be the case with the conventional reinforcements.

Punishment, by definition, reduces the probability of the response that precedes it. In addition, the punishing event elicits many responses, including emotional responses, which may become conditioned to the situation in which the punishment occurred. The offset of the punishment may function as a reinforcement for behaviors such as escape behaviors. Because of effects such as these, most forms of punishment are usually not the most desirable way to change human behavior.

Behavior modification often involves the reinforcement of desired behaviors and the extinction and/or punishment of undesired behaviors. One example of this approach is *contingency contracting,* in which there is a formal agreement among people about the reinforcement contingencies and the required behaviors. Contingency contracting provides for the systematic application of operant conditioning, builds more consistency into people's behavior, may cut down on the delay of reinforcement, and provides a structure for individualizing behavior modification programs. A *token economy* is a form of contingency contracting in which the person is rewarded with tokens that can later be exchanged for various reinforcements.

Recent research has shown that it is possible to condition animals to alter visceral responses such as heart rate, intestinal contractions, urine formation by the kidney, and blood flow to specific body areas. This suggests that the answers to the genesis and treatment of many psychosomatic illnesses may lie within operant conditioning. Related to this research is the work with biofeedback in which, via mechanical devices, humans are given feedback about the activity of body systems which usually provide little or no feedback. Through *biofeedback* procedures, people may learn voluntary control over heart rate, blood pressure, specific brain waves, and headaches.

A common form of feedback, one which is particularly important in education, is *knowledge of results (KR):* feedback about whether a person's response was correct or not. One important question is what the optimal delay of knowledge of results is. For example, for optimal long term learning, how long after a test should a student be given feedback about his performance on the test? *Programmed instruction* involves giving the student immediate knowledge of results as he actively works his way through a structured program designed to systematically shape his learning behavior.

SUGGESTED READINGS

Annett, J. *Feedback and Human Behavior.* Baltimore: Penguin, 1969.

Barber, T. X., DiCara, L. V., Kamiya, J., Miller, N. E., Shapiro, D., & Stoyva, J. (eds.) *Biofeedback and Self-Control, 1970.* Chicago: Aldine Atherton, 1971.

Honig, W. K. (ed.) *Operant Behavior: Areas of Research and Application.* New York: Appleton-Century-Crofts, 1966.

McGinnies, E., & Ferster, C. B. (eds.) *The Reinforcement of Social Behavior.* Boston: Houghton-Mifflin, 1971.

Reynolds, G. S. *A Primer of Operant Conditioning.* Glenview, Ill.: Scott, Foresman, 1968.

Skinner, B. F. *Science and Human Behavior.* Toronto: Macmillan, 1953.

Skinner, B. F. *Walden Two.* Toronto: Macmillan, 1948.

Tapp, J. T. (ed.) *Reinforcement and Behavior.* New York: Academic Press, 1969.

Whaley, D. L., & Malott, R. W. *Elementary Principles of Behavior.* New York: Appleton-Century-Crofts, 1971.

Williams, J. L. *Operant Learning: Procedures for Changing Behavior.* Belmont, Calif.: Wadsworth, 1973.

personality

The word "personality" comes from the Latin word *persona* meaning the mask worn by an actor in a drama to indicate his character. It is probably useful to consider a person's personality as the totality of the ways in which he behaves in various situations. Historically psychology has primarily conceptualized personality in terms of specific theories such as those of Freud, Jung, Adler, Rank, and Horney. Many of the constructs of the different theories are now part of common language (e.g., "anal character," "extrovert," "birth trauma"). Such theories have been useful for suggesting ideas to be experimentally tested and developed. They have also been useful in conceptualizing possible relationships between different behaviors. However, there are many problems with these classical theories.

The main problem is that most of the constructs of the different theories cannot be tested and measured independently. A person's behavior might easily be explained in terms of the interactions between different constructs of a specific theory, but such *post hoc* explanations have limited value if we cannot get at the individual constructs. For example, Freud's classic theory, including his constructs of ego, id, and superego, can explain almost any behavior *after* it happens. But how do we get an independent measure of the nature and functions of the id? The Freudian analyst might try to do this by techniques such as dream interpretation or word association. However, such procedures are confounded with other dynamic personality variables, do not meet the type of scientific rigor necessary to give them widespread usefulness, and are generally more a matter of artistic interpretation than logical measurement. It is sometimes argued that the human personality cannot be broken down into constituent parts, but must always be viewed as a whole. The experimental psychologist, however, generally assumes that it *can* be broken down. This in no way devalues the beauty of man or the complexity and richness of his experiences.

If we could measure and test the various constructs and assumptions of the different personality theories, we could begin a much needed evaluation and synthesis of the different ideas. But since many of the constructs are not readily measured and tested, many theories continue on with little change. A disadvantage of any particular theory is that much information may be distorted or lost in an attempt to fit the person into the theory. The classic personality theories are probably most useful in understanding the personality of the person who made up the theory and secondarily the personalities of a few of the people he counseled.

In this chapter we will look at personality from the viewpoint of learning. This approach basically involves two categories of phenomena: (1) those genetic and physiological variables that affect a person's behavior directly and/or that predispose him for certain types of learning, and (2) specific types of behavioral abnormalities that result from certain learning experiences. The vast majority of human behavior is learned by principles such as those discussed in the preceding chapters. Thus the best understanding, and probably also the best approach to change or treatment, of these behaviors is from the viewpoint of learning rather than from a personality theory. But there are individual differences resulting from such factors as genetic and physiological variables that affect what a person learns and how fast he learns it. A personality classification based on such variables would then be very useful in understanding and dealing with behavior. There are also a number of abnormalities, such as experimental neurosis and learned helplessness, whose genesis and treatment are being systematically researched. It may be that in a discussion or description of personality, reference to one of these phenomena would have heuristic and explanatory value.

GENETIC INFLUENCES ON PSYCHOPATHOLOGY

Psychologists tend to perceive behavior more in terms of learning than of instinct, while the opposite is often true of zoologists, particularly ethologists. Thus both groups, with different biases, are concerned with the *nature-nurture* controversy. That is, to what extent is behavior determined by hereditary influences (nature) and to what extent by environmental influences (nurture), such as learning? With simple organisms, where breeding and environment can be well controlled, it is often relatively easy to separate genetic variables from environmental variables.

But as the possibility of such control decreases and as the organism becomes more complex, it is harder to isolate the different variables. Human behavior is a highly complex interaction between nature and nurture in which a person's genetics affect his behavior and physical characteristics, which in turn affect the types of interactions he has with his environment and how other people respond to him, which then affects *his* behavior and aspects of his physical appearance (e.g., clothes style), and so forth. Such complex interactions are difficult to break down into nature and nurture components.

Dobzhansky (1972) has also argued that the fundamental peculiarity of human evolution, as opposed to the evolution of most other species, is that man has been selected for "trainability, educability, and consequent plasticity of behavior." Whereas for most species of animals it is *biologically* adaptive for all members of the species to have certain uniform behaviors under genetic control, man's evolutionary success is his ability to adapt to *cultural* variables. For man, adaptation by cultural changes is more effective than adaptation by genetic changes. But this adaptability in man makes it even harder to identify the role of genetic variables.

Animals such as mice (e.g., Bovet et al., 1969) have been selectively bred for a variety of "behavioral" characteristics. Mice have been bred for different degrees of vigor, aggressiveness, ability to win fights, and performance in mazes, while rats have been bred for different degrees of activity and fearfulness, and for maze performance. In the Tryon strains of rats, those rats that learned mazes well (maze bright) were mated with similarly bright rats, while slow maze learners (maze dull) were mated with similarly dull rats. After seven generations of such selective breeding there was little overlap in maze performance between the maze bright strain and the maze dull strain.

If characteristics such as fearfulness have a genetic component in rats (see Gray, 1971), we might expect something similar in humans, particularly in the case of psychopathy. Unfortunately in the area of mental health the criteria and diagnostic definitions of "illnesses" such as schizophrenia are so poorly defined that it is difficult to distinguish nature from nurture. But, drawing from Rosenthal (1971), we can suggest some possible relationships between genetics and psychopathology in man.

Schizophrenia

Of all the traditional clinical diagnostic categories, "schizophrenia" is one of the broadest and most poorly defined, so that it is very difficult to make any generalizations about people classified as schizophrenic. However, we do know that symptoms of schizophrenia usually include things such as unusual thought processes and associations, inappropriate or deteriorated emotions, ambivalence of feelings, detachment and inadequate adaptation to "reality," and lack of interest or will.

One way of investigating the possible role of genetics in schizophrenia is to study twins. Twins are either *monozygotic* (MZ), which means that they are from a single fertilized ovum (identical twins), or *dizygotic* (DZ), meaning that they come from two different fertilized eggs fraternal twins). If the two twins of each pair are raised in approximately the same way and in the same environment, then a comparison of the incidence of schizophrenia between MZ twins and DZ twins should give us some general idea of the role of genetics in schizophrenia. This is done by looking at the *concordance rate* for the two twins of each pair, i.e., the probability that they both display the same trait, in this case schizophrenia. In summarizing a number of such studies, Rosenthal (1971, p. 74) suggests that the concordance rate for MZ twins is usually 3 to 6 times as high as the rate for DZ twins, which offers "strong but not conclusive evidence of a genetic contribution to schizophrenia." However, the concordance rate for MZ twins is always less than 100 per cent, sometimes much less. Thus nongenetic factors play a large role in determining who develops schizophrenia. Also, it appears that the more severely schizophrenic one twin is, the more probable it is that the other twin will be schizophrenic.

Another way of trying to separate nature and nurture variables in schizophrenia is to compare the incidence of schizophrenia between parents and their children when the children were separated from the parents early in life and raised in other homes. Again, in summarizing such studies, Rosenthal (1971, p. 84) concludes that "the evidence has turned up so consistently and strongly in favor of the genetic hypothesis that this issue must now be considered closed."

An important question is whether the genetic factor actually produces the schizophrenic behavior per se, or if it produces a predisposition to *learn* those behaviors called schizophrenic.

Manic-Depressive Psychosis

When a person has an "attack" of *mania* he feels elated, more energetic and lively, or perhaps irritable and impatient. In more extreme cases he may be incoherent, very irritable, and extremely active. With attacks of *depression* the person is sluggish, has a low energy level, poor appetite, and disturbed sleeping habits; he may also have feelings of worthlessness or of being evil. A person classified as *manic-depressive* drifts from the normal state into the manic or depressive state. Some go primarily into the manic state, some into primarily the depressive state, and some people cycle between the manic and depressive states.

Studies of manic-depressive twins have not generated data as clear as that from studies on schizophrenia, but it appears that the concordance rate for MZ twins is higher than that for DZ twins (Rosenthal, (1971, p. 119).

Overall, Rosenthal (1971, p. 153) concludes that "the genetic studies — with their sundry faults — provide much evidence for the view that schizophrenia and manic-depressive psychosis are valid, distinctive, genetic disorders, and that unless future studies provide evidence to the contrary, it would be foolhardy to dismiss them out of hand."

Criminality

Many characteristics such as physical appearance, I.Q., and psychological abnormalities, which probably have genetic components, often affect a person's interactions in the social environment and thus may help to determine whether he will become a criminal. One major area of investigation has been relating chromosome constitution to aggressiveness and crime. Females generally have two X chromosomes, while males usually have an X and a Y chromosome. However, it is estimated that somewhere between 0.05 and 0.4 per cent of all males have an extra Y chromosome; that is, their chromosome constitution is XYY. There are reports (Hook, 1973; Montagu, 1968) that this extra Y chromosome may make the person more aggressive, and that males may be more aggressive than females because the females have no Y chromosome. There are also reports that there is a higher frequency of XYY males among criminals than in the population at large. However, the absolute numbers being compared are small, and there are some procedural problems with the studies. Montagu points out that XYY males are usually taller, and argues that as children they might learn to be more aggressive because of the manner in which other children respond to their height.

The evidence relating an extra Y chromosome to aggression and crime is suggestive, but still very speculative. In a review of XYY males, Owen (1972) concluded that "no consistent personality or behavioral constellation has been successfully predicted from the XYY complement," while Hook (1973) concludes that "There is a definite association between the XYY genotype and presence in mental-penal settings, but both the nature and extent of this association are yet to be determined." "Mental-penal settings" include hospitals for the criminally insane and security wings in hospitals for the mentally retarded.

Other Psychopathologies

The data on genetic influences on neurosis is sparse and confusing, but "the overall evidence points to the likelihood that heredity plays a role in the development of psychoneurotic symptoms" (Rosenthal, 1971, p. 144). However, the genetic component in neurosis seems small, particularly in comparison to environmental factors.

A person's physiological response to alcohol may have a genetic component. Wolff (1972) has reported ethnic differences in reactivity to alcohol, independent of where the people lived. He found that Japanese, Taiwanese, and Koreans, after drinking amounts of alcohol that have no detectable effect on Caucasoids, showed mild to moderate symptoms of intoxication. Rosenthal (1971, p. 149) has reported studies that suggest that some aspects of drinking behavior may be heritable.

Intelligence

Although not a psychopathology, it seems relevant to mention the intelligence and race issue. Are some races of humans genetically more intelligent than others? The answer is that for many reasons no-one knows. First, it is not clear exactly what intelligence is, nor are we sure of the best ways to measure it. I.Q. tests are not as reliable or valid as desired and have strong cultural biases. Many of the items and terminology on traditional I.Q. tests favor one cultural group over another. A second problem is that defining and identifying members of a "pure" race is often a difficult task. The major problem, however, is that the post-birth experiences of members of different races are so different that it is almost impossible to factor out environmental influences. There is no way that a black and a white in the United States can have the same social learning experiences. Cultural differences, prejudices, different social environments, varying expectancies of success or failure, and different diets are just a few of the many confounding variables. Thus the race and intelligence issue is unresolvable at the present time, and perhaps this is socially and politically desirable (see Bodmer & Cavalli-Sforza, 1970).

PREPAREDNESS OF LEARNING

The behavior of simple organisms is controlled largely by instinct. As organisms become more complex, learning plays a larger and larger role until, in the case of human behavior, learning far surpasses instinct in importance. Yet man is still a biological animal, and the instinctual components of the behavior of the human species must still be accounted for.

Unfortunately in the last few years the pendulum has swung to the side of instincts. Several popular books have tried to account for large parts of human behavior in terms of just a few instincts such as territoriality and bonding. But such oversimplifications are merely crude analogies that have not given appropriate weight to the role of learning. It may be fun to draw parallels between human behavior and the behavior of apes, but one must be careful about pushing this too far.

Seligman (Seligman, 1970; Seligman & Hager, 1972) has pointed out how animals can learn some things more easily than others. For example, Thorndike had no trouble training cats to pull strings to get out of puzzle boxes, but he had considerable trouble trying to train them to scratch or lick themselves to get out of the boxes. Seligman argues that we must consider how evolutionarily prepared the animal is to learn different responses. In the case of Thorndike's cats it would be evolutionarily advantageous for cats to be able to learn to associate manipulating objects with escape. But there seems to be little evolutionary pressure for the cats to quickly associate licking with escape. For how often in the natural world is licking related to escape? Similarly, Chapter 5 discussed how rats can be conditioned to associate gastric upset to taste stimuli more easily than to audio-visual stimuli, while avoidance reactions produced by electric shock were more easily conditioned to audio-visual stimuli than to taste stimuli.

Seligman suggests a *preparedness dimension*, a continuum which specifies for different types of learning the evolutionary constraints on the animal's ability to acquire the particular learning. At one end of the continuum are those behaviors for which the animal is *prepared*. This means that the biology and genetics of the animal facilitate this particular type of learning. At the other end of the continuum are those behaviors for which the animal is *contraprepared*—i.e., the animal's biology and genetics impede the learning. Different types of learning lie at different points on the continuum. Near the middle of the continuum is the neutral point at which the animal is *unprepared*—his natural history has no bearing on the learning. Instinct, according to this formulation, is an extreme form of preparedness. Similarly, rats are prepared to associate taste with illness, but perhaps contraprepared to associate taste with electric shock.

Seligman suggests that prepared associations are relatively inflexible and resistant to extinction, to such a degree that the behavior may acquire some autonomy in itself. Also, the learning does not involve cognitive processes, whereas unprepared associations are more flexible in nature, extinguish more readily, and often are mediated by consciousness, attention, and expectations.

It is not clear exactly what kinds of things humans are prepared to learn, although Seligman suggests that language acquisition might be one example. Seligman (1971) has also argued that man is prepared to learn certain phobias, such as fear of snakes, spiders, or heights. This would explain why such phobias are so common, are acquired so rapidly, are so resistant to extinction, and why they are probably outside conscious control. (The point about conscious control will be elaborated on in the next chapter.)

Gray (1971, p. 15), on the other hand, argues that man has an innate fear of snakes that does not develop until the child is several years old, although Gray allows for a possible learning component. Similarly fear of the dark and of some animals, such as dogs, may have an innate basis, according to Gray.

PHYSIOLOGICAL BASES OF SCHIZOPHRENIA

What is physiologically different about people classified as schizophrenic? Which of these differences might have been a cause or a partial cause of the person becoming schizophrenic? How can you tell whether a variable was really a partial cause or was actually a result of schizophrenia? That is, if there is a brain chemistry difference between schizophrenics and normals, did the difference in brain chemistry produce schizophrenia or did schizophrenia produce the difference in brain chemistry?

Questions such as these have led researchers and theorists in a host of different directions looking for physiological bases of schizophrenia. There has been considerable research into the biochemical differences in the blood and brain of schizophrenics and possible enzyme deficits or abundances that might result in abnormal experiences and behaviors (e.g., Mandell et al., 1972). We will consider here just a sample of the research on the bases of schizophrenia, remembering that "schizophrenia" is a very broad, poorly defined category.

Mednick (1971) studied over 200 Danish children whose mothers were schizophrenic. Of the children in this group who later became schizophrenic it was observed that for 70 per cent of them their mothers had experienced complications during pregnancy or birth (e.g., oxygen deficiency, prolonged labor). Also the galvanic skin response (GSR) of these children did not habituate as fast as that of normals to irritating noise, and they took longer to extinguish a conditioned GSR. This suggested to Mednick that the birth complications damaged the body's ability to regulate stress-response mechanisms (perhaps through damage to the hippocampus); this deficit then may lead to schizophrenia. For example, these children may be more sensitive to threats and stress, and may learn avoidance responses, such as the thinking of bizarre thoughts. However, birth complications did not produce these results in children whose mothers were not schizophrenic, suggesting that the effect requires an interaction between birth complications and a genetic variable related to schizophrenia.

In the previous chapter we discussed the fact that areas of the brain when electrically stimulated produce a reinforcing effect, and that these areas may underlie reinforcement in general. Stein and Wise (1971) have offered a model of schizophrenia that is based on deficiencies in these reward systems. They noted that two primary symptoms of schizophrenia are a deficit in goal-directed thinking and a deficit in the capacity to experience pleasure. They suggest that both of these symptoms could result from impairment of one of the physiological reward systems. Stein and Wise believe that the aberrant metabolite that produces these deficits is 6-hydroxydopamine (6-H). 6-hydroxydopamine injected into rats will decrease the rate of self-stimulation in the relevant brain area (medial forebrain bundle). It may be that chlorpromazine, a drug often used in the treatment of schizophrenia, produces its effects by preventing the reward area from taking in 6-H. Chlorpromazine, then, would not be as useful after the reward area had suffered irreversible damage. Finally, a particularly odorous substance (trans-3-methyl-2-hexenonic acid) often found in the sweat of schizophrenics is a possible biochemical result from 6-H. A question about the Stein and Wise model is how many people classified as schizophrenic would have this particular type of deficit in experiencing pleasure (e.g., Watson, 1972).

Another possibility is that some schizophrenics are in a continuous state of overarousal (Depue & Fowles, 1973; Lang & Buss, 1965). Since performance, and probably also learning, is best at some optimal level of arousal, people who are continually overaroused would be deficient in simply learning to behave in the most productive manner. According to this theory, the effect of drugs such as chlorpromazine is to reduce the arousal level to some optimal point. Too much of the drug, however, would result in passing the optimal point and making the person's arousal level too low.

There is no single physiological explanation for the wide range of behaviors that are called schizophrenic: For any one individual, the explanation of his schizophrenic behavior may be a very complex interaction of many different variables including genetic, current physiological, and social factors. In the next section we will see a couple of the ways in which physiological and psychological variables interact.

PHYSIOLOGICAL-ENVIRONMENTAL INTERACTIONS

When investigating variables that affect behavior it would be nice if we could break them down into two distinct lists: *physiological variables*, related to the physical construction of the organism, and *environmental variables*, related to the experiences of the organism. But, in fact, these two sets of variables continuously interact, producing changes in each other in quite complex ways. Here we will consider a few of these interactions and their effects on personality.

Rosenzweig, Bennett, and Diamond (1972) have investigated the effects of different types of living environments on the brains of rats. They raised rats in three different environments: (a) an impoverished environment of simple cages with one rat per cage, (b) a standard environment of simple cages with about three rats per cage, and (c) an enriched environment with 12 rats per large cage plus playthings in the cage that were changed each day. The rats in the enriched environment showed greater brain changes than rats in the other two groups: after 4 to 10 weeks in the enriched environment they showed greater weight of the cerebral cortex, greater thickness of the cortex, greater total activity of acetylcholinesterase (the enzyme described in Chapter 2 that breaks down the transmitter substance acetylcholine) but less activity per unit of tissue weight, more glial cells, no more nerve cells per unit of tissue but larger nuclei and cell bodies (indicating higher metabolic activity), and increases in the ratio of RNA to DNA. The greatest brain differences were found in the occipital cortex (the visual cortex). The same effects of the enriched environment can be shown with adult rats, but they generally require a longer exposure to the enriched environment to get the maximum effect. Rats kept in an outdoor setting for a month show even greater brain changes than rats from an enriched environment.

How do such brain changes affect later behavior? Rosenzweig and his associates report that the experience in the enriched environment facilitates later learning, but the effects are often short-lived and depend on the measure of learning, the type of task to be learned, and the age at which the enriched experience is provided. The implications for humans are still quite speculative; it would be interesting to investigate questions such as whether musicians, as a group, would show an enhanced development of the auditory cortex.

Malnutrition has been clearly shown to retard mental development in nonhumans. There is also suggestive, although not conclusive, evidence (Warren, 1973) that malnutrition is a contributing factor to mental deficiency in humans, preventing the person from realizing his full genetic potential (see Kaplan, 1972). Malnutrition may produce this effect in two ways. First, malnutrition in childhood, from the prenatal period (via the intrauterine environment) through the first years of life, may impair physiological development and produce mental deficiency. Many of these effects are irreversible, although some may be reversible. The I.Q.'s of mentally retarded children have been raised 10 points by changing what they eat. Low income families are, of course, more affected than others because they often cannot provide adequate nutrition (especially adequate amounts of protein) for their children. The second way in which malnutrition impairs mental development is by indirectly impairing learning. For example, poorly nourished children may miss more days of school because of illness or may be distracted from learning in school as the result of being hungry. The eating habits of parents may thus lead to malnutrition and mental deficiency in their children, affecting a whole range of the children's behaviors, particularly learning potential. Kaplan pointed out that 75 per cent of pre-school children in South America, Asia, and Africa are underweight for their age; in 1968 more than 10 million Americans were affected by hunger and malnutrition.

Holmes and Masuda (1972) report on a series of investigations that relate psychological events to physical illness. Although many illnesses clearly have a physical cause, such as a virus, *when* a person acquires the illness, or perhaps even *whether* he acquires it, may be influenced by psychological variables. Holmes and Masuda suggest that events in life trigger illness because the effort required to cope with these events weakens resistance. For example, they found that colds were triggered by events such as a visit from a mother-in-law, a change in job, or the birth of a child. After the subjects recovered from their colds, simply talking about the particular event often renewed the cold symptoms. They were also able to relate life events to other illnesses, including tuberculosis, heart disease, skin disease, and hernias. The common theme to illness-triggering events is that they are important changes in the life pattern, either positive or negative. For American subjects (there are cultural differences) the top 10 events in terms of triggering illness are as follows, in order of decreasing importance: death of spouse, divorce, marital separation, jail term, death of close family member, personal injury or illness, marriage, being fired, marital reconciliation, and retirement. Thus it appears that coping with life changes reduces a person's resistance to illness, particularly if the person has not learned effective ways of coping with these changes.

INDIVIDUAL DIFFERENCES IN CONDITIONING

Since most behaviors are learned, the ease with which an individual can be conditioned is an important personality characteristic, particularly since it appears that there are individual differences in conditionability (Franks, 1964; Nebylitsyn & Gray, 1972). (Personality theories based on such differences will be discussed later in this section.) Assuming that there *are* individual differences in conditionability, the rate at which an individual is conditioned would be a combination of his conditionability and situational factors. A general issue, as Franks points out, is how useful the concept of a general factor of conditionability *is,* for if the situational factors can account for most of the differences in learning rate, then conditionability may be an insignificant factor. Much research is still required before this issue can be resolved.

In Chapter 3 we discussed how organisms seek out activities that involve a certain amount of complexity. Events that provide such complexity thus function as incentives and reinforcements and underlie a considerable amount of learning. Humans have a need for a certain amount of complexity. We need variation and seek it out through activities such as playing, reading, daydreaming, and the use of drugs. Maddi (1961) suggested that the need for variation is an aspect of personality and that "individuals show reliable differences in the intensity and quality of their variation-seeking." A moderate amount of this need for variety is probably desirable; people without such a need may acquire undesirable characteristics, such as rigid defensiveness. However, Maddi suggests that too much of this need may produce an undesirable degree of behavioral instability. Maddi also points out that there are great differences between individuals in the ways in which their need for variety is expressed. Some individuals seek out variation in a relatively passive manner, such as through reading, whereas others are more active.

From our previous discussion of complexity it is clear that a person's experiences affect the level of complexity that he seeks. Since we know that learning affects the level of variation-seeking in humans, and since we assume that a moderately high level of this need is desirable, it might be useful for parents and teachers to build a moderate level of this need into children. Maddi suggests that this might be accomplished by eliciting and rewarding unusual responses in the child and by introducing the child to a wide range of experiences.

Toward the end of his life Pavlov put considerable thought into how his research on conditioning and the nervous system might extend to personality and psychiatry (see Franks, 1970). The system in which animals respond to environmental stimuli such as sights and sounds and learn associations between these stimuli was called by Pavlov the *first signaling system*. Pavlov assumed that man, but no other animal, has a *second signaling system* in which words stand for the stimuli of the first signaling system. This second signaling system is responsible for language and speech and underlies attributes Pavlov considered uniquely human, such as the human forms of communication.

Pavlov believed that many psychological problems were due to an imbalance between the ideal amounts of excitation and inhibition in the nervous system. Thus treatment might consist of sleep therapy to protect a person from overstimulation or use of stimulant drugs to increase excitation in a chronically tired or apathetic person. Pavlov suggested that excessive or prolonged stimulation of the nervous system would produce *protective inhibition,* a form of inhibition which serves to protect the nervous system from too much strain. People with weak nervous systems—systems particularly sensitive to stimulation—are assumed to generate more protective inhibition than others. Such people with weak nervous systems are considered subject to schizophrenia, which, according to Pavlov, results from excessive protective inhibition in the cerebral cortex. Pavlov suggested that as a result of this protective inhibition, schizophrenics condition slower than normals.

Pavlov's psychological theorizing drew on neurophysiological concepts such as the irradiation of excitatory and inhibitory waves through the cortex. The neurophysiological aspects of the theories have not held up as more has been learned about cortical functioning, but many of Pavlov's observations and suggested relationships have proved valuable and may still generate useful ideas (see Nebylitsyn & Gray, 1972).

Eysenck (see Eysenck, 1967; Eysenck & Beech, 1971) has suggested a personality model with two basic dimensions: *neuroticism* and *introversion-extroversion*. People low on the neuroticism scale are usually calm, not easily aroused, and have fairly stable emotions, whereas people high on this scale are easily aroused, moody, restless, and have labile emotions. According to Eysenck, the neuroticism scale is a measure of an innate reactivity and lability of the autonomic nervous system. People high on the neuroticism scale presumably have a more labile, easily aroused autonomic system that is more susceptible to the conditioning of fear and neurotic disorders. These people react more strongly to emotion-arousing stimuli and experience an aversive reaction to more stimuli than people low on the neuroticism scale.

People on the introvert end of the introversion-extroversion scale are usually quiet, introspective, and reserved; they like a well-ordered life and keep their emotions under close control. People at the extrovert end of the scale are usually sociable, impulsive, and easygoing; they crave excitement and like change. It is assumed that the introvert has a higher state of cortical arousal, often a high excitatory state and a low inhibitory state, and that this cortical excitation inhibits lower brain centers and many behaviors, thus making the person more introverted. The high level of cortical arousal also presumably makes many forms of conditioning easier for the introvert than for the extrovert, again bringing more behavior under learned control. The introvert has a low sensory threshold which produces stimulus avoidance and makes more stimuli painful than is the case for the extrovert.

The extrovert, on the other hand, has a lower level of conditionability and a lower state of cortical arousal. This low excitatory and high inhibitory cortical state thus frees lower brain centers and inhibits fewer behaviors associated with these lower centers. (A parallel is that alcohol may depress cortical activity but disinhibit many behaviors.) The extrovert has a higher sensory threshold than the introvert, which results in stimulus hunger and a relative disregard of painful stimuli. Since the conscience is assumed to be a function of learning and the extrovert conditions more slowly than the introvert, the extrovert generally has less conscience.

Eysenck thus can classify a person's personality according to where its components fall along his two dimensions, and his research has revealed a number of generalities. Eysenck has found psychopaths and some criminals to be high on the neuroticism scale and highly extrovert, while hysterics are also high on neuroticism but are intermediate on the introversion-extroversion scale. There are considerable data supporting Eysenck's theory, but also considerable data that tend to refute it. Research on the relationship between conditionability and introversion-extroversion is somewhat ambiguous and is based on only a couple of different types of conditioning tasks. Thus Eysenck's theory should be considered tentative, and of course oversimplified, until we can factor out the host of other relevant, but generally confounding, variables relating personality and learning.

Janet Taylor Spence offered a theory relating anxiety, as a personality variable, to learning (J. T. Spence, 1963). She composed a questionnaire called the Manifest Anxiety Scale (MAS) consisting of about 50 items drawn from the personality questionnaire of the Minnesota Multiphasic Personality Inventory (MMPI). These items were judged by clinicians to be indicative of manifest anxiety. (Eysenck would say that MAS measures a combination of neuroticism and introversion).

People who differ in their scores on the MAS are assumed to differ in anxiety. This anxiety, according to the Hull and K. W. Spence theory, feeds into a general non-specific drive which energizes ongoing responses. It is then assumed that in simple learning situations in which there is a single or highly dominant response tendency, such as respondent conditioning or paired-associate learning with little intralist similarity of material, high MAS people will perform at a level superior to that of low MAS people. This is because the anxiety increases the drive, which then strengthens the correct responses. On the other hand, in tasks where there are many response tendencies and the correct response is relatively weak, high MAS people will show inferior performance to low MAS people, at least in the initial stages of learning. For here the anxiety increases the drive which energizes incorrect response tendencies as well as the correct response. An increase in the incorrect responses, particularly if they were somewhat dominant, will interfere with the correct response and impair performance. For example, a high MAS student might do worse than a low MAS student on a multiple choice test where the correct response is not immediately obvious and incorrect responses are interfering with recall of the correct response.

Psychological stress, however, affects more than just the drive level. J. T. Spence suggests that stress might also produce changes in effort, attention, and fear of failure, among other things. Thus, as psychological stress increases, performance might first improve as the result of increased effort and then decline as anxiety and irrelevant responses are aroused.

Predictions relating MAS and learning have been supported in a number of studies, but many other studies have failed to confirm them. J. T. Spence (1963, p. 13) responds that:

> This inconsistency in findings may in part be due to the fact that only a minor part of the performance differences among subjects is attributable to variations in MAS scores, other characteristics such as differences in learning ability among the subjects playing a more important role. In addition, our theory is undoubtedly incomplete in the variables it specifies, both with respect to task variables and to properties other than drive level which may differentiate groups with extremely high scores on the MAS from those with extremely low scores.

There are, of course, other interpretations of the data generated by studies of the J. T. Spence theory. For example, Saltz (1970) suggests that people shown to be highly anxious on the MAS scale show disruption of learning under conditions of failure-induced stress, but not necessarily under pain-induced stress, while people low on the MAS scale show disruption of learning under pain-induced stress, but not necessarily under failure-induced stress. According to Saltz, the MAS is not simply a measure of anxiety but is also a measure of whether a person is disrupted more by failure- or by pain-induced stress. The MAS "represents an index to the types of situations that constitute stress for different persons."

EXPERIMENTAL NEUROSIS

In the remainder of this chapter we will consider some learning analogues of abnormal behavior. That is, we will discuss learning experiences that produce behaviors that have marked similarities to some forms of psychological problems often dealt with in clinical situations. The similarities suggest that the psychological problem may have its roots in the corresponding learning experience. But it should be kept in mind that this is not necessarily so; much of the learning research has been done with animals and then extrapolated to humans, and there are always problems in oversimplifying such extrapolations.

When an animal is exposed to a strong conflict situation, he often ends up in a disturbed state known as *experimental neurosis* (Liddell, 1956; Masserman, 1967). This state is characterized by a wide range of behaviors that may include some of the following: excessive anxiety, avoidance of the experimental situation, trembling and tics, increase in blood pressure and heart rate, excessive vocalization, diarrhea, drastic changes in the animal's social interactions with other animals, and responding to imaginary stimuli (e.g., the monkey that brushes off insects that are not there).

One type of conflict that often produces experimental neurosis is known as *approach-avoidance conflict,* in which the animal is caught between tendencies to make a particular response and tendencies *not* to make the response. For example, in an early experiment in Pavlov's laboratory a dog was trained to salivate to a circle but not to an ellipse, a relatively easy discrimination for the dog. Then the experimenters gradually decreased the longer axis of the ellipse so that it approached being a circle. The dog had little trouble with the discrimination until the ratio of the semi-axes was 9 to 8. At this point the discrimination was quite difficult and the dog was in a conflict between salivating and not salivating to the ellipse. After three weeks with this conflict, the dog developed experimental neurosis. Now he no longer stood quietly in the test apparatus but struggled and howled. At this point he could no longer perform even the simplest of the circle-ellipse discriminations. Another approach-avoidance conflict that has produced experimental neurosis involved training a cat to approach a food dish for food and then shooting a puff of air in its face. The cat is caught in a conflict between approaching the dish for food and avoiding the dish because of the puff of air (Masserman, 1967). Similarly monkeys may develop experimental neurosis if toy snakes suddenly appear in the food box, as many monkeys appear to have an innate fear of snakes. Many of the behaviors of these experimental neuroses occur only in the presence of the test situation, whereas other behaviors carry over to different situations.

Masserman has also produced experimental neurosis with *approach-approach conflicts,* a situation where the animal has response tendencies to make approach responses toward two different and mutually exclusive goals. For example, a hungry female cat in heat might be forced to choose between food and a male cat, or a monkey might be made to choose between two favorite foods.

Although experimental neurosis is generally produced by a conflict situation, researchers have reported it following a range of other treatment procedures. Pavlov suggested five ways of producing this type of breakdown in his dogs (see Franks, 1970): (1) use of intense stimuli such as loud explosions or swinging the dog's platform; (2) increasing the interstimulus interval (ISI)—the time interval between the CS and UCS; (3) use of difficult discriminations such as the circle-ellipse described above; (4) continually changing which stimuli the dog should respond to and which he should not respond to; and (5) subjecting the dog to physical stresses such as disease, accident, or surgery.

Because the concept of neurosis has not been well specified at either the animal or human level, it is difficult to decide what types of breakdowns in animals should be called experimental neurosis or how similar animal neuroses are to human neuroses. However, the parallels between experimental neuroses in animals and neuroses in humans are quite striking and probably involve many common elements.

Masserman has investigated a number of ways of treating experimental neurosis in animals. One procedure consists in resolving the conflict by satisfying one of the needs, such as feeding a cat caught in an approach-avoidance conflict relative to its food dish. A second way is to force the animal to resolve the conflict, such as mechanically forcing the cat to approach the food dish after the air puff is gone. Exposing the neurotic animal to a normal animal modeling the desired behavior may facilitate breaking down the neurosis. On the negative side, Masserman did not find electroshock therapy to be a useful treatment procedure.

SUPERSTITION AND LEARNED HELPLESSNESS

In Chapter 6 we discussed the effects of contingent events such as reinforcement and punishment. We defined a *dependent* event to mean that the event occurs only if the animal makes a specified response or set of responses, but the environment also provides many non-dependent events — events that occur independent of what the person or animal is doing. If the non-dependent event is pleasant (a potential positive reinforcer), the occurrence of the event may result in *superstitious behavior;* whereas if the non-dependent event is aversive (a potential positive punishment), the event may result in *learned helplessness.* These two effects are discussed below.

Consider a hungry pigeon in a test apparatus in which at random intervals a grain of food drops into the food well. The food is presented aperiodically, independent of what the pigeon is doing; i.e., the food is *not* dependent on the pigeon's behavior. But the pigeon will be doing something when the food appears, so that *some* behavior will be reinforced. Through such chance reinforcements a number of behaviors may be accidentally reinforced. Eventually the response strength of one behavior will come to dominate and the pigeon will keep repeating this behavior, which will occasionally be reinforced by having the food presented non-dependently. Skinner (1948), who studied pigeons in such situations, found that the pigeons soon came to emit very stereotyped behaviors which he named *superstitions.* For example, one of Skinner's pigeons "learned" to turn counterclockwise in its effort to receive food, while another kept thrusting its head into one of the upper corners of the cage.

Since the animal in such a situation will not be reinforced each time he performs his superstitious behavior, the accidentally reinforced behaviors might extinguish before being reinforced. Thus, to develop superstitions the potential reinforcement must be presented at intervals shorter than the duration of complete extinction of the various superstitious behaviors. If this is done, the superstitious behavior will be reinforced on an intermittent schedule of reinforcement, which is likely to result in a long time to extinction.

It is easy to see human parallels of this type of behavior. A person playing a slot machine may alter the way he puts money in the machine and the way he pulls the handle if he thinks that doing these things a certain way will bring him luck. Independent of these behaviors the machine will occasionally pay off (reinforcement). Such a situation allows the person to develop a superstitious behavior, such as not looking at the machine while he pulls the handle. Observation of a gambling casino will reveal a large number of people displaying their superstitious behaviors at the slot machines. Each person's superstition may be unique to him, as each of Skinner's pigeons had a unique superstition.

Human superstitions are quite abundant. A college student in an elevator may keep pushing the button of his floor as if this would cause the elevator to move faster. A card player may pick up his cards one at a time as if to improve the hand he was dealt. A businessman may wear a "special" tie when going to an important meeting.

There are, however, a number of differences between human and animal superstitions. First, humans, as opposed to animals, often spend considerable time justifying why they are not reinforced each time they do their superstitious behavior. ("I have some questions about that so-called virgin we sacrificed to the volcano god." "I lost the golf match today because my lucky hat doesn't seem to work two days in a row.") Second, humans spend more time than animals trying to convince others to adopt their superstitious behaviors. Children often carry on many of the superstitions of their parents. Finally, as Herrnstein (1966) points out, "Human superstition, unlike that of animals, arises in a social context." The acquired superstitions in humans are not as arbitrary as those of animals. Rather they are molded by the person's culture. Thus, although it is possible to develop a superstition about Wednesday the 11th, it is more probable in our culture to be superstitious about Friday the 13th.

A group of investigators (Overmier & Seligman, 1967; Seligman, Maier, & Geer, 1968) studied the effects of non-dependent aversive events (electric shock) on dogs' behavior. First they periodically gave harnessed dogs electric shock that the dogs had no control over, as it was non-dependent. No response that a dog could make would enable it to terminate or avoid the shock. After this experience the dogs were put in an avoidance task where on cue the dogs could learn to cross a barrier to escape, and later learn to avoid, foot-shock. Normal dogs learn this avoidance task quite readily. However, a majority of the dogs that experienced the non-dependent shock made few escape responses and basically no avoidance responses. They would often just lie on the grid floor receiving shock rather than escaping across the barrier. To anthropomorphize, it is as if the dogs during the non-dependent shocks learned that there was nothing they could do that affected the occurrence of the shocks, so that when they were later in the avoidance task they didn't even try to do anything about the shocks, although in this situation they could have. The investigators labeled this phenomenon *learned helplessness*, a passive state resulting from the learning of independence between behavior and the presentation and/or withdrawal of aversive events. It should also be noted that other types of pretraining can also impair later learning of avoidance responses, such as pretraining on an escape procedure that reinforces long response latencies and interresponse times (Cohen, 1970).

Dogs showing learned helplessness in the avoidance task can be cured through a guidance procedure of physically forcing the animal to make the avoidance response. To do this the dog is put on a leash and literally dragged through the test apparatus when the cue for the avoidance response occurs. It seems that only by such physical force can the learned helplessness be readily overcome. Future research might find other cures.

Interestingly, if before the dogs are exposed to the non-dependent shocks they are put in a situation where they learn to press panels to turn off shock, then it is significantly less probable that they will later develop learned helplessness. Once the dogs have learned in the panel-press situation that shocks can be controlled, the experiences with non-dependent shocks do not affect their later learning of the avoidance task.

To date there have been only a few controlled studies with humans that have demonstrated a phenomenon similar to learned helplessness (Dweck & Reppucci, 1973; Thornton & Jacobs, 1971), but there are a number of human situations highly suggestive of learned helplessness (see Seligman et al., 1968). For example, prisoners in Nazi concentration camps often had no hope or control over what happened to them, and many became passively resigned to everything. Similarly some mental patients believe that they have no control over their environment, and their behavior is like that in learned helplessness. Seligman (1973) suggests that some forms of depression, particularly those that are set off by external events rather than those that are hormonally or genetically based, appear very similar to states of learned helplessness. It should be noted, however, that learned helplessness does not have to be as dramatic as these examples. Rather it seems that a more moderate form of learned helplessness is a characteristic of quite a number of people.

One of the most important principles for parents and teachers is to be consistent in their dealings with children, for the responses that a parent or teacher makes to a child should be a function of the child's behavior rather than of the adult's mood. A key part of many behavior modification programs, such as contingency contracting, is to build in consistency. If a child in dealing with a parent or teacher learns that there is little connection between what he does and how the person will respond to him, the child may develop some degree of learned helplessness.

By using the information gained from the dog studies, we might be able to immunize humans against developing learned helplessness (Seligman, 1969). This would consist of providing children with many experiences in which they clearly had control over parts of their environment; that is, they would learn a correlation between their behaviors and different environmental events. With such pretraining, and particularly if they have consistent parents, children might be less affected by the nondependent aversive events that happen in everyone's life.

FRUSTRATION-FIXATION

Similar to learned helplessness is the type of fixated behavior observed in rats following frustration (Feldman & Green, 1967; Maier, 1949). These experiments, originated by N. R. F. Maier, used a Lashley jumping stand. In this apparatus a rat is placed on a small platform and jumps toward one of two windows. If he chooses correctly the window opens and he goes through to an area where he receives a reinforcement, such as food. If the rat chooses the incorrect window he hits himself on the closed window and falls four feet into a net. Rats that are not interested in jumping off the platform at the windows are goaded into jumping with electric shock or a blast of air. This apparatus has been used for a variety of learning tasks, such as discrimination learning where the rat learns to jump to the darker of the two windows regardless of whether it is on the left or right side on any one trial. Usually there are two sets of cues to which the animal may respond: position (left vs. right) and brightness (dark vs. light).

Maier exposed some rats to an insolvable discrimination task on the Lashley jumping stand. There was no "correct" response; half of the rats' responses to any cue were randomly reinforced and the other half were randomly punished. The usual result of this frustrating experience was that the rats would adopt a stereotyped response to a position, such as always jumping to the left window. Maier called this stereotyped way of responding *fixation*. Maier then exposed the fixated rats to a solvable discrimination problem in which, for example, the dark door, regardless of position, was correct. Although 15 to 20 per cent of the fixated rats solved this problem, a task that normal rats learn fairly readily, the *majority* of the fixated rats continued their fixated behavior throughout training. The fixated behavior is usually a positional response. However, if rats first learn a discrimination, such as going to the dark door, *before* the frustration, then they may later fixate the earlier discrimination and always jump to the dark door even though this is no longer correct.

The fact that a rat fixates a response (e.g., always jumping left) in a solvable discrimination (e.g., dark is correct) does not mean that on the perceptual side he cannot learn the discrimination. In fact the fixated rats often do seem to have learned the discrimination. This is evidenced by the fact that the response latencies are usually shorter when the fixated response is the correct response (dark door on left) than when incorrect (dark door on right). Also, when making an incorrect fixated response the rat will often turn his body during the jump in such a way as to minimize hurting himself on the window, but in a way so that he couldn't possibly go through the window if it were correct. A rat fixated to the left can even be shown the right window wide open for him to jump through and he will still jump left. Again, to anthropomorphize, it is as if the fixated rat "knows" what the correct response is but can't break his fixation.

The rats' fixated behavior is not alterable by simple reinforcement procedures, and punishment seems only to increase the fixation. Rather, breaking the fixation, like breaking learned helplessness, involves guidance. The rat must be physically forced to make the correct response by having his jump physically guided from the platform.

There are many explanations for the frustration-fixation effect. Feldman and Green (1967) suggest that the rat during the insolvable discrimination is in a double "go-no go" conflict, an approach-avoidance conflict to each of the two responses. The approach, or "go," consists of the food reward on half the trials plus the tendency to escape or avoid the goad shock. The avoidance, or "no go," is based on the punishment that the rat receives on half the trials. This double conflict holds true for both the spatial dimension and the brightness dimension. There is also conflict about which of these two dimensions to respond to. According to Feldman and Green the stereotyped response that develops is due in large part to a general avoidance of one of the stimuli, which then "pushes" the animal toward the other.

Extrapolating from rat fixations to parallels in human behavior is difficult for a number of reasons. First, Maier's ideas on frustration-fixation have not been adequately followed up by research on humans despite the wealth of relevant ideas that Maier has suggested. Second, fixation is just one of a number of different possible results of frustration, other classic results being aggression and anxiety. Finally, human behavior is so complex that it is difficult to factor out fixated behaviors from other high probability behaviors.

However, it does seem likely that a number of human behaviors, such as some forms of compulsions, obsessions, and ritualistic acts, may be examples of fixations that follow a particularly bad frustrating situation. Also, successful treatment of human compulsions by implosive therapy often involves physically helping the person to make a response that he is avoiding, which parallels the "guidance" that is used to break fixations. Perhaps some compulsions are a combination of conditioned anxiety and response fixations. It also may be that frustration is the common element to a number of phenomena such as fixation, learned helplessness, and experimental neuroses.

APPROACH-AVOIDANCE CONFLICTS

Approach-avoidance conflicts have been discussed in the preceding sections in relation to experimental neurosis and frustration-fixations. In this section we will discuss some of the experimental analyses of such conflicts, primarily those by Neal Miller and his associates (Dollard & Miller, 1950; N. E. Miller, 1959). The following is a fairly common experimental procedure for studying approach-avoidance conflicts: Rats are first trained to run down an alley for food. Then they receive shock in the goal box where they previously received the food. The rats are now in an approach-avoidance conflict relative to the goal box, a conflict between the response tendency to approach the goal for food and the response tendency to avoid the goal because of the shock.

The general findings are that both the tendency to approach the goal and the tendency to avoid it increase as the goal becomes closer. However, the strength of the avoidance tendency increases more rapidly as the goal is neared than does the approach tendency. The avoidance gradient is thus said to have a steeper slope. These relationships are shown in Figure 7–1. Although the rest of our discussion will center on this figure, two qualifications should be made. First, the gradients usually are not linear, but for the types of conclusions that we will draw, the deviations from linearity do not seem critical. Second, the gradients need not intersect as they do in the figure; one gradient could be completely higher than the other and never intersect it. But the non-intersection case is not interesting for our purposes.

Note that the point of intersection of the two gradients occurs at some distance X from the goal. Now assume that the figure is for one of the rats in the food-shock conflict. When this rat is farther than X from the goal, the approach tendency is stronger than the avoidance tendency. Hence the rat moves toward the goal. However, when the rat is nearer than X to the goal, the avoidance tendency is stronger than the approach tendency. In this case the rat moves away from the goal. At X, of course, the tendencies balance out. All of this results in the rat's tending to fluctuate around a distance about X from the goal, but in a state of conflict.

A human parallel would be the young child at the beach who is both fascinated by the ocean (approach tendency) and afraid of the waves

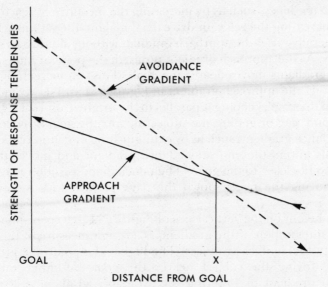

Figure 7-1 Approach-avoidance conflict.

(avoidance tendency). The child may run back and forth from the edge of the water, vacillating around a point where his gradients cross.

One of Freud's important contributions to psychology was his emphasis on behavior as often being the result of a conflict, an example being the conflict between approach tendencies of the id and avoidance tendencies from the superego. Using our approach-avoidance conflict model we may also look at Freud's idea of *displacement,* the shift of energy from one outlet to another. Consider a small boy who is punished by his father. The boy may wish to strike the father, but past experiences have built in inhibitions against this, so the boy displaces his aggression and hits the family dog. From the conflict model we can see the boy in a conflict between the approach tendency to hit his father and the avoidance tendency of fear of the father. Again, we would expect vacillation at distance X from the father. But this instance involves psychological distance rather than physical distance. That is, in Figure 7-1 the bottom axis would now be a dimension of stimulus similarity, rather than simple physical distance. Moving along this dimension from the goal of father, we may pass points corresponding to mother, brother, sister, dog, cat, and teddy bear. In our case of the boy hitting the dog, the intersection of the gradients occurs at an X-psychological distance from the father at a point corresponding to the dog.

There are basically two ways of resolving an approach avoidance conflict (i.e., getting the subject to the goal). First, we can increase the approach tendency, such as by increasing the incentive to reach the goal and/or increasing the relevant drive (e.g., making the rat more hungry). This generally raises the approach gradient without altering its slope significantly. As the approach gradient is raised, the point of intersection of the two gradients moves nearer the goal. (This can be seen by laying a pencil along the approach gradient in Figure 7–1 and slowly moving the pencil up the page, keeping it parallel to the original approach gradient.) The second way of getting the subject nearer the goal is by decreasing the avoidance gradient, such as by extinguishing or counterconditioning fear. This lowers the entire avoidance gradient and moves the intersection point closer to the goal. (The pencil demonstration may be used again, moving the pencil down the page parallel with the avoidance gradient.)

The height on the vertical axis of Figure 7–1 that corresponds to the point of intersection of the gradients is a rough measure of the amount of anxiety the conflict produces. The higher the point, the greater the anxiety. Moving the subject nearer the goal, by either raising the approach gradient or lowering the avoidance gradient, will raise the point of intersection and thus the anxiety. However, raising the approach gradient will raise the point of intersection more than lowering the avoidance gradient will. Thus in many practical situations it may be preferable to lower the avoidance gradient through procedures such as desensitization.

MASOCHISM

In Chapter 5 we discussed how a stimulus may become a conditioned reinforcer if it is paired with a reinforcer. It may also be possible for a stimulus that is naturally aversive to become a conditioned reinforcer, *if* the reinforcing effect is dominant to the aversive effect. If this should be true, we could have an animal working for a stimulus because of its conditioned reinforcing properties even though the stimulus is aversive. This is relatively easy to do, such as producing a dog that will bar-press to receive electric shock because the shock had previously been paired with receiving food. In this situation, the conditioned reinforcing properties of the shock, if no longer paired with food, should soon extinguish. This type of situation may be an experimental analogue of masochism, although there are other analogues and theories (see Dreyer & Renner, 1971).

Ayllon and Azrin (1966) demonstrated this effect in an experiment with three female schizophrenics. The subjects were first trained to pull either of two levers for tokens that could later be exchanged for back-up reinforcements. After a number of such sessions an annoying buzzer was made contingent on pulling one of the levers. This caused the subjects to emphasize pulling the other lever, and the buzzer was thus demonstrated to be punishing. Then the buzzer and tokens were paired by having one lever produce the buzzer and tokens and the other lever produce nothing. After this pairing the subjects were given two buttons to push. One button produced the buzzer, while neither button yielded any tokens. In this situation the subjects preferred to press the button that produced the aversive buzzer, even though they received no tokens. The buzzer here seems to have become a conditioned reinforcer.

Following are some naturalistic examples of this phenomenon. A mother spanks her child, but afterward, so that the child will not feel a loss of love, the mother hugs and cuddles the child. This relatively common practice may produce masochistic tendencies by pairing spanking and caressing, particularly if the mother is more loving after a spanking than she usually is. Or a student's antics in the classroom may result in punishment from the teacher but social rewards from his peers. If this pairing occurs often enough and if the social rewards are powerful enough, the student may soon work simply for the conditioned reinforcement of the punishment from the teacher.

REPRESSION

Often, unwanted thoughts that create anxiety are kept out of consciousness. This effect, known as *repression,* can be thought of as the inhibiting of the response of thinking particular thoughts that make the person uncomfortable or unhappy (Dollard & Miller, 1950). If the thought produces anxiety, then repression of the response will be anxiety-reducing, and thus repression is reinforced. Repression is simply an avoidance response.

In this chapter we have discussed a few of the learning-related variables and phenomena that probably should be part of a conceptualization of personality. Much more could be included, and this chapter is just a sample. What will be relevant in the future will depend in part on the directions taken by learning-oriented personality theorists.

SUMMARY

In this chapter personality is discussed from the viewpoint of learning, under two main divisions: (1) those genetic and physiological variables that affect a person's behavior directly or predispose him for certain types of learning; (2) specific types of behavioral abnormalities that result from certain learning experiences.

Human behavior is a highly complex interaction between hereditary influences *(nature)* and environmental influences *(nurture)* including learning. Therefore it is difficult to separate these two classes of variables, especially when trying to relate them to poorly defined classifications of behavior, such as schizophrenia. There are environmental effects on the physiology of an organism which then affect the organism's learning and behavior. Rats that are kept in more enriched environments have brains that are, among other things, larger and heavier. These brain differences, although reversible, may affect learning. Malnutrition clearly retards mental development in nonhumans and probably contributes to mental deficiency in humans as well. On the other hand, there is research suggesting that the severity of a person's physical illness, or even whether he acquires the illness at all, may be due to psychological variables, primarily major changes in the person's life.

There is considerable evidence that there is a genetic component in some forms of mental illness, such as schizophrenia and manic-depressive psychosis. There is also a possible genetic factor in some forms of criminality, in psychoneurosis, and in alcoholism. There is no valid evidence that any particular race is genetically more intelligent than any other race. Research into possible physiological bases of schizophrenia has suggested biochemical imbalances in blood or brain, enzyme imbalances, inability to regulate stress-response mechanisms, impairment of a physiological reward system, and a continual state of overarousal. There are probably several different physiological deficits that may lead to behaviors we call schizophrenic.

Man as a species has apparently been selected in the evolutionary scheme to adapt culturally rather than genetically. Adaptation by cultural changes is more effective for humans than adaptation by genetic changes. Man may also be evolutionarily prepared to learn certain things, such as language, and perhaps some phobias, such as fear of snakes.

An account of personality should include individual differences as they relate to learning, for example, individual differences in the ease with which a person can be conditioned. Several theorists have suggested personality variables that relate to what and how the person will learn: Maddi suggested that people differ in their need for variation and in the types of stimulus complexity that they seek. Pavlov argued that many psychological problems are due to an imbalance between the ideal amounts of excitation and inhibition in the nervous system, which then affects learning. Eysenck proposed a personality classification of basically two dimensions—neuroticism and introversion-extroversion—and he related these dimensions to learning. Spence related anxiety, as measured by the Manifest Anxiety Scale (MAS), to learning by suggesting that anxiety feeds into a general non-specific drive.

The chapter concludes with a number of learning paradigms and behavioral abnormalities suggestive of some common human psychological problems. The topics include experimental neurosis, superstition, learned helplessness, frustration-fixation, approach-avoidance conflicts, masochism, and repression.

SUGGESTED READINGS

Dollard, J., & Miller, N. E. *Personality and Psychotherapy.* New York: McGraw-Hill, 1950.

Kimble, G. A. *Hilgard and Marquis' Conditioning and Learning.* New York: Appleton-Century-Crofts, 1961, Chapter 14.

Lundin, R. W. *Personality: A Behavioral Analysis.* New York: Macmillan, 1969.

Maher, B. A. *Principles of Psychopathology: An Experimental Approach.* New York: McGraw-Hill, 1966.

Rosenthal, D. *Genetics of Psychopathology.* New York: McGraw-Hill, 1971.

chapter eight

behavior, cognitions, and consciousness

Considerable work in comparative psychology and zoology has been devoted to behavioral comparisons between man and other animals. Comparative differences are often useful in helping us to understand possible evolutionary trends and the development of specific types of brain functioning. Man often uses such comparisons to argue for his own superiority over other animals, a position of some question if we use criteria such as how an animal treats a fellow of his species. Man created a phylogenetic scale and modestly placed himself at the top, and some people hold the curious belief that man is the final product of evolution. Similarly many people argue that dogs are more intelligent than cats because dogs are better at learning to do what man wants them to do, a somewhat egocentric approach to the concept of "intelligence." To appreciate some of the legitimate differences between man and the other animals we will first briefly mention some of the research on chimpanzees.

In some extremely important field work Jane Goodall (Lawick-Goodall, 1971) lived for several years with wild chimpanzees in the rain forests of Tanzania. It took her considerable time and patience to gradually approach and be accepted by the chimps. But after she was finally accepted she was able to observe and record the behavior of chimps in their natural settings, behavior which proved to be much more complex than had been expected. The chimps showed a wide range of identifiable emotions, including fear, rage, shock, confusion, amusement, worry, and embarrassment. They would often dance and play games. When a new fruit tree was discovered they would hug each other and slap each other on the back. And they often organized hunting parties with complex plans to catch their prey.

Perhaps most important of Goodall's observations relates to the chimps' use of tools. Before these observations, toolmaking was generally considered to be unique to man. Other animals, such as some birds, might *use* tools, but only man was assumed capable of *making* the tools he used. Goodall observed that the chimps did in fact make and use tools. They would chew leaves to make sponges in order to sop water out of a branch. When they desired some termites they might poke twigs or blades of grass into termite nests and then withdraw them with termites on them. To maintain man's uniqueness as toolmaker, some anthropologists now say that for an implement to be a tool it has to be made according to a regular pattern.

One set of chimpanzee experiments has involved raising the chimps in homes, like humans (Kellogg, 1968). These experiments tell us what types of human behaviors chimps might be capable of. Home-raised chimps easily learned to wear clothes, sleep in beds, drink from glasses, eat with silverware, open doors, work faucets, and play catch. They matured faster than humans in eye-hand coordination and locomotion. The chimps enjoyed photographs and motion pictures. However, attempts at teaching the chimps to speak more than a few words always failed.

Trying to teach chimps to speak, however, may not be a fair test of their language capabilities, for chimps are generally not vocal animals unless disturbed. Therefore some researchers are investigating language learning in chimps with non-vocal language. Gardner and Gardner (1969) taught their chimp to use sign language with specific hand gestures for words such as "more," "open," and "please." As soon as the chimp had a vocabulary of eight to ten words she started using combinations of words such as "gimme tickle." She invented the phrase "open food drink" when she wanted the refrigerator opened, yet had no word for "refrigerator." Premack (1970), on the other hand, taught his chimp a language of more than 120 words, where the words were plastic figures put on a board. This chimp was shaped to be able to understand and construct sentences such as "Mary give apple Sarah." Premack systematically demonstrated that he could produce in his chimp a range of language properties previously considered to be unique to human communication.

Although chimps may be capable of language learning in ways qualitatively similar to man, it is the *amount* of language usage that provides large differences between the behavior of humans and nonhumans, for through his language man creates a culture which acquires an autonomy that supersedes the individuals. When an animal dies, most of what he has learned dies with him; other members of his species must keep starting from the beginning again. But much of man's learning is incorporated into the culture's memory storage (e.g., books, articles, folk-tales) which other men can draw on. The culture in turn takes an active role in the socializing and conditioning of its members, as through its mores, laws, and schools. Current evolution is clearly more cultural than biological. Early antagonists of Darwin, such as Paul Kammerer, disliked the idea that natural selection seemed purposeless. They prefered a model of man in which what a man masters and learns might be passed on biologically. Their mistake was that the type of evolution they wanted probably occurs at a *cultural* level, not at a biological level.

It it weren't for language, man would essentially have no culture. Take away culture and all that is derived from it and the differences between man and chimp would be considerably reduced. Although the preceding discussion is oversimplified, language is clearly a key variable in the complexity of man's behavior. Pavlov was so impressed by the importance of language that he suggested that with the advent of language a new principle of neural action was introduced.

As language becomes internalized into processes such as "thinking" and "reasoning," we enter the domain of consciousness. Of all of the proposed differences between man and the other animals, from disparate areas such as psychology, philosophy, and theology, some of the strongest and potentially most important arguments relate to differences in consciousness. Furthermore, an understanding of the nature of consciousness and how it interrelates with learning underlies some of the key issues of psychology, particularly those related to therapy and self-discovery and to the relationship between awareness and performance.

NATURE OF CONSCIOUSNESS

Consciousness is a nebulous, poorly defined construct. It refers to a subjective experience within the organism in which the organism is aware of some event such as sensory input or the associative processing of his brain. Each person has some idea of the nature of consciousness from his own personal experiences, and we generally assume that other people have similar conscious experiences. However, we cannot know for sure, for at the current scientific level our only measure of the content of consciousness of another person is what the person tells us.

Much of our knowledge about consciousness comes from *introspection*—looking inward. We assume here that the mind has the ability to observe itself. Hebb (1968, 1969) has questioned this assumption and suggested that much of introspection may be fantasy. That is, a person may be aware of a sense impression or a memory trace that has been elicited and has the illusion that he is observing the working of his mind.

The type of illusions that may arise can be seen in the imagery of consciousness. For example, if a group of people are told to close their eyes and to imagine seeing the word "Louisiana," most people will report that they have a clear image of the word in their mind. But if asked to quickly spell the word backward, which they should be able to do if they really had a true image of the word, they usually have trouble. Similarly the reader might stop here and recall some specific activity he has done, such as diving into a swimming pool or working in a garden. When they "recall" such memories, people often have images that they never actually observed, such as seeing themselves doing the activity from the perspective of another person. For example, my memories of a recent bicycle ride include images of myself riding the bicycle as seen from the front door of my house. Hebb's recollection of a certain field involved a visual image of the field as seen from 30 feet in the air, although he had never seen the field from this point.

Because the nature of consciousness is currently so subjective and is not directly measurable, many psychologists, particularly those influenced by Skinner, do not consider it a phenomenon worth pursuing and generally do not include consciousness as a construct in their psychological models. If we are measuring consciousness by means of verbal report, then let us restrict our discussions to the verbal report rather than postulating a consciousness that precedes verbal report. This approach has proven extremely productive and powerful. Someone like Skinner can generally adequately account for the complexities of human behavior without appealing to such elusive phenomena as consciousness. The only fault with such an approach is that many people may consider it worthwhile to study consciousness for its own sake. Many theorists give great importance to the nature and functions of consciousness.

The ambiguity about consciousness becomes even greater when we move from humans to nonhumans, for it is very difficult to extrapolate from our subjective experiences to those of nonhuman animals, and the animal doesn't tell us much by verbal report. There are basically two approaches to the issue of whether animals have consciousness. The first, popular among many theologians and anthropologists, is that consciousness is a property that emerges only when the nervous system reaches a certain complexity, and this minimum level of complexity appears to have been reached only by man. Thus man has consciousness and other animals do not. According to this view, consciousness is a threshold phenomenon; it does not occur at all until some threshold value of nervous system complexity has been reached. One wonders whether a future computer network will reach the level of complexity necessary for consciousness.

The second approach to consciousness assumes that consciousness occurs in varying degrees in different animals, depending on the complexity of their nervous systems. Thus nonhumans have some consciousness, but theirs is probably much less complex and sophisticated than that of humans. A large part of most human consciousness is visual images, since vision is one of the most important senses to man, and language symbols such as words. Animals don't use symbols as much as man; not that they necessarily cannot use symbols, but symbols are not that important in their life, so they don't learn them. Therefore we might expect the consciousness of animals to be relatively symbol-free. Animal consciousness is probably dominated by sequences of sense impressions emphasizing the sense modes that are important to the animal's particular species. It is also probable that man's greater use of symbols and language in his reasoning is the basis for the major behavioral differences between man and other animals.

It is sometimes suggested that only man has self-awareness — awareness of himself as an object. It is not clear exactly what self-awareness is, but some experiments with chimps suggest that they may have something akin to self-awareness, if self-recognition in a mirror implies a primitive concept of self. Gallup (1971) exposed jungle-born chimpanzees to mirrors. At first they responded to their images as if they were other chimps. By the third day, however, the chimps used the mirrors to inspect parts of their bodies they could not see and to make faces at themselves. One time, after the chimps were anesthetized so that they were unconscious, Gallup applied to each chimp an odorless dye to the upper ridge of one eyebrow and the top half of the opposite ear. When the chimps awoke they didn't know that they had the dye on them until they saw themselves in the mirror. They then became agitated and started touching the dyed areas. Thus it appears that chimps have at least some concept of self.

Differences in consciousness are generally considered related to differences in the complexity of the nervous system. But exactly what aspects of the nervous system account for these various differences? Pure size is not the answer, for an elephant's brain is larger than a man's. The brain of the porpoise is larger and more convoluted than man's brain. To develop a complete explanation for the differences between humans and nonhumans, we will probably have to examine variables such as the specific types of neurons, how the neurons are organized, and the types and efficiency of neural transmission. Right now the structural differences between the brains of man, chimp, and porpoise seem too superficial to account for the large differences in capabilities.

MIND-BODY PROBLEM

One of the major unresolved philosophical issues is the *mind-body problem* (Eacker, 1972; Tibbetts, 1973). The "body" here refers to the unthinking, observable substance that constitutes the form and figure of a person. The "mind," on the other hand, has no substance, and is generally defined in terms of its functions, primarily thinking. That is, it is the mind which thinks and is conscious. The mind-body problem is the question of how two entities as different as mind and body can influence each other.

The approach of *monism* assumes that mind and body are simply two aspects of the same underlying reality; in other words, there is just one entity which is observed, conceptualized, and described from different perspectives. This is essentially the position of Skinner, who assumes that the same laws of behavior apply to events inside a man as outside; it is just harder to measure and observe the internal events. As Skinner (1972) argues:

> What we feel when we have feelings and what we observe through introspection are nothing more than a rather miscellaneous set of collateral products or by-products of the environmental conditions to which behavior is related. (We do not act because we feel like acting, for example; we act and feel like acting for a common reason to be sought in our environmental history.) Do I mean to say that Plato never discovered the mind? Or that Aquinas, Descartes, Locke, and Kant were preoccupied with incidental, often irrelevant by-products of human behavior? Or that the mental laws of physiological psychologists like Wundt, or the stream of consciousness of William James, or the mental apparatus of Sigmund Freud have no useful place in the understanding of human behavior? Yes, I do. And I put the matter strongly because, if we are to solve the problems that face us in the world today, this concern for mental life must no longer divert our attention from the environmental conditions of which human behavior is a function.

Munn (1971, p. 12) defined a person's mind as "the integrated totality of the conscious and unconscious processes involved in acquiring, storing, and utilizing information in his interactions with his environment."

The opposite of monism is *dualism,* in which the mind and body are considered separate entities which may or may not interact. There are many forms of dualism, three of which are discussed below:

1. According to *interactionism,* the mind and body are different substances which causally interact with each other. For example, Descartes suggested that the mind and body interact through the mediation of the pineal body, a small gland in the brain of unknown function.

2. The position of *parallelism* is that the mind and body do not interact but simply run in parallel. Bodily and mental events may correspond, but they are not causally connected to each other.

3. The position of *epiphenomenalism* assumes that the phenomena of the mind accompany the functions of the body but have no important effect on the body. Consider a futuristic robot that has been programmed to behave according to specified laws, but which is complex enough so that its behavior is modifiable by experience. That is, the robot's behav-

ior is determined, but it can also learn. Assume also that we can some-how give the robot an awareness or consciousness of its own behavior, including awareness of some of the processes of the mediating circuitry inside itself. Now if the robot's programming and the current stimulus situation determine its behavior as well as what goes into the robot's awareness, but the awareness has no effect on the behavior, then the robot's mind is an epiphenomenon. The mind receives input from the body but does not send output to the body. The robot could also be programmed to be aware of a response that it is about to make just before it actually makes the response. Then, even though its behavior is determined, the robot might have the belief it has free will since it has the illusion of deciding to make a response before actually making it. The reader might consider what differences he thinks exist between us and the robot.

Physiological studies have produced a number of observations that bear on the relationship between brain and consciousness. In Chapter Two we discussed split-brain studies in humans, studies in which the corpus callosum connecting the two hemispheres is severed. This produces a person with essentially two brains: the major hemisphere (usually the left hemisphere), which contains the basic areas related to speech, and the minor hemisphere, which is incapable of producing speech. The major hemisphere has the kind of consciousness that we usually experi-ence, particularly consciousness whose content is speech-related. But there may also be an independent and different stream of consciousness in the minor hemisphere. Sperry's (1968) studies of the functioning of the minor hemisphere "suggest the presence of ideas and a capacity for mental association and at least some simple logic and reasoning." For ex-ample, from a number of items, the minor hemisphere consciousness can identify a wrist watch as being the most like a wall clock, suggesting some concept of timepieces. The minor hemisphere can also use sym-bols, as is indicated by its ability to do simple arithmetic problems. Sperry also notes that the minor hemisphere "is able to comprehend both writ-ten and spoken words to some extent, although this comprehension can-not be expressed verbally." For example, it can match actual objects to the written name of the object. The minor hemisphere also displays emotions, as when the subject is surprisingly shown a picture of a nude.

Sperry concludes that "Observations like the foregoing lead us to favor the view that in the minor hemisphere we deal with a second con-scious entity that is characteristically human and runs along in parallel with the more dominant stream of consciousness in the major hemi-sphere." Ornstein (1973) suggests that the left (dominant) hemisphere generally is "predominantly involved with analytic thinking, especially language and logic" and "seems to process information sequentially," whereas the right hemisphere is "primarily responsible for our orienta-tion in space, artistic talents, body awareness, and recognition of faces" and "integrates material in a simultaneous, rather than linear fashion." More generally, Sperry (1969) considers consciousness to be an emergent property of the simple neural constituents. Consciousness is assumed to exert a holistic form of causal control over brain activity.

Humans with damage to the frontal cortex often show a form of perseverative behavior, a tendency to keep repeating a way of responding, even after the particular responses are no longer appropriate. That is, they often do not adapt as fast as normals to changing contingencies. However, observation of frontally damaged humans shows that they often know what the correct response *should* be (as, for example, in a card-sorting task), but they can't make the response (B. Milner, 1964). To oversimplify, it is as if the part of the brain which "knows" what the correct response is, and can often verbalize it, had inadequate control over the part of the brain that moves the body in making the response. This latter part then has a tendency to perseverate responses. There is some slightly suggestive evidence for similar phenomena in rats with lesions of the caudate nucleus, a brain area which in rats has some functional similarities to the frontal cortex in man (Mikulas & Isaacson, 1965).

MEDIATION

Earlier we emphasized the importance of contiguity in learning and performance. Many times events are associated together, not through simple contiguity but through the *mediation* of a common event to which they are both associated. Thus if A is associated with C, and B is associated with C, then the person may associate A and B through the mediation of C. The concept of mediation has proven powerful to psychology (e.g., Kjeldergaard, 1968), since it allows us to explain complex associations and behavior patterns in terms of contiguity and mediation. Deese and Hulse (1967, p. 316) give three of the basic forms of mediation: (1) *chaining* involves learning A-B and B-C and then testing for the association A-C; (2) *stimulus equivalence* involves learning A-B and C-B and then testing for A-C; (3) *response equivalence* involves learning B-A and B-C and testing for A-C. In all cases, A and C became associated through the mediation of B.

A lot takes place within an organism between the stimulus situation that the organism is exposed to and the response that he makes to the situation. Some theorists disregard what goes on within the organism, some theorists fill the organism with various assumed variables and constructs, and some theorists put volition within the organism. It is also possible to argue that between stimulus and response there is a complex sequence of mediation of the types discussed above. That is, through learning the nervous system develops a complex web of mediated associations that interconnect stimuli and responses. In test situations subjects are often aware of the mediational processes involved, but it is also well established that mediation can occur without awareness (Kjeldergaard, 1968).

Much or all of thinking might simply be mediational processes, some of which we are conscious of. The consciousness may or may not have any effect on the mediation. It is also possible that sometimes our thinking is consciousness of mediational processes other than the ones actually determining our behavior.

AWARENESS AND VERBAL CONDITIONING

Much of our learning occurs without our being aware of what we are learning or even that we are learning at all. A person might be able to remember where a shoe repair shop is in his town because he has passed it a number of times, but it is possible that when passing the shop the person may not have paid any attention to it or been consciously aware it was there. When walking along with someone we may adjust our pace to accommodate them and not be aware that we are doing so. Later, when starting a walk with the same person, we might immediately assume the learned pace, again without being aware. The above types of learning may, of course, involve awareness, but they need not; for awareness can only accommodate a small part of our behavior and the variables affecting the behavior. If we had to be aware of everything we learn, our learning capabilities would be cut down significantly and we would be much less efficient at coping with a changing environment. This is particularly true when the relevant stimuli are subtle environmental cues or internal stimuli.

Similarly, many behaviors that may have required (or produced) awareness at one time may now no longer have a conscious component. Consider learning to drive a car. When first learning to stop at a stopsign, the beginner may have to be aware of putting in the clutch, braking, shifting gears, and then simultaneously releasing the clutch and pressing the accelerator. After the person acquires more experience, he can do all of this without being aware of it, as when his awareness is involved in a conversation with a passenger. Yet even after these behaviors are no longer conscious, learning may still be taking place as the driver becomes more and more skilled at using the car.

Not everyone, however, agrees with what has just been said. Some theorists believe that awareness is necessary for learning, at least some forms of learning. Most of the relevant research and arguments have revolved around the role of awareness in verbal conditioning.

The verbal conditioning and awareness studies essentially began with an experiment by Greenspoon (1955). Greenspoon told his subjects to just continually say individual words. After getting a baseline of how many plural nouns the subject ordinarily says in such a situation, an attempt was made to increase the rate of plural nouns through reinforcement. This was accomplished by the experimenter subtly saying "mmm-hmm" after each plural noun. The overall result of the reinforcement was small in magnitude, but significant in effect. The reinforcements doubled the rate of the subjects' saying plural nouns. The reader can easily repeat this experiment with a friend if the reader is careful not to make his "mmm-hmm's" obvious.

After the conditioning sessions were over, Greenspoon questioned his subjects about how aware they were about what was going on. Those subjects who could correctly describe the reinforcement contingency were not included in the final analysis given above. Thus it appeared that people's verbal behavior could be conditioned without their being aware of the conditioning. This launched a massive number of experiments and theories relating awareness and verbal conditioning (e.g., Dulany, 1968; Greenspoon & Brownstein, 1967; Holz & Azrin, 1966; Marlatt, 1972; Spielberger & DeNike, 1966). The experiments involved conditioning a variety of types of verbal behavior, such as types of verbs or specific pronouns to complete sentences, with subtle reinforcements, such as "good" or a nod of the head.

Awareness during these experiments is generally measured by verbal report of the subject, either oral or written. Verbal report is a highly questionable measure of awareness, but it is not clear what a better alternative might be. A major problem is that verbal behavior can be considered just another behavior that follows the same laws of learning as any other behavior. That is, verbal behavior can be conditioned in ways that often make it suspect as a reliable measure. It seems somewhat paradoxical that studies demonstrating the conditioning of verbal behavior use verbal behavior as a measure of the awareness of the conditioning.

Another problem is the question of exactly what it is that the subject is supposed to be aware of. Is awareness simply being cognizant that something is going on? What if the subject is generally aware of the contingency, but his hypothesis is not quite right? For example, the subject might believe that the experimenter is saying "good" after all nouns that end in "s" when in fact the experimenter will reinforce *any* plural noun. A determination of awareness is often harder than it seems. Most experimenters consider a subject aware when he can state the correct reinforcement contingency. Marlatt (1972) suggests that the "concept of awareness should be defined as the degree of congruence between the subject's own perception of the purpose of the experiment and the experimenter's purpose."

Numerous studies have been reported demonstrating verbal conditioning without awareness, and many other studies have found conditioning only when the subjects were aware; thus, the controversy is yet unresolved. In attempting to account for such discrepancies, Spielberger and DeNike (1966) suggested that many of the measures of awareness used in some experiments were not sensitive enough. In their research they used more detailed questioning about awareness and assessed for awareness at different intervals during the conditioning itself, rather than assessing after the last conditioning trial. They found that only those subjects who were judged to be aware showed any performance gains during conditioning. Also, the subjects were judged aware at that point of the conditioning at which performance gains began. Thus it seemed that awareness was necessary for verbal conditioning, and previous studies that did not find this did not use sensitive enough measures of awareness. According to Spielberger and DeNike the verbal conditioning studies are essentially problem solving tasks in which the subject learns to be aware of a correct response-reinforcement contingency.

There are some problems with the Spielberger and DeNike approach. First, to say that a person *learns* to be aware is at least allowing for some type of learning without awareness. Second, a measure of awareness might be considered sensitive enough only if it shows awareness to precede or correspond to performance changes. A researcher who believes that awareness is necessary for learning might discount those findings that don't match his bias by saying that the measure used was not sensitive enough. Third, and most important, is that the procedures that Spielberger and DeNike used to determine awareness may have facilitated the subject's becoming aware. Perhaps the subjects would not have been aware if they hadn't been questioned so much.

Thus the problem is how to question the subject in enough detail so that you have a reasonable measure of awareness, but at the same time to do this in a manner that does not make the subject aware. Rosenfeld and Baer (1969, 1970) seem to have found a way. In their first experiment (1969) they told a graduate student that he would be an interviewer whose job was to reinforce mannerisms in a subject who was the interviewee. This was accomplished by the interviewer's asking questions of the interviewee and then reinforcing by head-nodding whenever the interviewee rubbed his chin. In fact, the interviewee was a "double-agent" working for Rosenfeld and Baer. The interviewee was reinforcing the interviewer for certain verbal responses such as "yeah." The reinforcement the interviewee used was his own chin-rubbing, which was reinforcing to the interviewer since this was the response he was trying to produce.

During the time-outs between conditioning trials, the interviewer could be questioned in detail about the experiment without making him suspect that he was the actual subject of the experiment, for he believed that he was conditioning the interviewee, rather than the other way around. Using this approach it was possible to demonstrate that the verbal responses of the interviewer could be reinforced and altered in rate without the interviewer being aware.

In a variation on this approach, Rosenfeld and Baer (1970) had their subjects believe that they were experimenters who were reinforcing fluent pronunciation of nouns by people speaking over an intercom. In fact, the supposed "people" were a double-agent multitrack tape recorder which reinforced the subjects with fluent nouns whenever the subjects made certain types of verbal requests for the next noun. Again, verbal conditioning without awareness was demonstrated.

Like Spielberger and DeNike, Marlatt (1972) views the verbal conditioning studies as problem-solving tasks. According to Marlatt, the subject at first does not know how to perform successfully in the task. He gradually gains information through sources such as instructions, verbal reinforcement, and models. Awareness might result from any combination of these sources of information. Marlatt suggests that the reinforcement serves two functions: (1) it has informational properties which may feed into awareness; and (2) it has incentive properties that may affect the person's intentions regarding performance. That is, reinforcement in verbal conditioning tasks is a form of feedback and hence may have any of the properties of feedback discussed in Chapter Six.

There seems to be sufficient reason and evidence to suggest that verbal conditioning may occur without awareness. Awareness may often occur in such tasks, but it does not seem to be a prerequisite for conditioning. On the other hand, procedures aimed to make the subject more aware may often facilitate learning through effects on processes such as attention and the values assigned to different stimuli. For discussion let us assume, like Spielberger, that changes in performance occur only after awareness occurs. If this were true, would it prove that awareness is necessary for learning in verbal conditioning? Again the answer is no. First of all there is the old problem of going from correlation to causation. That is, just because awareness and performance changes may be correlated does not tell you which caused which or if perhaps both are effects from some third source.

More important is the fact that information relating awareness to *performance* changes may be irrelevant to the issue of whether awareness is necessary for *learning* (Mikulas, 1970). For example, it may be that during the early conditioning trials learning is gradually taking place, but it is not displayed in performance because it is below some threshold value. When the strength of learning reaches this threshold, performance gains occur. Now awareness might also occur at the point, or just before the point, when learning reaches the threshold. The awareness may then be a result of the learning or it may be independent of the learning.

An important implication of the verbal conditioning literature is that it makes us a little suspicious of the reliability of verbal report as a measure of something else, such as internal states, attitudes, or other behaviors. We have noted how the parent, teacher, or therapist might, intentionally or otherwise, reinforce the person he is interacting with to talk in a certain fashion that may more reflect the first person's bias rather than what the report is supposed to measure in the second person. For example, a therapist who relies on his patient's verbal report may reinforce his patients to talk in ways that fit the therapist's theoretical orientation. Many examples of so-called insight may be nothing more than the products of a subtle shaping program. And much of this learning may occur without the patient's being aware of it.

INTERACTIONS OF COGNITIONS AND BEHAVIORS

For the purpose of discussion let us consider two different systems of human activity — a behavioral system and a cognitive system. The behavioral system includes the output of the person: what he does, both skeletally and autonomically, as well as overtly and covertly. The behavioral system encompasses how the person responds to a situation, including internal responses such as physiological reactions. The cognitive system includes the subjective conscious experience that accompanies and perhaps precedes the behaviors. The cognitive system is the seat of consciousness, awareness, insight, and the evaluative component of attitudes.

Important questions for anyone concerned with change processes are: (1) Do changes in the cognitive system result in changes in the behavioral system? and (2) Do changes in the behavioral system result in changes in the cognitive system?

Unfortunately there is currently no way of measuring the cognitive system independently of the behavioral system, for we can't know about another person's cognitions except through some behavior such as verbal report. One approach to this dilemma is to deny the existence of the cognitive system or to discount questions about it as being meaningless. Another possibility is that all aspects of the cognitive system will eventually reduce to the behavioral system. For purposes of this discussion, however, we will assume that there are two systems, realizing that the cognitive system is always measured via the behavioral system.

Thus, when talking about the interactions between changes in the cognitive system and changes in the behavioral system, what we will really be considering are the interactions between changes in the cognitive system, as measured by specific behaviors, and changes in behaviors other than those used to measure the cognitions. Obviously if the two sets of behaviors are very similar they will change in similar ways as the result of response generalization. Our interest will be more in those situations where the behaviors are dissimilar. For example, when considering whether changing a person's attitudes toward a minority group will change the way the person acts toward members of this group, we really are asking a question such as the following: "How do changes in Fred's behavior of checking rating scales about the minority group (presumed to measure attitudes) correlate with changes in Fred's behavior of helping a member of the minority group to get a home in Fred's neighborhood?"

Changing the Cognitive System

There is no question that a person's behaviors generally match his cognitions; a person generally does those things that he consciously intends to do. But how effective is it to change cognitions in an attempt to change behaviors? Consider attitudes first.

Attitudes have basically two components: an emotional component in the behavioral system and an evaluative component in the cognitive system. The evaluative component includes the subjective associations and classifications that a person has toward some stimulus complex. The cognition "a woman's place is in the home" is an example of the cognitive part of an attitude that many people are currently trying to alter. The basic problem is to determine how changes in attitudes correlate with changes in the general behavioral system. It is assumed by educators, politicians, and other influence agents that changing attitudes is an effective way to produce changes in a number of behaviors. However, there is little support for this assumption, particularly for long term effects.

The general finding is that although it may be relatively easy to change attitudes, unless general behaviors are altered independently in the same direction, the attitudes will drift back to where they were before. The attitudes of a white racist might be altered so that he will say that he likes blacks, but if his general behavior isn't independently altered to make him act toward blacks in a more favorable manner, there is a good chance that his attitude will change back to that of a racist.

In an early review Festinger (1964) concluded that attitude change is "inherently unstable and will disappear or remain isolated unless an environmental or behavioral change can be brought about to support or maintain it." In a later, very extensive review Wicker (1969) noted that "Taken as a whole, these studies suggest that it is considerably more likely that attitudes will be unrelated or only slightly related to overt behaviors than that attitudes will be closely related to actions." Wicker could find "little evidence to support the postulated existence of stable, underlying attitudes within the individual which influence both his verbal expressions and his actions."

A number of common examples support these conclusions. Many smokers are well informed about the hazards of smoking and believe this information, but this does not stop their smoking; the same is true for many alcoholics. After pointing out how research in psychotherapy has neglected the relationships between attitudes and behavior, Ludwig (1968) suggested that constructive attitude change with alcoholics might merely produce a more insightful drunk.

It is possible to think of situations in which changes in attitudes seem to produce long term general changes in behavior. If these situations are investigated carefully, however, it is usually possible to identify variables apart from the attitude change which deal with the behavioral system directly. Perhaps in addition to changing a person's attitudes one also reinforces him for acting in a different way. The person might also be exposed to salient models or required to role-play new behaviors. In some situations following attitude change the person might be sent out on specific behavioral assignments requiring him to act in new ways which may then be reinforced by the social environment. It is also possible that during the attitude change procedure the person is exposed to counterconditioning of new responses in place of old responses, either overt responses or mediating responses in a response chain. Many of these variables affecting the behavioral system are often artifacts of attempting to alter attitudes. A more powerful approach is to develop a systematic learning program that attempts to directly alter the behavioral system. Such an approach goes under many names, one of which is *behavior modification*.

A trend among many social psychologists is to no longer merely alter attitudes but to also directly change the related behaviors in the same direction. For example, Zimbardo and Ebbesen (1970, p. 85) conclude that "changes in attitude are not necessarily accompanied by changes in behavior. Furthermore, when changes in behavior do occur, they are rarely, if ever, general or enduring." Their solution to this problem is to wed learning theory and social psychology into "social learning," which add to the attitude change techniques the behavior change techniques of respondent conditioning, operant conditioning, and modeling. "When would the social learning approach expect verbal statements to match nonverbal behavior? Essentially it would predict a match whenever a person expects similar consequences for both kinds of behavior." (Zimbardo & Ebbesen, 1970, p. 92).

A general area that is based on the assumption that cognitive change produces behavioral change is insight-oriented psychotherapy. Here it is assumed that providing the patient with insight or awareness about the nature and etiology of his problems will result in changes in his behavior and correction of these problems. A person might spend hundreds of hours with a psychotherapist working through events of his psychosexual history, interpreting the symbols of his dreams and fantasies, and learning to perceive his behavior from the theoretical orientation of the therapist. Out of such a process, or from some other insight-oriented psychotherapy, new cognitions arise. But do such cognitive changes produce general behavioral changes? The answer appears to be no.

Eysenck (1952) searched the published literature and could find no evidence that patients given psychotherapy improved significantly more than patients given no formal psychotherapy. Although there were some methodological problems with some of the evidence that Eysenck presented, his challenge still stands. There is still a conspicuous absence of well-controlled studies demonstrating that psychotherapy as practiced by professional therapists is more effective than treatment by nonprofessionals such as ministers and friends.

In his presidential address to the Division of Clinical Psychology of the American Psychological Association, Hobbs (1962) suggested that "Insight is not a cause of change but a possible result of change. It is not a source of therapeutic gain, but one among a number of possible consequences of gain." Similarly London (1969, p. 53) concludes that "Insight therapy is clearly a poor means of symptom control; after almost 70 years of use, there are still few indications that uncovering motives and expanding self-understanding confer much therapeutic power over most troubling symptoms."

As with attitudes, it appears that in therapeutic settings, changing cognitions is an inefficient way to change behaviors. This is not surprising since simply understanding a problem doesn't necessarily mean that the person has the skills to overcome it. His behaviors may be too strongly conditioned. Consider a person with a fear of snakes. He might know that the snake we are going to show him is harmless and locked in a glass case. He knows there is no reason to be afraid of this snake. But when we put him near the case with the snake in it, he will be anxious. The anxiety is beyond his cognitive control. The reader can probably identify things that make him anxious, such as heights, speaking before groups, or certain insects. Do you think that being aware of the irrationality of your fear, its etiology, or its symbolic meaning is going to reduce your fear significantly? Probably not. It would be better to condition the anxiety out with procedures such as desensitization, discussed in Chapter Five.

The author worked with a case of a sexually impotent man who, following psychotherapy, "knew" and "understood" his impotence in terms of his puritan childhood and was "aware" of the irrationality of his anxiety in his present marriage. But the man was still impotent. However, over a period of a couple of months it was possible to countercondition out his anxiety and countercondition in the desired sexual response.

Many people, because of their conditioning history, have strong negative emotional responses to blacks. For some people, unfortunately not enough, their emotional reactions to the blacks are contradictory to their social-religious philosophy. But since their philosophy (cognitions) is insufficient to alter their conditioned emotions, they continue to respond emotionally to blacks and avoid discussing or thinking about this discrepancy with their philosophy, as awareness of the discrepancy is unpleasant. Again, counterconditioning seems called for.

This doesn't mean that a person who goes through insight-oriented psychotherapy will show no behavioral changes. There is too much evidence for such behavioral changes. However, the behavioral changes which do result probably are not due to cognitive changes per se. Rather they are due to the role of learning variables such as reinforcement, extinction, modeling, role-playing, counterconditioning, and behavioral assignments. The psychotherapist may provide the patient with discrimination training, alter incentives to which the person responds, or produce respondent conditioning through complex language-mediated associations.

Whatever the changes in the behavioral system, they are probably based on the principles of conditioning. Unfortunately many therapists produce such changes as an unintentional side effect of trying to alter cognitions. This makes such behavioral changes quite inefficient. The advocate of behavior modification argues that the therapist would be significantly more effective if he applied a systematic conditioning program to alter the behavioral system, rather than trying to produce behavioral changes indirectly by altering the cognitive system. Of course sometimes the goal is cognitive changes for the sake of cognitive change alone, but that is a different issue than is being discussed here.

Elsewhere the author (Mikulas, 1972a, p. 9) has argued that "The assumption of psychology is that there is a set of laws that describes factors that determine a person's behavior. If a person's behavior is changed, regardless of what the procedure is called (e.g., behavior modification, analysis, influence, nondirective counseling), the change must be based on these laws. And the closer the treatment program comes to utilizing these laws, the more effective it is. It is not known exactly what these basic laws are, but the experimental psychologist believes that the information from the experimental laboratory is the best approximation we have at present."

Cognitions as Mediators

Having made the preceding generalizations about cognitive change and behavior change, we can now qualify some of the points with the following useful (albeit oversimplified) discussion of the possible role of cognitions as mediators in response chains. Here we will speak of cognitions as responses when more technically we mean the processes which are the substrates of the subjective cognitions.

We can think of the behavior of a person as being the end of a chain of responses initiated by the stimulus situation. That is, the initial stimuli elicit some response which leads to a second response which leads to a third response and so forth through the nervous system, until we come to the final behaviors. (The reader might prefer to use some other word than "response" for such mediating chains; the terminology is not important here.) This response chain will generally have several branches that produce different overt behaviors, as well as side branches which do not lead to overt behavior. If a cognition is a link in a direct path leading to a specific overt behavior, then altering the cognition may break the chain and alter the behavior. However, the cognition may be part of a chain that does not lead to an overt behavior, in which case altering the cognition will not change any overt behaviors. Or the cognition may be a link in chains for some behaviors, such as verbal behavior, but not be a link in the chain for the behavior we wish to alter. To the extent that this analogy is correct, it is not surprising that changing cognitions will seldom change a range of overt behaviors.

Two actual case examples will illustrate the different roles of cognitions as mediators. The first case was a young man who had a phobia about being around more than one or two people and an unrealistic fear of social criticism. When in the presence of a number of people, he became anxious. The anxiety then led to cognitions about social criticism. After desensitization eliminated the anxiety, the related cognitions dropped out, as the chain was broken. Between treatment sessions the subject often found himself in the presence of a number of people without realizing that this was a situation that used to cause anxiety. In this case, simply altering the cognitions would not have helped the anxiety, since it was the anxiety that produced the cognitions.

A second, somewhat similar, case involved a female secretary who had irrational fears concerning people talking about her. A group of her co-workers standing by someone's desk elicited the cognition "They are talking about me," which then elicited anxiety. In her case, simply eliminating the anxiety would not alter the cognitions. Therefore the behavioral technique of coverant control was used to alter the unwanted thoughts; this broke the chain and eliminated the anxiety.

In practice, response chains are not as simple as they might appear from the preceding discussion, and most cases are not as simplistic as the two given as examples. Rather, a good practitioner would often use a combination of techniques, such as desensitization and coverant control. Overall it seems that cognitions more often change following changes in overt behaviors than the other way around.

Earlier it was mentioned that thoughts could be altered by coverant control. This approach is based on the logic that a thought is a response that follows the same laws of conditioning as any other response. The main difference is that it is a covert rather than an overt response. The word "coverant" is a contraction of "covert operant" and *coverant control* is the application of operant conditioning to thoughts (Homme, 1965; Mahoney, 1970). By systematically reinforcing desired thoughts to occur in specific situations, we can replace undesired thoughts with desired thoughts. This is often worth doing just for itself, as with a depressive person who continually has negative thoughts about himself. To the extent that some of the undesired thoughts lead to undesired behaviors, coverant control may break the response chain.

It is also possible to use respondent conditioning procedures to alter the affect elicited by thoughts or words (DiCaprio, 1970; Hekmat & Vanian, 1971). This again may be a useful way to break response chains.

Behavior modification is increasingly developing procedures that alter behavior by breaking the response chain at some point *before* the final behavior is reached. This gives more generality to the treatment procedures as well as laying the groundwork for teaching people self-control over many different problematic behaviors, for self-control is very often merely the ability to alter a response chain before the overt behaviors occur. Moving back in the response chain may also provide a basis for synthesis between behavior modification and some cognitive theories, if such a synthesis is desired.

Changing the Behavioral System

Earlier it was argued that changing the cognitive system generally is ineffective in changing the behavioral system. The next question is whether changing the behavioral system produces changes in the cognitive system. The answer appears to be yes, often.

Ayllon and Michael (1959) treated a female patient who refused to eat and who made delusional statements such as that the food was poisoned. Treatment consisted of the staff's spilling food on her when she was spoon-fed and reinforcing her when she fed herself. Although no attempt was made to deal directly with her delusions, they disappeared as she began to feed herself and found that she was not poisoned.

Cautela (1965) described three cases in which desensitization was used to treat phobias. Although Cautela made no attempt to make the patient aware of the etiology of his anxiety, the patient gave "insightful-like" statements as the desensitization became effective. In one case a 29 year old nurse felt great anxiety when in social situations, but had no idea what caused the fear. Near the end of the desensitization to social situations she "realized" her fear was that people would think she was emotionally unstable because she came from a broken home. It may be unimportant whether this is a "valid" insight, since following treatment she was functioning adequately.

In an extensive study Bandura, Blanchard, and Ritter (1969) treated snake phobias with various combinations of desensitization and modeling. Although no attempt was made to deal directly with attitudes, attitudes were assessed by general attitude scales and adjective rating scales. As the treatment procedures altered the subjects' phobic behavior, there was a corresponding change in the subjects' attitudes toward snakes, which became more favorable.

The three studies just discussed are a sample of a number of reports suggesting that changing the behavioral system often changes the cognitive system. Exactly why and in which situations this happens is not known, although it may be nothing more than generalization from the responses of the assumed behavioral system to those responses presumed to measure cognitions. Another theory is that getting the person to behave in a new way may provide a set of new learning experiences that alters the cognitions.

It is likely that there is a psychological need for consistency between cognitions and behaviors. Since the behavioral system is generally dominant to the cognitive system, when there is a discrepancy between cognitions and behaviors it is the cognitions that usually change to match the behaviors. If a person has a snake phobia and negative attitudes toward snakes, simply changing his attitudes will create a discrepancy between his new attitudes and his old phobic behavior. This discrepancy will be reduced by the attitudes changing back to match the phobic behavior. However, as described in a study above, if the phobic *behavior* is changed, the discrepancy between attitudes and behaviors will cause the attitudes to change to match the new behaviors. An interesting question is whether this postulated psychological need to reduce the discrepancy between cognitions and behaviors is a learned need.

Along this line the human mind has a tendency to construct reasons for behaviors that are better explained in other ways. Delgado (1969, p. 115) describes a patient who was forced to turn his head by electrical stimulation of a part of the brain called the internal capsule. Although the stimulation produced simple movement, the patient seemed to need to justify why he was turning his head: "I am looking for my slippers," "I heard a noise," or "I was looking under the bed." It may be that the stimulation elicited hallucinations, but more probably the cognitive system had to "justify" activities of the behavioral system.

When the author was a graduate student, he and other students conditioned one of the Michigan psychology faculty, such conditioning being a popular pastime among psychology students around the country. When the professor was in one half of the room the students were somewhat more attentive and interested, took more notes, and asked more questions. Because these things were reinforcing to the professor, he spent most of his time lecturing from this half of the room. Then this half of the room divided into two quarters and the professor was reinforced only for being in the quarter nearest the windows. This type of shaping was continued until the professor gave most of his lectures standing right next to the windows. Although this was far from a controlled experiment, a couple of observations are of interest. First, the professor was not aware that he was being conditioned, even after he was told. Second, the professor offered good "reasons" for what he did, such as being able to see the blackboard better from the window wall because it reduced the glare on the board.

The reader might ask himself how many of the reasons we have for our behaviors could simply be justifications for behaviors that are better explained in terms of variables that we are not aware of, and which may be completely unrelated to our reasons.

LEVELS OF FREEDOM

Philosophers and social scientists, among others, have spent considerable time debating whether man has any free will or whether all of his behaviors are completely determined. The issue is unresolvable for the simple reason that anytime someone offers a situation in which a person seems to be acting out of free will it can always be argued that the behavior *is* determined, but that we aren't scientifically sophisticated enough to be able to identify the relevant variables. Apparent acts of volition might be simple illusions, conscious links in a determined mediation chain, or legitimate expressions of free will. Whatever the answer, there is practical value in considering the different levels of freedom.

The lowest level of freedom is that experienced by the person who is a complete pawn of his external environment. His mannerisms, appearance, and philosophy are under the tight control of variables such as social reinforcers and modeling cues. His emotions are outside of his control and are readily elicited by environmental stimuli. His behavior is quite predictable to the trained observer. The highest level of freedom is that of the person whose behavior, as much as possible, is under the control of those internal variables which, rightly or wrongly, are identified with acts of volition. This is the person who is aware of the external influences on his behavior and how they interact with his internal variables to yield his final behavior. This person has learned control over his emotions and can manipulate the environment to alter his own behavior. He is aware of more alternatives and how to take advantage of them. Very few people, of course, exist at either end of this continuum of levels of freedom; most people are somewhere in-between.

I do not mean to argue that as a person moves into higher levels of freedom his behavior is less determined (although this may be true). The behavior might be just as determined, but the relevant variables may be more internal than external; the determined mediating chains may be more complex; different parts of the mediating chain may be gaining access to consciousness; or the mind may be creating an illusion. Skinner (1971, 1972) argues that variables inside the person follow the same deterministic laws of behavior as variables outside the person. The important point, however, is that many people value moving toward higher levels of freedom. At these higher levels many people feel more free and autonomous, and hence happier. Therapy and many religions are often aimed at helping the person reach higher levels of freedom.

In a therapy situation a person is often at such a low level of freedom that he feels completely overwhelmed and often isn't really sure what he wants. As a crude parallel the reader might consider how his own thinking effectiveness is impaired when he is absorbed in a problem that makes him quite anxious. A person at a low level of freedom cannot adequately introspect, make important decisions, or objectively observe his own behavior. Environmental control over his actions, emotions, and thoughts is too strong. Therefore he is a poor candidate for cognitively oriented therapies such as existential psychology or non-directive approaches.

Behavior modification, however, may be used to raise a person into higher levels of freedom, for such modification is geared toward dealing with the variables that control behavior, and the locus of control can easily be switched from external to internal variables. That is, through behavior modification a person whose behaviors were under undesired environmental control can learn self-control of these same behaviors (see Goldfried & Merbaum, 1973). A person who feels uncontrolled anxiety in certain situations can with behavior modification learn to eliminate this anxiety and feel relaxed in the same situations. A person who does not have the "will power" to keep from overeating can, through behavior modification, learn self-control of his eating, whereas before his eating was controlled by the environment.

Thus behavior modification is probably the most effective way for moving toward higher levels of freedom. When the subject reaches a high enough level of freedom, the therapist may wish to interweave a cognitively oriented therapy, although it is not always clear when, how, or why this should be done.

Similarly many people who wish to evolve as individuals or explore the reaches of their consciousness are not at a level of freedom where this is possible. The environment exerts too much control over their thoughts and behaviors. There are innumerable free-thinking, liberated, unbiased, mind-exploring individuals who look, talk, live, and think essentially just like their free-thinking, liberated, unbiased, mind-exploring friends. They may be spinning their wheels until they move into a higher level of freedom.

STATES OF CONSCIOUSNESS

Consciousness is often considered a relatively unitary phenomenon. However, some researchers such as Tart (1972a, 1972b) argue that there are qualitatively different states of consciousness. According to Tart, a state of consciousness is an "overall patterning of psychological functioning." Although properties of different states of consciousness may overlap, Tart suggests that significantly different states may result from a variety of different situations, including sleep, hypnosis, meditation, and being under the influence of such drugs as alcohol, marijuana, and LSD.

According to Tart, the laws of one state do not necessarily apply in another state. That is, the principles of one state of consciousness, such as principles of organization, information-processing, and subjective experience, may be qualitatively different from the corresponding principles in a different state of consciousness. Thus it would be difficult, if not impossible, to "understand" or "explain" the nature of one state of consciousness from the perspective of a different state of consciousness. This results in what Tart calls *state-specific sciences*, sciences based entirely on the principles of one relatively common state of consciousness. Within our Western scientific tradition the "ordinary-consciousness science" is the only state-specific science we have developed, although there have been some attempts to chart the properties of different states of consciousness (Fischer, 1971; Tart, 1969).

There is considerable evidence that different states of consciousness do exist. There are the reports of people such as mystics and drug users who claim to have experienced qualitatively different states of consciousness. Aldous Huxley (1954) graphically described his early experiences with the hallucinogenic drug mescaline. Huxley also often put himself into different states of consciousness, including one he called "Deep Reflection" (Erickson, 1965). Much of Huxley's creative work was done while he was in these different states.

Other possible evidence of different states of consciousness comes from our attempts to understand the nature of such phenomena as sleep and dreams. Psychotherapists and occultists, among others, have struggled to learn the laws and meanings of the sleep-dream state. The current explosion of drug usage, particularly marijuana, has filled our culture with psychological perspectives and attitudes, styles of dress and behavior, and humor that "fit" better into the marijuana state than into the traditional consciousness state. Some forms of music, such as acid rock, are created by, performed by, intended for, and best liked by drug users.

It may be that there is just one general form of consciousness which underlies *all* of the different states of consciousness. These states then are simply slices of the whole which seem qualitatively different because we do not understand or perceive the general continuums that underlie them. However, even if this is true, it may still be useful to talk in terms of different states.

Many reasons have been offered for why it is desirable to experience different states of consciousness. For some people it is another window through which to view an ultimate reality underlying all consciousness. For others it is a way of gaining new perspectives on some part of life and experiencing new ways of thinking and perceiving. For some, like Huxley, it facilitates creativity.

Robert Louis Stevenson commanded the "brownies" of his mind to furnish him with stories while he slept. Poincaré described mathematical ideas rising in clouds while he lay in bed awaiting sleep. Kekule developed his theory of molecular constitution as the result of images he had during dreamlike reveries (Green et al., 1971).

Green, Green, and Walters (1971) have observed that experienced meditators often generate theta waves in their EEG when in a state of reverie. Believing that a state of reverie is associated with creativity, they hope to train people to be more creative by teaching them to put themselves in the state associated with low frequency alpha and theta waves and to learn to use the experiences that they encounter in this state.

MENTAL ILLNESS AS A STATE OF CONSCIOUSNESS

The concept of mental illness is a social-political fiction. There is no such thing as a person who *is* mentally ill; there are only people who *behave* in ways that deviate enough from a culture's norms that the culture classifies them as mentally ill. The arbitrariness of this approach may be seen in cultural anthropology, which shows that for almost any behavior that our culture considers mentally ill or abnormal there exists (or has existed) a culture where the same behavior is the norm or is highly esteemed. Homosexuality is generally considered abnormal or perverse in our culture, but in some of the early Greek cultures it was considered superior to heterosexuality. Cannibalism is an abnormality in our culture, but not in the New Guinea culture discussed in Chapter Five. Most of the major religious leaders of the past, if they threatened our society today, would probably be put into mental hospitals.

With the exception of people whose abnormal behavior is due to major organic dysfunction, just about anyone who is classified as mentally ill is a person who, because of his particular conditioning history, has learned a set of behaviors that the people in power consider abnormal. Treatment, then, should consist of providing a controlled set of new learning experiences, as with behavior modification, so that the person learns behaviors that the society considers normal. Such an approach, as is true of any treatment, counseling, or influence, raises ethical questions about altering a person's behavior toward arbitrary norms.

It is also possible that many people who are called mentally ill have experienced different states of consciousness. If they could utilize these experiences and perhaps integrate them into the "ordinary conscious" state, then they might be artists, mystics, prophets, or play some other social role within the range of "normalcy." However, if they are overwhelmed by their experiences in the different states or have trouble moving back into the ordinary consciousness, they may be considered mentally ill.

Barron (1972) has shown a number of similarities between creative people and schizophrenics. He found that creative writers are unusually open to non-rational experiences. Half of the male writers he studied reported sensory experiences of things that weren't there. Half of all the writers reported intense experiences of mystical communion. Twenty per cent of the writers reported dreams that proved prophetic. When given the Minnesota Multiphasic Personality Inventory (MMPI), the writers were well above the general population on measures of schizophrenic tendency and depression, moderately high on measures of hysteria and psychopathic deviation, but also well above average in ego strength. Barron found that creative artists and schizophrenics both report odd sensations such as ringing in the ears or peculiar odors, high levels of tension and restlessness, and a proneness to impulsive outbursts. However, creative artists "seem to be able to incorporate psychotic-like experiences and tendencies in a matrix of rationality, very high conceptual intelligence, honesty, and personal effectiveness."

Many of the proponents of the *radical therapies* (see Ruitenbeek, 1972), particularly under the influence of R. D. Laing (1967), view many forms of mental illness as an adventure into a different state of consciousness. Treatment, according to Laing and his supporters, should not consist of trying to force a person right back into ordinary consciousness; rather, the person should be helped and guided during his journey in inner space so that he is not overcome but profits from his experiences in this state. Then the person is gradually guided back to ordinary consciousness, hopefully in a way that facilitates the integration of the different states.

LEVELS OF CONSCIOUSNESS

Does it make any sense to say that one state or level of consciousness is "higher" than another? Perhaps not, but many psychologists, mystics, and theologians explicitly or implicitly assume that the different levels of consciousness can be rank-ordered along some dimension of importance. Maslow (1970) describes "plateau-experiences" and "peak-experiences" that correspond to different levels of consciousness. A *plateau-experience* is a feeling of exceptional serenity and calm, usually with a cognitive element. It may involve marvelling and enjoying a simple experience in a new way. Plateau-experiences may be achieved through hard work and require the experience of living. A *peak-experience* is an exceptional, emotional, climactic experience. It may have no cognitive element but be purely emotional. It is a "first-time" experience, a rebirth. During a peak-experience the person may perceive the universe as a unified whole. Maslow believed that other high-level conscious experiences, such as mystical experiences, are examples of peak-experiences interpreted within a particular framework such as religion.

Maslow considered it important and desirable that an individual have plateau-experiences and hopefully peak-experiences. However, he was not particularly enlightening on how to attain these experiences. Perhaps a first step would be raising a person's level of freedom.

DeRopp (1968, p. 51) offers the following five approximate levels of consciousness, which correspond closely to levels of consciousness proposed by many other writers in this area:
1. Deep sleep without dreams
2. Sleep with dreams
3. Waking sleep (identification)
4. Self-transcendence (self-remembering)
5. Objective consciousness (cosmic consciousness)

Waking sleep is the ordinary state of consciousness in which man is lost in whatever he happens to be doing, feeling, and thinking. At this level man has no inner unity or real will; he is at one of the lower levels of freedom. Some people are able to move into the next higher level of consciousness — self-transcendence — in which they discover their selves, have an objective awareness of self, and feel a detachment from the physical body. At the highest level of consciousness, objective consciousness, one becomes conscious of the cosmos and experiences an apparent understanding of the life and order of the universe. This ultimate stage of cosmic consciousness (see Bucke, 1901) is considered by many to be the most important experience that one can have. It is the final goal of many Oriental religions and mystical practices.

A person practicing meditation may try to move into the higher states of consciousness (see Davis, 1962). The following is a possible sequence of stages experienced by a person undergoing one type of meditation. First the meditator learns to control his attention, for example, by focusing it on his breathing. Then he learns to let his "mind" run free without thinking. Here he experiences wide ranges of sensations as he opens the gates of consciousness. Later he learns to "observe" the functioning of his mind—not "think" about it, as only the mind can think. At this point he starts to develop a subjective concept of his self as being different from either his body or his mind. Finally, with much practice and patience, he begins to have glimpses of cosmic consciousness. If the meditator is particularly adept, he will be able to stay in this final state of consciousness for longer and longer periods of time.

THE QUEST

For a multitude of different reasons, a large number of people are involved in the quest of expanding the domain of their consciousness. The composite perceptions and ideas that a person forms from several different states of consciousness may be a better approximation to some ultimate "reality" than the perceptions and ideas from a single state of consciousness.

There are innumerable ways by which people pursue the quest of altered consciousness, including yoga, meditation, hypnosis, mind control, brain wave conditioning, use of hallucinogenic drugs, alchemy, ritualistic magic, and the use of symbol systems such as the Quabalah, Tarot, and I Ching. Different routes are suited for different experiences for different people at different times. Each route has its own unique experiences and traps.

What is common to most of the routes is the assumption that man's consciousness and knowledge may be greatly expanded during adventures through inner space, often guided by an intuitive validity mechanism that helps assign importance to various experiences. Huxley (see introduction to Prabhavananda & Isherwood, 1944) has summarized the Highest Common Factor of many of the routes of the quest into what he calls the *Perennial Philosophy.* As the core of the Perennial Philosophy Huxley gives the following four fundamental doctrines:

> *First:* the phenomenal world of matter and individualized consciousness—the world of things and animals and men and even gods—is the manifestation of a Divine Ground within which all partial realities have their being, and apart from which they would be nonexistent.
> *Second:* human beings are capable of not merely knowing *about* the Divine Ground by inference; they can also realize its existence by a

direct intuition, superior to discursive reasoning. This immediate knowledge unites the knower with that which is known.

Third: man possesses a double nature, a phenomenal ego and an eternal Self, which is the inner man, the spirit, the spark of divinity within the soul. It is possible for a man, if he so desires, to identify himself with the spirit and therefore with the Divine Ground, which is of the same or like nature with the spirit.

Fourth: man's life on earth has only one end and purpose: to identify himself with his eternal Self and so to come to unitive knowledge of the Divine Ground.

Currently one of the more popular routes of the quest is the use of hallucinogenic drugs, although, of course, there are many other reasons why people use these drugs. Much has been written about drug experiences in inner space (Cohen, 1965; Huxley, 1954; Watts, 1962; Weil, 1972). The main advantage of drugs for exploring inner space is the speed with which they get people to states of consciousness they might not be aware of or had trouble reaching by other means. This rate, however, is also the greatest danger: The drugs may cause the user to be bombarded by experiences he cannot handle or assimilate properly. Without proper assimilation, the experiences will be useless in the non-drug state. For this reason many people prefer more systematic and controlled approaches, such as meditation, as ways to move into inner space.

In an important sequence of books, Carlos Castaneda (1969, 1971, 1972) describes his experiences over a period of about 12 years during which he was an apprentice to a Yaqui Indian sorcerer named Don Juan. Through a combination of hallucinogenic drugs and ritualistic magic, Don Juan carefully exposed Castaneda to different states of consciousness in which Castaneda experienced a number of extraordinary phenomena. Castaneda learned that the laws of reality of one state of consciousness do not always correspond to the laws of reality of another state.

We all learn to see the world from one perspective, to see it in one particular way. Don Juan tried to teach Castaneda to perceive without interpretation. To do this he first taught Castaneda other ways to see, from the perspective of other states of consciousness. First Castaneda learned the different realities (or states of consciousness) and the laws that go with them. Later he learned that none of the realities is correct by itself, but that the true reality is a composite, forming a reality basic to all the other realities.

A parallel but less dramatic effect is often reported by users of marijuana. When a person first experiences the effects of marijuana his feelings, perceptions, and thoughts may to a certain extent be outside his control. This is because the skills of ordinary consciousness may not immediately transfer to this novel state, owing to state-dependent learning, if no other reason. However, many experienced users of marijuana gradually learn to function in the marijuana-induced state with the same skills as they use in the ordinary state. They can then keep themselves "straight" at "will" or immerse themselves in a passive experience, to mention just two possibilities. With experience and work, the marijuana user can learn to move freely between the different states, gradually building up a composite reality drawing on the perspectives from both states. Other users of marijuana, however, are content to passively experience the effects of the marijuana-induced state without learning how to use the state for their advantage.

SUMMARY

Of the many behavioral differences that have been proposed for man versus the other animals, one of the major differences centers around man's use of *language*. Although animals such as chimpanzees are capable of learning to use a language in ways very similar to man, only man naturally makes extensive use of symbolic languages. This use of language has created *cultures* which store what men learn, build upon this information, and socialize and condition the members of the culture, causing human evolution to be more cultural than biological.

One of the proposed differences between man and the other animals is based on the nature of *consciousness*, much of which in man is internalized language. Consciousness is a nebulous, poorly defined construct referring to a subjective experience within an organism; it is some form of awareness of external and internal events. Any person can know only about his own experiences and can only assume that at least some other people have similar experiences, without ever being absolutely sure of this assumption. It is also not clear what function, if any, consciousness serves. This is illustrated by the unresolved *mind-body problem*, which questions the relationship between the mind — an entity with no substance which thinks and is conscious — and the body, which is the substance underlying the form and figure of the person. How can two such different entities influence one another?

Introspection, or looking inward, is a popular but unreliable way of studying consciousness, for introspection yields "memory" images that could not have been observed, as well as distorted information and images and thoughts that are simple conditioned responses. Much of thinking and general information processing of the brain appears to be based on mediated chains of associations, some of which may or may not have conscious elements.

If we cannot be sure whether another person has consciousness (we can only extrapolate from the way they act and what they say), we certainly cannot know whether animals have consciousness. However, some people argue that only man has a nervous system that is complex enough for consciousness, while others argue that consciousness occurs in varying degrees in animals, depending on the complexity of the nervous system. Physiological studies suggest that each of the two hemispheres of the brain of man is capable of some form of consciousness, although usually only the left hemisphere has much language-related consciousness. Other human physiological studies, such as those with subjects with frontal cortex damage, may help to determine where different aspects of consciousness are localized.

Much of human learning takes place without awareness, which is necessary since a person could not attend to and be conscious of everything that he learns. Similarly many behaviors that may have at one time demanded awareness, such as the mechanics of driving a car, eventually no longer require awareness, except at special times. Considerable research relating awareness and learning has been done in the area of verbal conditioning, where there is controversy over whether or not awareness is necessary for conditioning. A major problem has been to develop and implement a procedure for assessing awareness which is sensitive enough to detect awareness when it occurs but does not itself make the subject aware. Another problem is that many experiments have correlated changes in awareness with changes in *performance,* which may not tell us how awareness relates to *learning.* Overall the evidence suggests that it is possible for verbal conditioning to take place without the subject's being aware of the learning contingencies.

For purposes of discussion we may think of there being two different systems interacting in human activity: (1) a *behavioral system* which includes the output of the person—what he does both skeletally and autonomically, as well as overtly and covertly; and (2) a *cognitive system* involving the conscious experience that accompanies and perhaps precedes behavior, including such constructs as consciousness, awareness, insight, and the evaluative component of attitudes. The major question is whether changes in one of the systems produce changes in the other system. Changing the cognitive system, as by changing attitudes or by insight-oriented psychotherapy, seems an ineffective way to change behaviors other than those behaviors used as measures of the cognitions. The exception is when the cognitive changes alter a *mediation chain* that leads to a number of different behaviors. On the other hand, changing the behavioral system often produces changes in the cognitive system, perhaps because the behavioral system is dominant to the cognitive system.

It appears that there exist qualitatively different *states of consciousness* which result from procedures such as sleep, meditation, and the use of certain drugs. Although the different states may overlap in their properties, they are based on different overall patternings of psychological functioning. Because of these differences, the laws based on our ordinary consciousness may not apply to the other states of consciousness. It is also possible that some forms of creativity and mental illness may be related to experiences in other states of consciousness. Experiencing different states is sought by many people as a way to broaden their perspectives about some underlying reality.

Psychologists, mystics, and theologians also speak of different *levels* of consciousness, the highest level being cosmic consciousness in which one experiences an apparent understanding of the order of the universe. People who purport to have experienced higher levels of consciousness argue for the value of such experiences in many areas, including improvement of psychological functioning and religious understanding.

SUGGESTED READINGS

Lilly, J. C. *The Center of the Cyclone.* New York: Julian Press, 1972.
Munn, N. L. *The Evolution of the Human Mind.* Boston: Houghton-Mifflin, 1971.
Ornstein, R. E. (ed.) *The Nature of Human Consciousness.* San Francisco: W. H. Freeman, 1973.
Ornstein, R. E. *The Psychology of Consciousness.* San Francisco: W. H. Freeman, 1972.
Razran, G, *Mind in Evolution.* Boston: Houghton Mifflin, 1971.
Tart, C. T. (ed.) *Altered States of Consciousness.* New York: Wiley, 1969.
Wooldridge, D. E. *Mechanical Man.* New York: McGraw-Hill, 1968.

Adams, H. B. A case utilizing sensory deprivation procedures. In Ullmann, L. P., & Krasner, L. (eds.) *Case studies in Behavior Modification.* New York: Holt, Rinehart & Winston, 1965.

Adams, J. A. Response feedback and learning. *Psychological Bulletin, 70:*486–504, 1968.

Agranoff, B. W. Memory and protein synthesis. *Scientific American,* June, 1967.

Albert, D. J. Memory in mammals: evidence for a system involving nuclear ribonucleic acid. *Neuropsychologia, 4:* 79–93, 1966.

Allport, G. W., & Postman, L. F. The basic psychology of rumor. *Transactions of the New York Academy of Sciences, Series II, 8:*61–81, 1945.

Annett, J. *Feedback and Human Behavior.* Baltimore: Penguin, 1969.

Armus, H. L. Conditioning of the sensitive plant, *Mimosa pudica.* Unpublished manuscript.

Aronson, E. *The Social Animal.* San Francisco: W. H. Freeman, 1972.

Atkinson, R. C. Computerized instruction and the learning process. *American Psychologist, 23:* 225–239, 1968.

Ausubel, D. P., Stager, M., & Gaite, A. J. H. Retroactive facilitation in meaningful verbal learning. *Journal of Educational Psychology, 59:*250–255, 1968.

Ayllon, T., & Azrin, N. H. Punishment as a discriminative stimulus and conditioned reinforcer with humans. *Journal of the Experimental Analysis of Behavior, 9:* 411–419, 1966.

Ayllon, T., & Azrin, N. H. *The Token Economy.* New York: Appleton-Century-Crofts, 1968.

Ayllon, T., & Michael, J. The psychiatric nurse as a behavioral engineer. *Journal of the Experimental Analysis of Behavior, 2:* 323–334, 1959.

Bachrach, A. J. Some applications of operant conditioning to behavior therapy. In Wolpe, J., Salter, A., & Reyna, L. J. (eds.) *The Conditioning Therapies.* New York: Holt, Rinehart & Winston, 1964.

Baddeley, A. D. Retrieval rules and semantic coding in short-term memory. *Psychological Bulletin, 78:*379–385, 1972.

Baer, D. M. Let's take another look at punishment. *Psychology Today,* October, 1971.

Bandura, A., Blanchard, E. B., & Ritter, B. Relative efficacy of desensitization and modeling approaches for inducing behavioral, affective, and attitudinal changes. *Journal of Personality and Social Psychology, 13:* 173–199, 1969.

Barrett, R. J., Leith, N. J., & Ray, O. S. Kamin effect in rats: index of memory or shock-induced inhibition? *Journal of Comparative and Physiological Psychology, 77:* 234–239, 1971.

Barron, F. The creative personality: akin to madness. *Psychology Today,* July, 1972.

Bates, M. *Gluttons and Libertines.* New York: Random House, 1958.

Baum, M. Extinction of avoidance responding through response prevention (flooding). *Psychological Bulletin, 74:* 276–284, 1970.

Berlyne, D. E. *Conflict, Arousal, and Curiosity.* New York: McGraw-Hill, 1960.

Berlyne, D. E. Arousal and reinforcement. In Levine, A. (ed.) *Nebraska Symposium on Motivation.* Lincoln: University of Nebraska Press, 1967.

Best, R. M. Encoding of memory in the neuron. *Psychological Reports, 22*: 107–115, 1968.

Bexton, W. H., Heron, W., & Scott, T. H. Effects of decreased variation in the sensory environment. *Canadian Journal of Psychology, 8*: 70–76, 1954.

Bishop, M. P., Elder, S. T., & Heath, R. G. Intracranial self-stimulation in man. *Science, 140*: 394–396, 1963.

Bodmer, W. F., & Cavalli-Sforza, L. L. Intelligence in race. *Scientific American*, October, 1970.

Bolles, R. C. Interactions with motivation. In Marx, M. H. (ed.) *Learning: Interactions*. Toronto: Macmillan, 1970.

Bolles, R. C. Reinforcement, expectancy, and learning. *Psychological Review, 79*:394–409, 1972.

Booth, D. A. Vertebrate brain nucleic acids and memory retention. *Psychological Bulletin, 68*: 149–177, 1967.

Booth, D. A. Neurochemical changes associated with learning and memory retention. In Ungar, G. (ed.) *Molecular Mechanisms in Memory and Learning*. New York: Plenum Press, 1970.

Bourne, L. E., Jr., Ekstrand, B. R., & Dominowski, R. L. *The Psychology of Thinking*. Englewood Cliffs, N. J.: Prentice-Hall, 1971.

Bovet, D., Bovet-Nitti, F., & Oliverio, A. Genetic aspects of learning and memory in mice. *Science, 163*: 139–149, 1969.

Bower, G. H. How to . . . uh . . . remember! *Psychology Today*, October, 1973.

Bower, G. H., & Miller, N. E. Rewarding and punishing effects from stimulating the same place in the rat's brain. *Journal of Comparative and Physiological Psychology, 51*: 669–674, 1958.

Braud, L. W., & Braud, W. G. Biochemical transfer of relational responding (transposition). *Science, 176*: 942–944, 1972.

Broadbent, D. E. Flow of information within the organism. *Journal of Verbal Learning and Verbal Behavior, 2*: 34–39, 1963.

Broadhurst, P. L. Emotionality and the Yerkes-Dodson law. *Journal of Experimental Psychology, 54*:345–352, 1957.

Brown, J. S. *The Motivation of Behavior*. New York: McGraw-Hill, 1961.

Brown, R., & Lennenberg, E. A study in language and cognition. *Journal of Abnormal and Social Psychology, 49*: 454–462, 1954.

Bruner, J. S. Social psychology and perception. In Maccoby, E. E., Newcomb, T. M., & Hartley, E. L. (eds.) *Readings in Social Psychology*. New York: Holt, Rinehart & Winston, 1958.

Bruner, J. S., & Postman, L. On the perception of incongruity: a paradigm. *Journal of Personality, 18*: 206–223, 1949.

Bucke, R. M. *Cosmic Consciousness*. New York: E. P. Dutton, 1901.

Budzynski, T., Stoyva, J., & Adler, C. Feedback-induced muscle relaxation: application to tension headache. *Journal of Behavior Therapy and Experimental Psychiatry, 1*: 205–211, 1970.

Burns, B. D. The production of afterbursts in isolated unanesthetized cerebral cortex. *Journal of Physiology, 125*: 427–446, 1954.

Butter, M. J. Differential recall of paired associates as a function of arousal and concreteness-imagery levels. *Journal of Experimental Psychology, 84*:252–256, 1970.

Cameron, D. E., & Solyom, L. Effects of ribonucleic acid on memory. *Geriatrics, 16*: 74–81, 1961.

Campbell, B. A., & Church, R. M. (eds.) *Punishment and Aversive Behavior*. New York: Appleton-Century-Crofts, 1969.

Campbell, D., Sanderson, R. E., & Laverty, S. G. Characteristics of a conditioned response in human subjects during extinction trials following a single traumatic conditioning trial. *Journal of Abnormal and Social Psychology, 68*: 627–639, 1964.

Cantor, M. B. Signaled reinforcing brain stimulation facilitates operant behavior under schedules of intermittent reinforcement. *Science, 174*: 610–613, 1971.

Carroll, J. B. (ed.) *Language, Thought, and Reality: Selected Writings of Benjamin Lee Whorf*. Cambridge, Mass.: Massachusetts Institute of Technology Press, 1956.

Castaneda, C. *The Teachings of Don Juan: A Yaqui Way of Knowledge*. New York: Ballantine Books, 1969.

Castaneda, C. *A Separate Reality*. New York: Simon & Schuster, 1971.

Castaneda, C. *Journey to Ixtlan.* New York: Simon & Schuster, 1972.

Cautela, J. H. Desensitization and insight. *Behaviour Research and Therapy, 3:* 59–64, 1965.

Chomsky, N. *Review of Verbal Behavior* by B. F. Skinner. *Language, 35:* 26–58, 1959.

Chorover, S. L., & Schiller, P. H. Reexamination of prolonged retrograde amnesia in one-trial learning. *Journal of Comparative and Physiological Psychology, 61:* 34–41, 1966.

Church, R. M. The varied effects of punishment on behavior. *Psychological Review, 70:* 369–402, 1963.

Clairborn, W. L. Expectancy effects in the classroom: a failure to replicate. *Journal of Educational Psychology, 60:* 377–383, 1969.

Cohen, P. S. Interference effects of escapable shock upon subsequent acquisition of escape-avoidance responding. *Journal of Comparative and Physiological Psychology, 71:* 484–486, 1970.

Cohen, S. *The Beyond Within.* New York: Atheneum Press, 1965.

Cole, M., & Maltzman, I. (eds.) *A Handbook of Contemporary Soviet Psychology.* New York: Brooks Cole, 1969.

Cotter, L. H. Operant conditioning in a Vietnamese mental hospital. *American Journal of Psychiatry, 124:* 23–28, 1967.

Coughlin, R. C., Jr. The aversive properties of withdrawing positive reinforcement: a review of recent literature. *Psychological Reports, 22:* 333–354, 1972.

Cravens, R. W., & Renner, K. E. Conditioned appetitive drive states: empirical evidence and theoretical status. *Psychological Bulletin, 73:* 212–220, 1970.

Damianopoulos, E. N. S-R contiguity and delay of reinforcement as critical parameters in classical aversive conditioning. *Psychological Review, 74:* 420–427, 1967.

Davis, R. E. *This Is Reality.* Lakemont, Georgia: CSA Press, 1962.

Dawson, R. G. Retrograde amnesia and conditioned emotional response incubation reexamined. *Psychological Bulletin, 75:* 278–285, 1971.

Deese, J., & Hulse, S, H, *The Psychology of Learning.* New York: McGraw-Hill, 1967.

Delgado, J. M. R. *Physical Control of the Mind.* New York: Harper & Row, 1969.

Dember, W. N. *The Psychology of Perception.* New York: Holt, Rinehart & Winston, 1960.

Dember, W. N., & Earl, R. W. Analysis of exploratory, manipulatory, and curiosity behavior. *Psychological Review, 64:* 91–96, 1957.

Depue, R. A., & Fowles, D. C. Electrodermal activity as an index of arousal in schizophrenics. *Psychological Bulletin, 79:* 233–238, 1973.

DeRopp, R. S. *The Master Game.* New York: Dell, 1968.

Deutsch, J. A. Neural basis of memory. *Psychology Today,* May, 1968.

Deutsch, J. A. The cholinergic synapse and the site of memory. *Science, 174:* 788–794, 1971.

Deutsch, J. A., & Howarth, C. I. Some tests of a theory of intracranial self-stimulation. *Psychological Review, 70:* 444–460, 1963.

DiCaprio, N. S. Essentials of verbal satiation therapy: a learning-theory–based behavior therapy. *Journal of Counseling Psychology, 70:* 419–424, 1970.

DiCara, L. V. Learning in the autonomic nervous system. *Scientific American,* January, 1970.

Dobzhansky, T. Genetics and the diversity of behavior. *American Psychologist, 27:* 523–530, 1972.

Dollard, J., & Miller, N. E. *Personality and Psychotherapy.* New York: McGraw-Hill, 1950.

Dreyer, P., & Renner, K. E. Self-punitive behavior—masochism or confusion? *Psychological Review, 78:* 333–337, 1971.

Dulany, D. E. Awareness, rules, and propositional control: a confrontation with S-R behavior theory. In Dixon, T. R., & Horton, D. L. (eds.) *Verbal Behavior and General Behavior Theory.* Englewood Cliffs, N. J.: Prentice-Hall, 1968.

Dunham, P. J. Punishment: method and theory. *Psychological Review, 78:* 58–70, 1971.

Dweck, C. S., & Reppucci, N. D. Learned helplessness and reinforcement responsibility in children. *Journal of Personality and Social Psychology, 25:* 109–116, 1973.

Eacker, J. N. On some elementary philosophical problems of psychology. *American Psychologist, 27:* 553–565, 1972.

Eccles, J. C. *The Physiology of Nerve Cells.* Baltimore: Johns Hopkins Press, 1957.

Eccles, J. C. *The Physiology of Synapses.* New York: Academic Press, 1964.

Eccles, J. C. Possible ways in which synaptic mechanisms participate in learning, remembering, and forgetting. In Kimble, D. P. (ed.) *The Anatomy of Memory.* Palo Alto, Calif.: Science and Behavior Books, 1965.

Egger, M. D., & Miller, N. E. Secondary reinforcement in rats as a function of information value and reliability of the stimulus. *Journal of Experimental Psychology, 64*: 97–104, 1962.

Eisenberger, R. Explanation of rewards that do not reduce tissue needs. *Psychological Bulletin, 77*: 319–339, 1972.

Ekstrand, B. R. Backward (R-S) associations. *Psychological Bulletin, 65*: 50–64, 1966.

Erickson, M. H. A special inquiry with Aldous Huxley into the nature and character of various states of consciousness. *American Journal of Clinical Hypnosis, 8*: 17–33, 1965.

Eysenck, H. J. The effects of psychotherapy: an evaluation. *Journal of Consulting Psychology, 16*: 319–324, 1952.

Eysenck, H. J. *The Biological Basis of Personality.* Springfield, Ill.: Charles C Thomas, 1967.

Eysenck, H. J., & Beech, R. Counterconditioning and related methods. In Bergin, A. E., & Garfield, S. L. (eds.) *Handbook of Psychotherapy and Behavior Change: An Empirical Analysis.* New York: Wiley, 1971.

Feldman, R. S., & Green, K. F. Antecedents to behavior fixations. *Psychological Review, 74*: 250–271, 1967.

Ferster, C. B., & Skinner, B. F. *Schedules of Reinforcement.* New York: Appleton-Century-Crofts, 1957.

Festinger, L. Behavioral support for opinion change. *Public Opinion Quarterly, 28*: 404–417, 1964.

Fischer, R. A cartography of the ecstatic and meditative states. *Science, 174*: 897–904, 1971.

Fiske, D. W., & Maddi, S. R. *Functions of Varied Experience.* Homewood, Ill.: Dorsey Press, 1961.

Fjerdingstad, E. J., Nissen, Th., & Røigaard-Petersen, H. H. Effect of ribonucleic acid (RNA) extracted from the brain of trained animals on learning in rats. *Scandinavian Journal of Psychology, 6*: 1–6, 1965.

Flexner, J. B., Flexner, L. B., Stellar, E., de la Haba, G., & Roberts, R. B. Inhibition of protein synthesis in brain and learning and memory following puromycin. *Journal of Neurochemistry, 9*: 595–605, 1962.

Flexner, L. B., & Flexner, J. B. Intracerebral saline: effect on memory of trained mice treated with puromycin. *Science, 159*: 330–331, 1968.

Franks, C. M. Individual differences in conditioning and associated techniques. In Wolpe, J., Salter, A., & Reyna, L. J. (eds.) *The Conditioning Therapies.* New York: Holt, Rinehart & Winston, 1964.

Franks, C. M. Pavlovian conditioning approaches. In Levis, D. J. (ed.) *Learning Approaches to Therapeutic Behavior Change.* Chicago: Aldine, 1970.

Gaito, J. DNA and RNA as memory molecules. *Psychological Review, 70*: 471–480, 1963.

Gaito, J., & Bonnett, K. Quantitative versus qualitative RNA and protein changes in the brain during behavior. *Psychological Bulletin, 75*: 109–127, 1971.

Galambos, R. A glia-neural theory of brain function. *Proceedings of the National Academy of Sciences, 47*: 129–136, 1961.

Gallinek, A. Fear and anxiety in the course of electroshock therapy. *American Journal of Psychiatry, 113*: 428–434, 1956.

Gallistel, C. R. Motivating effects in self-stimulation. *Journal of Comparative and Physiological Psychology, 62*: 95–101, 1966.

Gallup, G. G. Chimps and self-concept. *Psychology Today,* March, 1971.

Garcia, J., & Koelling, R. A. Relation of cue to consequence in avoidance learning. *Psychonomic Science, 4*: 123–124, 1966.

Gardner, R. A., & Gardner, B. T. Teaching sign language to a chimpanzee. *Science, 165*: 664–672, 1969.

Gazzaniga, M. S. The split brain in man. *Scientific American,* February, 1967.

Gellhorn, E., Kessler, M., & Minatoya, H. Influence of Metrazol, insulin, hypoglycemia, and electrically induced convulsions of re-establishment of inhibited conditioned reflexes. *Proceedings of the Society of Experimental Biological Medicine, 50:* 260–262, 1942.

Gibson, E. J. A systematic application of the concepts of generalization and differentiation to verbal learning. *Psychological Review, 47:* 196–229, 1940.

Gibson, E. J. *Principles of Perceptual Learning and Development.* New York: Appleton-Century-Crofts, 1969.

Girden, E., & Culler, E. Conditioned responses in curarized striate muscle in dogs. *Journal of Comparative Psychology, 23:* 261–274, 1937.

Glassman, E. The biochemistry of learning: an evaluation of the role of RNA and protein. *Annual Review of Biochemistry, 38:* 605–646, 1969.

Glickman, S. E., & Schiff, B. B. A biological theory of reinforcement. *Psychological Review, 74:* 81–109, 1967.

Goldfried, M. R., & Merbaum, M. (eds.) *Behavior Change Through Self-Control.* New York: Holt, Rinehart & Winston, 1973.

Goldstein, H., Krantz, D. L., & Rains, J. D. (eds.) *Controversial Issues in Learning.* New York: Appleton-Century-Crofts, 1965.

Goldwater, B. C. Psychological significance of pupillary movements. *Psychological Bulletin, 77:* 340–355, 1972.

Gray, J. *The Psychology of Fear and Stress.* New York: McGraw-Hill, 1971.

Green, A. M., Green, E. E., & Walters, E. D. Psychophysiological training for creativity. Paper presented at American Psychological Association, Washington, D. C., 1971.

Greenspoon, J. The reinforcing effect of two spoken sounds on the frequency of two responses. *American Journal of Psychology, 68:* 409–416, 1955.

Greenspoon, J., & Brownstein, A. J. Awareness in verbal conditioning. *Journal of Experimental Research in Personality, 2:* 295–308, 1967.

Greenwald A G Sensory feedback mechanisms in performance control: with special reference to the ideo-motor mechanism. *Psychological Review, 77:* 73–99, 1970.

Gregory, R. L. *Eye and Brain.* New York: McGraw-Hill, 1966.

Gregory, R. L. Visual illusions. *Scientific American,* November, 1968.

Griffith, J. S., & Mahler, H. R. DNA-ticketing theory of memory. *Nature, 223:* 580–582, 1969.

Grossman, S. P. *A Textbook of Physiological Psychology.* New York: Wiley, 1967.

Gurowitz, E. M. *The Molecular Basis of Memory.* Englewood Cliffs, N. J.: Prentice-Hall, 1969.

Haber, R. N. Nature of the effect of set on perception. *Psychological Review, 73:* 335–351, 1966.

Hailman, J. P. How an instinct is learned. *Scientific American,* December, 1969.

Hake, D. F., & Azrin, N. H. Conditioned punishment. *Journal of the Experimental Analysis of Behavior, 8:* 279–293, 1965.

Hartry, A. L., Keith-Lee, P., & Morton, W. D. Planaria: memory transfer through cannibalism reexamined. *Science, 146:* 274–275, 1964.

Hearn, M. T., & Evans, D. R. Anger and reciprocal inhibition therapy. *Psychological Reports, 30:* 943–948, 1972.

Heath, R. G. Electrical self-stimulation of the brain of man. *American Journal of Psychiatry, 120.* 571–577, 1963.

Hebb, D. O. *Organization of Behavior.* New York: Wiley, 1949.

Hebb, D. O. The distinction between "classical" and "instrumental." *Canadian Journal of Psychology, 10:* 165–166, 1956.

Hebb, D. O. Distinctive features of learning in the higher animal. In Delafresnaye, J. F. (ed.) *Brain Mechanisms and Learning.* London: Oxford University Press, 1961.

Hebb, D. O. Concerning imagery. *Psychological Review, 75:* 466–477, 1968.

Hebb, D. O. The mind's eye. *Psychology Today,* May, 1969.

Hebb, D. O. *Textbook of Psychology.* Philadelphia: W. B. Saunders Company, 1972.

Hekmat, H., & Vanian, D. Behavior modification through covert semantic desensitization. *Journal of Consulting and Clinical Psychology, 36:* 248–251, 1971.

Hendry, D. P. (ed.) *Conditioned Reinforcement.* Homewood, Ill.: Dorsey Press, 1969.

Herrnstein, R. J. Superstition: a corollary of the principle of operant conditioning. In Honig, W. K. (ed.) *Operant Behavior: Areas of Research and Application.* New York: Appleton-Century-Crofts, 1966.

Herrnstein, R. J. Method and theory in the study of avoidance. *Psychological Review, 76:* 49–69, 1969.

Hess, E. H. Imprinting. *Science, 130:* 133–141, 1959.

Hilgard, E. R., & Bower, G. H. *Theories of Learning.* New York: Appleton-Century-Crofts, 1966.

Hobbs, N. Sources of gain in psychotherapy. *American Psychologist, 17:* 741–747, 1962.

Holland, J. G. Teaching machines: an application of principles from the laboratory. *Journal of the Experimental Analysis of Behavior, 3:* 275–287, 1960.

Holmes, T. H., & Masuda, M. Psychosomatic syndrome. *Psychology Today,* April, 1972.

Holz, W. C., & Azrin, N. H. Conditioning human verbal behavior. In Honig, W. K. (ed.) *Operant Behavior: Areas of Research and Application.* New York: Appleton-Century-Crofts, 1966.

Homme, L. E. Perspectives in psychology-XXIV. Control of coverants, the operants of the mind. *Psychological Record, 15:* 501–511, 1965.

Hook, E. B. Behavioral implications of the human XYY genotype. *Science, 179:* 139–150, 1973.

Hoppe, R. A. Religious belief and the learning of paired associates. *Journal of Social Psychology, 78:* 275–279, 1969.

Horn, G., Rose, S. P. R., & Bateson, P. P. G. Experience and plasticity in the central nervous system. *Science, 181:* 506–514, 1973.

Hubel, D. H. The visual cortex of the brain. *Scientific American,* November, 1963.

Hull, C. L. *Principles of Behavior.* New York: Appleton-Century-Crofts, 1943.

Huxley, A. *The Doors of Perception.* New York: Harper & Row, 1954.

Hyden, H. The question of a molecular basis for the memory trace. In Pribram, K. H., & Broadbent, D. C. (eds.) *Biology of Memory.* New York: Academic Press, 1970.

Hyden, H., & Egyhazi, E. Nuclear RNA changes of nerve cells during a learning experiment in rats. *Proceedings of the National Academy of Sciences, 48:* 1366–1373, 1962.

Hyden, H., & Egyhazi, E. Glial RNA changes during a learning experiment with rats. *Proceedings of the National Academy of Sciences, 49:* 618–624, 1963.

Hyden, H., & Egyhazi, E. Changes in RNA and base composition in cortical neurons of rats in a learning experiment involving transfer of handedness. *Proceedings of the National Academy of Sciences, 52:* 1030–1035, 1964.

Ittelson, W. H., & Cantril, H. *Perception: A Transactional Approach.* New York: Doubleday, 1954.

Ittelson, W. H., & Kilpatrick, F. B. Experiments in perception. *Scientific American,* August, 1951.

Jacobs, B. L., & Sorenson, C. A. Memory disruption in mice by brief posttrial immersion in hot or cold water. *Journal of Comparative and Physiological Psychology, 68:* 239–244, 1969.

Jarvik, M. E., & Kopp, R. Transcorneal electroconvulsive shock and retrograde amnesia in mice. *Journal of Comparative and Physiological Psychology, 64:* 431–433, 1967.

John, E. R. High nervous functions: brain functions and learning. *Annual Review of Physiology, 23:* 451–484, 1961.

John, E. R. *Mechanisms of Memory.* New York: Academic Press, 1967.

John, E. R. Switchboard versus statistical theories of learning and memory. *Science, 177:* 850–864, 1972.

John, E. R., Chesser, P., Bartlett, F., & Victor, I. Observation learning in cats. *Science, 159:* 1489–1491, 1968.

John, E. R., Shimokochi, M., & Bartlett, F. Neural readout from memory during generalization. *Science, 164:* 1519–1521, 1969.

Johnston, J. M. Punishment of human behavior. *American Psychologist, 27:* 1033–1054, 1972.

Jones, J. E. Contiguity and reinforcement in relation to CS-UCS intervals in classical aversive conditioning. *Psychological Review, 69:* 176–186, 1962.

Kamin, L. J. Retention of an incompletely learned avoidance response: some further analysis. *Journal of Comparative and Physiological Psychology, 56*: 713–718, 1963.

Kandel, E. R. Nerve cells and behavior. *Scientific American,* August, 1970.

Kandel, E. R., & Spencer, W. A. Cellular neurophysiological approaches in the study of learning. *Physiological Reviews, 48*: 65–134, 1968.

Kandel, E. R., & Tauc, L. Heterosynaptic facilitation in neurons of the abdominal ganglion of Aplysia depilans. *Journal of Physiology, 181*: 1–27, 1965.

Kaplan, B. J. Malnutrition and mental deficiency. *Psychological Bulletin, 78*: 321–334, 1972.

Katkin, E. S. *Instrumental Autonomic Conditioning.* New York: General Learning Press, 1971.

Katz, J. J., & Halstead, W. C. Protein organization and mental function. *Comparative Psychology Monographs, 20*: 1–38, 1950.

Kazdin, A. E., & Bootzin, R. R. The token economy: an evaluative review. *Journal of Applied Behavior Analysis, 5*: 343–372, 1972.

Kelley, H. H. The warm-cold variable in first impressions of persons. *Journal of Personality, 18*: 431–439, 1950.

Kellogg, W. N. Chimpanzees in experimental homes. *Psychological Record, 18*: 489–498, 1968.

Keppel, G. Retroactive and proactive inhibition. In Dixon, T. R., & Horton, D. L. (eds.) *Verbal Behavior and General Behavior Theory.* Englewood Cliffs, N. J.: Prentice-Hall, 1968.

Kettlewell, N. M., & Papsdorf, J. D. The effects of an interpolated ITI stimulus on classical conditioning of the nictitating membrane response of the rabbit. *Psychonomic Science, 9*: 257–258, 1967.

Kimble, D. P. (ed.) *The Anatomy of Memory.* Palo Alto, Calif: Science and Behavior Books, 1965.

Kimble, G. A. *Hilgard and Marquis' Conditioning and Learning.* New York: Appleton Century-Crofts, 1061.

Kimura, D. The asymmetry of the human brain. *Scientific American,* March, 1973.

Kjeldergaard, P. M. Transfer and mediation in verbal learning. In Dixon, T. R., & Horton, D. L. (eds.) *Verbal Behavior and General Behavior Theory.* Englewood Cliffs, N. J.: Prentice-Hall, 1968.

Kleinsmith, L. J., & Kaplan, S. Paired-associate learning as a function of arousal and interpolated interval. *Journal of Experimental Psychology, 65*: 190–193, 1963.

Laing, R. D. *The Politics of Experience.* New York: Ballantine Books, 1967.

Landauer, T. K. Reinforcement as consolidation. *Psychological Review, 76*: 82–96, 1969.

Lang, P. J. The mechanics of desensitization and the laboratory study of fear. In Franks, C. M. (ed.) *Behavior Therapy: Appraisal and Status.* New York: McGraw-Hill, 1969.

Lang, P. J. Autonomic control. *Psychology Today,* October, 1970.

Lang, P. J., & Buss, A. H. Psychological deficit in schizophrenia. II. Interference and activation. *Journal of Abnormal Psychology, 70*: 77–106, 1965.

Lashley, K. S. In search of the engram. *Symposia of the Society for Experimental Biology, 4*: 454–482, 1950.

Lawick-Goodall, J. van. *In the Shadow of Man.* Boston: Houghton-Mifflin, 1971.

Lenzer, I. Differences between behavior reinforced by electrical stimulation of the brain and conventionally reinforced behavior: an associative analysis. *Psychological Review, 78*: 103–118, 1972.

Lett, B. T. Delayed reward learning: disproof of the traditional theory. *Learning and Motivation, 4*: 237–246, 1973.

Lewis, D. J. Sources of experimental amnesia. *Psychological Review, 76*: 461–472, 1969.

Liddell, H. S. *Emotional Hazards in Animals and Men.* Springfield, Ill.: Charles C Thomas, 1956.

Lloyd, D. P. C. Post-tetanic potentiation of response in monosynaptic reflex pathways of the spinal cord. *Journal of General Physiology, 33*: 147–170, 1949.

Locke, E. A., Cartledge, N., & Koeppel, J. Motivational effects of knowledge of results: a goal-setting phenomenon? *Psychological Bulletin, 70*: 474–485, 1968.

Logan, F. A. A micromolar approach to behavior theory. *Psychological Review, 63*: 63–73, 1956.

LoLordo, V. M. Positive conditioned reinforcement from aversive situations. *Psychological Bulletin, 72*: 193–203, 1969.

London, P. *Behavior Control*. New York: Harper & Row, 1969.

Lorente de No, R. Analysis of the activity of the chains of internuncial neurons. *Journal of Neurophysiology, 1*: 207–244, 1938.

Ludwig, A. M. Relationship of attitude to behavior: preliminary results and implications for treatment evaluation studies. In Shlien, J. M. (ed.) *Research in Psychotherapy, Vol. 3.* Washington, D. C.: American Psychological Association, 1968.

Luttges, M., Johnson, T., Buck, C., Holland, J., & McGaugh, J. An examination of "transfer of learning" by nucleic acid. *Science, 151*: 834–837, 1966.

Lynch, J., & Paskewitz, D. On the mechanisms of the feedback control of human brain wave activity. *Journal of Nervous and Mental Disease, 153*: 205–217, 1971.

MacCorquodale, K. B. F. Skinner's *Verbal Behavior:* a retrospective appreciation. *Journal of the Experimental Analysis of Behavior, 12*: 831–841, 1969.

Maddi, S. R. Exploratory behavior and variation-seeking in man. In Fiske, D. W., & Maddi, S. R. (eds.) *Functions of Varied Experience.* Homewood, Ill.: Dorsey Press, 1961.

Madsen, C. H., Jr., Becker, W. C., & Thomas, D. R. Rules, praise, and ignoring: elements of elementary control. *Journal of Applied Behavior Analysis, 1*: 139–150, 1968.

Mahoney, M. J. Toward an experimental analysis of coverant control. *Behavior Therapy, 1*: 510–521, 1970.

Maier, N. R. F. *Frustration*. New York: McGraw-Hill, 1949.

Malmo, R. B. Measurement of drive: an unsolved problem in psychology. In Jones, M. R. (ed.) *Nebraska Symposium on Motivation.* Lincoln: University of Nebraska Press, 1963.

Maltzman, I., Kantor, W., & Langdon, B. Immediate and delayed retention, arousal, and the orienting and defensive reflexes. *Psychonomic Science, 6*: 445–446, 1966.

Mandell, A. J., Segal, D. S., Kuczenski, R. T., & Knapp, S. The search for the schizococcus. *Psychology Today,* October, 1972.

Marlatt, G. A. Task structure and the experimental modification of verbal behavior. *Psychological Bulletin, 78*: 335–350, 1972.

Martin, E. Verbal learning theory and independent retrieval phenomena. *Psychological Review, 78*: 314–332, 1971.

Maslow, A. H. *Religions, values, and peak-experiences.* New York: Viking Press, 1970.

Massaro, D. W. Preperceptual images, processing time, and perceptual units in auditory perception. *Psychological Review, 79*: 124–145, 1972.

Masserman, J. H. The neurotic cat. *Psychology Today,* November, 1967.

Masters, W. H., & Johnson, V. E. *Human Sexual Inadequacy.* Boston: Little, Brown & Co., 1970.

McConnell, J. V. Memory transfer through cannibalism in planarians. *Journal of Neuropsychiatry, 3*: 42–48, 1962.

McConnell, J. V., & Shelby, J. M. Memory transfer experiments in invertebrates. In Ungar, G. (ed.) *Molecular Mechanisms in Memory and Learning.* New York: Plenum Press, 1970.

McGaugh, J. L. Time-dependent processes in memory storage. *Science, 153*: 1351–1358, 1966.

McGaugh, J. L., & Herz, M. J. *Memory Consolidation.* San Francisco: Albion, 1972.

McGaugh, J. L., & Petrinovich, L. F. Effects of drugs on learning and memory. *International Review of Neurobiology, 8*: 139–191, 1965.

McGeoch, J. A. *The Psychology of Human Learning.* New York: Longmans, 1942.

Mednick, S. A. Birth defects and schizophrenia. *Psychology Today,* April, 1971.

Melton, A. W. Implications of short-term memory for a general theory of memory. *Journal of Verbal Learning and Verbal Behavior, 2*: 1–21, 1963.

Melton, A. W., & Irwin, J. McQ. The influence of degree of interpolated learning on retroactive inhibition and the overt transfer of specific responses. *American Journal of Psychology, 53*: 173–203, 1940.

Mikulas, W. L. Awareness and verbal conditioning. *Psychological Reports, 26*: 472, 1970a.

Mikulas, W. L. Interactions of attitudes and associative interference in classroom learning. *Journal of Experimental Education, 39*: 49–55, 1970b.

Mikulas, W. L. *Behavior Modification: An Overview.* New York: Harper & Row, 1972a.

Mikulas, W. L. Criticisms of behavior therapy. *Canadian Psychologist, 13*: 83–104, 1972b.

Mikulas, W. L., & Isaacson, R. L. Impairment and perseveration in delayed tasks due to bilateral lesions of the caudate nucleus in rats. *Psychonomic Science, 3*: 485–486, 1965.

Miller, G. A. The magical number seven, plus or minus two: some limits on our capacity for processing information. *Psychological Review, 63*: 81–97, 1956.

Miller, G. A., Galanter, E. H., & Pribram, K. H. *Plans and the Structure of Behavior.* New York: Holt, Rinehart & Winston, 1960.

Miller, N. E. Liberalization of basic S-R concepts: Extensions to conflict behavior, motivation, and social learning. In Koch, S. (ed.) *Psychology, A Study of a Science, Vol. 2.* New York: McGraw-Hill, 1959.

Miller, N. E. Implications for theories of reinforcement. In Sheer, D. E. (ed.) *Electrical Stimulation of the Brain.* Austin: University of Texas Press, 1961.

Miller, N. E. Some reflections on the law of effect produce a new alternative to drive reduction. In Jones, M. R. (ed.) *Nebraska Symposium on Motivation.* Lincoln: University of Nebraska Press, 1963.

Miller, N. E. Learning of visceral and glandular responses. *Science, 163*: 434–445, 1969.

Miller, N. E., & Dollard, J. C. *Social Learning and Imitation.* New Haven: Yale University Press, 1941.

Miller, R. R., & Springer, A. D. Amnesia, consolidation, and retrieval. *Psychological Review, 80*: 69–79, 1973.

Milner, B. Some effects of frontal lobectomy in man. In Warren, J. M., & Akert, K. (eds.) *The Frontal Granular Cortex and Behavior.* New York: McGraw-Hill, 1964.

Milner, P. M. The cell assembly: Mark II. *Psychological Review, 64*: 242–257, 1957.

Moan, C. E., & Heath, R. G. Septal stimulation for the initiation of heterosexual behavior in a homosexual male. *Journal of Behavior Therapy and Experimental Psychiatry, 3*: 23–30, 1972.

Montagu, A. Chromosomes and crime. *Psychology Today,* October, 1968.

More, A. J. Delay of feedback and the acquisition and retention of verbal materials in the classroom. *Journal of Educational Psychology, 60*: 339–342, 1969.

Morganstern, K. P. Implosive therapy and flooding procedures: a critical review. *Psychological Bulletin, 79*: 318–334, 1973.

Morrell, F. Electrophysiological contributions to the neural basis of learning. *Physiological Reviews, 41*: 443–494, 1961.

Mowrer, O. H. On the dual nature of learning—a re-interpretation of "conditioning" and "problem-solving." *Harvard Educational Review, 17*: 102–148, 1947.

Munn, N. L. *The Evolution of the Human Mind.* Boston: Houghton-Mifflin, 1971.

Nebylitsyn, V. D., & Gray, J. A. (eds.) *Biological Bases of Individual Behavior.* New York: Academic Press, 1972.

Nielson, H. C. Evidence that electroconvulsive shock alters memory retrieval rather than memory consolidation. *Experimental Neurology, 20*: 3–20, 1968.

Nodine, C. F. Temporal variables in paired-associate learning: the law of contiguity revisited. *Psychological Review, 76*: 351–362, 1969.

Norman, D. A. *Memory and Attention.* New York: Wiley, 1969.

Ochs, S. *Elements of Neurophysiology.* New York: Wiley, 1965.

O'Leary, K. D., & Drabman, R. Token economy programs in the classroom: a review. *Psychological Bulletin, 75*: 379–398, 1971.

Olds, J. Hypothalamic substrates of reward. *Physiological Reviews, 42*: 554–604, 1962.

Olds, J., & Milner, P. Positive reinforcement produced by electrical stimulation of septal area and other regions of rat brain. *Journal of Comparative and Physiological Psychology, 47*: 419–427, 1954.

Ornstein, R. E. Right and left thinking. *Psychology Today,* May, 1973.

Ost, J. W. Consolidation disruption and inhibition in classical conditioning. *Psychological Bulletin, 72*: 379–383, 1969.

Overmier, J. B., & Seligman, M. E. P. Effects of inescapable shock upon subsequent escape and avoidance responding. *Journal of Comparative and Physiological Psychology, 63*: 28–33, 1967.

Overton, D. High education. *Psychology Today,* November, 1969.

Owen, D. R. The 47, XYY male: a review. *Psychological Bulletin, 78*: 209–233, 1972.

Paivio, A. Mental imagery in associative learning and memory. *Psychological Review, 76*: 241–263, 1969.

Penfield, W. The permanent record of the stream of consciousness. *Proceedings of the 14th International Congress of Psychology,* 1954, pp. 47–69.

Penfield, W., & Jasper, H. *Epilepsy and the Functional Anatomy of the Brain.* Boston: Little, Brown & Co., 1954.

Peterson, L. R. Short term verbal memory and learning. *Psychological Review, 73*: 193–207, 1966.

Pevzner, L. Z. Nucleic acid changes during behavioral events. In Gaito, J. (ed.) *Macromolecules and Behavior.* New York: Appleton-Century-Crofts, 1966.

Pomerantz, J. R., Kaplan, S., & Kaplan, R. Satiation effects in the perception of single letters. *Perception and Psychophysics, 6*: 129–132, 1969.

Prabhavananda, S., & Isherwood, C. *The Song of God: Bhagavad-Gita.* Hollywood, Calif.: Vedanta Society, 1944.

Premack, D. Reinforcement theory. In Levine, D. (ed.) *Nebraska Symposium on Motivation.* Lincoln: University of Nebraska Press, 1965.

Premack, D. A functional analysis of language. *Journal of the Experimental Analysis of Behavior, 14*: 107–125, 1970.

Pribram, K. H. The neurophysiology of remembering. *Scientific American,* January, 1969.

Pribram, K. H. *Languages of the Brain: Experimental Paradoxes and Principles in Neuropsychology.* Englewood Cliffs, N. J.: Prentice-Hall, 1971a.

Pribram, K. H. The brain. *Psychology Today,* September, 1971b.

Pryor, K. Behavior modification: the porpoise caper. *Psychology Today,* December, 1969.

Rachman, S., & Hodgson, R. J. Experimentally induced "sexual fetishism": replication and development. *Psychological Record, 18*: 25–27, 1968.

Rachman, S., & Teasdale, J. *Aversion Therapy and Behavior Disorders: An Analysis.* Coral Gables, Fla.: University of Miami Press, 1969.

Razran, G. *Mind in Evolution.* Boston: Houghton-Mifflin, 1971.

Renner, K. E. Delay of reinforcement: a historical review. *Psychological Bulletin, 61*: 341–361, 1964.

Rescorla, R. A. Pavlovian conditioning and its proper control procedures. *Psychological Review, 74*: 71–80, 1967.

Rescorla, R. A. Pavlovian conditioned inhibition. *Psychological Bulletin, 72*: 77–94, 1969.

Rescorla, R. A. Second-order conditioning: implications for theories of learning. In McGuigan, F. J., & Lumsden, D. B. (eds.) *Contemporary Approaches to Conditioning and Learning.* Washington, D. C.: Winston & Sons, 1973.

Rescorla, R. A., & Solomon, R. L. Two-process learning theory: relationships between Pavlovian conditioning and instrumental learning. *Psychological Review, 74*: 151–182, 1967.

Reuttenberg, A., & Kay, K. E. Effect of one electroconvulsive seizure on rat behavior. *Journal of Comparative and Physiological Psychology, 59*: 285–288, 1965.

Rosenfeld, H. M., & Baer, D. M. Unnoticed verbal conditioning of an aware experimenter by a more aware subject: the double-agent effect. *Psychological Review, 76*: 425–432, 1969.

Rosenfeld, H. M., & Baer, D. M. Unbiased and unnoticed verbal conditioning: the double agent robot procedure. *Journal of the Experimental Analysis of Behavior, 14*: 99–107, 1970.

Rosenthal, D. *Genetics of Psychopathology.* New York: McGraw-Hill, 1971.

Rosenthal, R. The Pygmalion effect lives. *Psychology Today,* September, 1973.

Rosenthal, R., & Jacobson, L. F. Teacher expectations for the disadvantaged. *Scientific American,* April, 1968.

Rosenzweig, M. R., Bennett, E. L., & Diamond, M. C. Brain changes in response to experience. *Scientific American,* June, 1972.

Rosenzweig, M. R., Møllgaard, K., Diamond, M. C., & Bennett, E. L. Negative as well as positive synaptic changes may store memory. *Psychological Review, 79*: 93–96, 1972.

Rozin, P., & Kalat, J. W. Specific hungers and poison avoidance as adaptive specializations of learning. *Psychological Review, 78*: 459–486, 1971.

Ruitenbeek, H. M. (ed.) *Going Crazy.* New York: Bantam, 1972.

Russell, I. S., & Ochs, S. Localization of a memory trace on one cortical hemisphere and transfer to the other hemisphere. *Brain, 86*: 37–54, 1963.

Russell, W. R., & Nathan, P. W. Traumatic amnesia. *Brain, 69*: 280–300, 1946.

Sabatasso, A. P., & Jacobson, L. I. Use of behavioral therapy in the reinstatement of verbal behavior in a mute psychotic with chronic brain syndrome: a case study. *Journal of Abnormal Psychology, 76*: 322–324, 1970.

Salter, A. *Conditioned Reflex Therapy.* New York: Capricorn Books, 1949.

Saltz, E. Manifest anxiety: have we misread the data? *Psychological Review, 77*: 568–573, 1970.

Saltz, E. *The Cognitive Bases of Human Learning.* Homewood, Ill.: Dorsey Press, 1971.

Sargent, J. D., Green, E. E., & Walters, E. D. Preliminary report on the use of autogenic feedback training in the treatment of migraine and tension headaches. Unpublished manuscript, 1972.

Sassenrath, J. M., & Yonge, G. D. Effects of delayed information feedback and feedback cues in learning on delayed retention. *Journal of Educational Psychology, 60*: 174–177, 1969.

Schachter, S., & Singer, J. E. Cognitive, social and physiological determinants of emotional state. *Psychological Reviews, 69*: 379–399, 1962.

Schneider, A. M. Control of memory by spreading cortical depression: a case for stimulus control. *Psychological Review, 74*: 201–215, 1967.

Schneider, A. M., & Ebbesen, E. Interhemisphere transfer of lever pressing as stimulus generalization of the effects of spreading depression. *Journal of the Experimental Analysis of Behavior, 10*: 193–197, 1967.

Schoenfeld, W. N. (ed.) *The Theory of Reinforcement Schedules.* New York: Appleton-Century-Crofts, 1970.

Schoenfeld, W. N., & Farmer, J. Reinforcement schedules and the "behavior stream." In Schoenfeld, W. N. (ed.) *The Theory of Reinforcement Schedules.* New York: Appleton-Century-Crofts, 1970.

Schwartz, G. E. Voluntary control of human cardiovascular integration and differentiation through feedback and reward. *Science, 175*: 90–93, 1972.

Seligman, M. E. P. For helplessness: can we immunize the weak? *Psychology Today,* June, 1969.

Seligman, M. E. P. On the generality of the laws of learning. *Psychological Review, 77*: 406–418, 1970.

Seligman, M. E. P. Phobias and preparedness. *Behavior Therapy, 2*: 307–320, 1971.

Seligman, M. E. P. Fall into helplessness. *Psychology Today,* June, 1973.

Seligman, M. E. P., & Hager, J. L. The sauce bearnaise syndrome. *Psychology Today,* August, 1972.

Seligman, M. E. P., Ives, C. E., Ames, H., & Mineka, S. Conditioned drinking and its failure to extinguish: avoidance, preparedness, or functional autonomy? *Journal of Comparative and Physiological Psychology, 71*: 411–419, 1970.

Seligman, M. E. P., & Johnston, J. C. A cognitive theory of avoidance learning. In McGuigan, F. J., & Lumsden, D. B. (eds.) *Contemporary Approaches to Conditioning and Learning.* Washington, D. C.: Winston & Sons, 1973.

Seligman, M. E. P., Maier, S. F., & Geer, J. H. Alleviation of learned helplessness in the dog. *Journal of Abnormal Psychology, 73*: 256–262, 1968.

Senden, M. von. *Space and Sight: the Perception of Space and Shape in the Congenitally Blind Before and After Operation.* Translated by P. Heath. London: Methuen, 1960.

Shapiro, D., & Schwartz, G. E. Biofeedback and visceral learning: clinical applications. *Seminars in Psychiatry, 4*: 171–184, 1972.

Shapiro, D., Tursky, B., Gershon, E., & Stern, M. Effects of feedback and reinforcement on the control of human systolic blood pressure. *Science, 163*: 588–590, 1969.

Sheffield, F. D. A drive-induction theory of reinforcement. In Haber, R. N. (ed.) *Current Research in Motivation.* New York: Holt, Rinehart & Winston, 1966a.

Sheffield, F. D. New evidence on the drive-induction theory of reinforcement. In Haber,

R. N. (ed.) *Current Research in Motivation.* New York: Holt, Rinehart & Winston, 1966b.

Shulman, H. G. Similarity effects in short-term memory. *Psychological Bulletin, 75:* 399–415, 1971.

Skinner, B. F. "Superstition" in the pigeon. *Journal of Experimental Psychology, 38:* 168–172, 1948.

Skinner, B. F. *Verbal Behavior.* New York: Appleton-Century-Crofts, 1957.

Skinner, B. F. Teaching machines. *Science, 128:* 969–977, 1958.

Skinner, B. F. Pigeons in a pelican. *American Psychologist, 15:* 28–37, 1960.

Skinner, B. F. *Beyond Freedom and Dignity.* New York: Knopf, 1971.

Skinner, B. F. Humanism and behaviorism. *The Humanist, 32:* No. 4: 18–20, 1972.

Slamecka, N. J., & Ceraso, J. Retroactive and proactive inhibition of verbal learning. *Psychological Bulletin, 57:* 449–475, 1960.

Smith, W. M. Feedback: real-time delayed vision of one's own tracking behavior. *Science, 176:* 939–940, 1972.

Solomon, R. L. Punishment. *American Psychologist, 19:* 239–253, 1964.

Solomon, R. L., & Turner, L. H. Discriminative classical conditioning in dogs paralyzed by curare can later control discriminative avoidance responses in the normal state. *Psychological Review, 69:* 202–219, 1962.

Spear, N. E. Retrieval of memory in animals. *Psychological Review, 80:* 163–194, 1973.

Spear, N. E., Gordon, W. C., & Chiszar, D. A. Interaction between memories in the rat: effect of degree of prior conflicting learning on forgetting after short intervals. *Journal of Comparative and Physiological Psychology, 78:* 471–477, 1972.

Spence, J. T. Learning theory and personaltiy. In Wepman, J. M., & Heine, R. W. (eds.) *Concepts of Personality.* Chicago: Aldine, 1963.

Spence, K. W. *Behavior Theory and Learning.* Englewood Cliffs, N. J.: Prentice-Hall, 1960.

Spence, K. W., & Norris, E. B. Eyelid conditioning as a function of the inter-trial interval. *Journal of Experimental Psychology, 40:* 716–720, 1950.

Sperling, G. The information available in brief visual presentations. *Psychological Monographs, 74:* No. 498, 1960.

Sperry, R. W. Hemisphere deconnection and unity in conscious awareness. *American Psychologist, 23:* 723–733, 1968.

Sperry, R. W. A modified concept of consciousness. *Psychological Review, 76:* 532–536, 1969.

Spevack, A. A., & Suboski, M. D. Retrograde effects of electroconvulsive shock on learned responses. *Psychological Bulletin, 72:* 66–76, 1969.

Spielberger, C. D., & DeNike, L. D. Descriptive behaviorism versus cognitive theory in verbal operant conditioning. *Psychological Review, 73:* 306–326, 1966.

Staats, A. W. *Learning, Language, and Cognition.* New York: Holt, Rinehart & Winston, 1968. a, p. 34.

Stampfl, T. G., & Levis, D. J. Essentials of implosive therapy: a learning-theory-based psychodynamic behavior therapy. *Journal of Abnormal Psychology, 72:* 496–503, 1967.

Stein, L., & Wise, C. D. Possible etiology of schizophrenia: progressive damage to the noradrenergic reward system by 6-hydroxydopamine. *Science, 171:* 1032–1036, 1971.

Sturges, P. T. Information delay and retention: effect of information feedback and tests. *Journal of Educational Psychology, 63:* 32–43, 1972.

Sussman, H. M. What the tongue tells the brain. *Psychological Bulletin, 77:* 262–272, 1972.

Sweet, R. C. RNA "memory pills" and memory: a review of clinical and experimental status. *Psychological Record, 19:* 629–644, 1969.

Tart, C. T. (ed.) *Altered States of Consciousness.* New York: Wiley, 1969.

Tart, C. T. Scientific foundations for the study of altered states of consciouness. *Journal of Transpersonal Psychology, 3:* 93–124, 1972a.

Tart, C. T. States of consciousness and state-specific sciences. *Science, 176:* 1203–1210, 1972b.

Terhune, J. G., & Premack, D. On the proportionality between the probability of not running and the punishment effect of being forced to run. *Learning and Motivation, 1*: 141–149, 1970.

Thompson, C. I., & Neely, J. E. Dissociated learning in rats produced by electroconvulsive shock. *Physiology and Behavior, 5*: 783–786, 1970.

Thompson, R., & McConnell, J. V. Classical conditioning in the planarian, Dugesia Dorotouphala. *Journal of Comparative and Physiological Psychology, 48*: 65–68, 1955.

Thompson, T., & Grabowski, J. G. *Reinforcement Schedules and Multioperant Analysis.* New York: Appleton-Century-Crofts, 1972.

Thornton, J. W., & Jacobs, P. D. Learned helplessness in human subjects. *Journal of Experimental Psychology, 87*: 367–372, 1971.

Tibbetts, P. The mind-body problem: empirical or conceptual issue? *Psychological Record, 23*: 111–120, 1973.

Tolman, E. C. There is more than one kind of learning. *Psychological Review, 56*: 144–155, 1949.

Trowill, J. A., Panksepp, J., & Gandelman, R. An incentive model of rewarding brain stimulation. *Psychological Review, 76*: 264–281, 1969.

Underwood, B. J. Interference and forgetting. *Psychological Review, 64*: 49–60, 1957.

Underwood, B. J. Attributes of memory. *Psychological Review, 76*: 559–573, 1969.

Ungar, G. (ed.) *Molecular Mechanisms in Memory and Learning.* New York: Plenum Press, 1970.

Valenstein, E. S. Problems of measurement and interpretation with reinforcing brain stimulation. *Psychological Review, 71*: 415–437, 1964.

Vanderplas, J. Perception and learning. In Marx, M. H. (ed.) *Learning: Interactions.* Toronto: Macmillan, 1970.

Verhave, T. The inspector general is a bird. *Psychology Today,* November, 1967.

Walker, E. L. The duration and course of the reaction decrement and the influence of reward. *Journal of Comparative and Physiological Psychology, 49*: 167–176, 1956.

Walker, E. L. Action decrement and its relation to learning. *Psychological Review, 65*: 129–142, 1958.

Walker, E. L. Psychological complexity as a basis for a theory of motivation and choice. In Levine, D. (ed.) *Nebraska Symposium on Motivation.* Lincoln: University of Nebraska Press, 1964.

Walker, E. L. Arousal and the memory trace. In Kimble, D. P. (ed.) *The Organization of Recall.* New York: New York Academy of Sciences, 1967.

Walter, T. L., & Mikulas, W. L. Long term discriminative operant behavior and food-storing in rats. *Journal of Psychology, 73*: 41–44, 1969.

Warren, N. Malnutrition and mental development. *Psychological Bulletin, 80*: 324–328, 1973.

Watson, C. G. Relationships of anhedonia to learning under various contingencies. *Journal of Abnormal Psychology, 80*: 43–48, 1972.

Watson, J. B., & Rayner, R. Conditioned emotional reactions. *Journal of Experimental Psychology, 3*: 1–14, 1920.

Watts, A. *The Joyous Cosmology.* New York: Pantheon Books, 1962.

Waugh, N. C., & Norman, D. A. Primary memory. *Psychological Review, 72*: 89–104, 1965.

Weil, A. *The Natural Mind.* Boston: Houghton-Mifflin, 1972.

Weiner, B. Effects of motivation on the availability and retrieval of memory traces. *Psychological Bulletin, 65*: 24–37, 1966.

Weiner, B. Motivational factors in short-term retention. II. Rehearsal or arousal? *Psychological Reports, 20*: 1203–1208, 1967.

Weiner, B., & Walker, E. L. Motivational factors in short-term retention. *Journal of Experimental Psychology, 71*: 190–193, 1966.

Weiskrantz, L. Experimental studies of amnesia. In Whitty, C. W. M., & Zangwill, O. L. (eds.) *Amnesia.* London: Butterworths, 1966.

Wicker, A. W. Attitudes versus actions: the relationship of verbal and overt behavioral responses to attitude objects. *Journal of Social Issues, 25*: No. 4: 41–78, 1969.

Wiener, N. *Cybernetics or Control and Communication in the Animal and Machine.* New York: Wiley, 1948.

Wilson, G. T., & Davison, G. C. Processes of fear-reduction in systematic desensitization: animal studies. *Psychological Bulletin. 76*: 1–14, 1971.

Wolff, P. H. Ethnic differences in alcohol sensitivity. *Science, 175*: 449–450, 1972.

Wolpe, J. *Psychotherapy by Reciprocal Inhibition.* Stanford: Stanford University Press, 1958.

Wolpe, J. *The Practice of Behavior Modification.* Elmsford, N. Y.: Pergamon Press, 1969.

Yates, A. J. Delayed auditory feedback. *Psychological Bulletin, 60*: 213–232, 1963.

Yerkes, R. M., & Dodson, J. D. The relation of strength of stimulus to rapidity of.habit-formation. *Journal of Comparative and Neurological Psychology, 18*: 459–482, 1908.

Zimbardo, P., & Ebbesen, E. B. *Influencing Attitudes and Changing Behavior.* Reading, Mass.: Addison-Wesley, 1970.

Zinkin, S., & Miller, A. J. Recovery of memory after amnesia induced by electroconvulsive shock. *Science, 155*: 102–104, 1967.

name index

229

topic index